bar

store

refuse

kitchen

bar

servery

first aid

women   men

cenery store

upper workshop

women   men

dis.

hall

stage door

foyer   recep.

coats   vid st.   chair st.

main entrance

LEVEL ONE

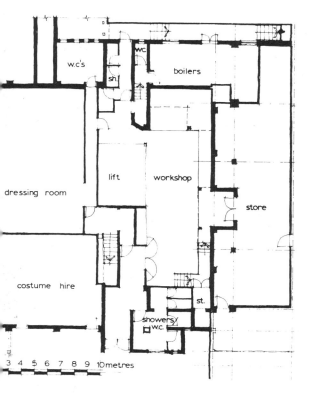

w.c's

wc

sh.

boilers

lift   workshop

store

dressing room

Architect's drawings
by Ken Davis produced
in March 1993
showing the floor
plans of the lower
two levels. The upper
two levels are shown
on the back endpaper.

costume hire

st.

showers
w.c.

3 4 5 6 7 8 9 10metres

GROUND LEVEL

Life's Not a Rehearsal

LIFE'S
NOT A REHEARSAL

The Autobiography of
Margaret Durdant-Hollamby MBE

Founder of The Stag Theatre, Sevenoaks

With a Preface by RICHARD BRIERS

DURDANT-HOLLAMBY

First published in Great Britain 1998
by Durdant-Hollamby
Vine Lodge, Hollybush Lane, Sevenoaks, Kent

Copyright © 1998 Margaret Durdant-Hollamby

ISBN 0 9532362 0 X

Typeset in Great Britain
by Gatehouse Wood, Limpsfield, Oxted, Surrey
and printed in Great Britain
by Antony Rowe Ltd, Chippenham, Wiltshire

To John, Kim, Noel and Barry

It is also written with love for those
who will not find their names mentioned in these pages
but who know that they too are part of the story.

Contents

List of Illustrations

Acknowledgements

My thanks can never be properly expressed to all those
who helped create this story. Suffice it to say
that I shall not forget the never-ending encouragement
and friendship which I have experienced over the years.

As to this book, I thank Kim, Noel and Barry,
and Christopher and Margaret Holgate, for love,
support and advice beyond the call of duty.

I acknowledge with thanks the use of photographs
by the following amongst others: Adscene Publishing,
Sidney Harris, Kensington Press Agency, Kent Messenger,
Derek Medhurst, Rod Nipper, Prospect Contract
Furnishings, Sevenoaks Chronicle and Peter Walker.

Preface

When Margaret asked me to appear on stage in Sevenoaks nine years ago one of the things she made clear was that The Stag was yet another theatre 'struggling for its very existence'.

It is with great delight therefore that I write this introduction knowing that The Stag Theatre has thrived and that the dreams and aspirations of so many have been fulfilled – both amateur and professional.

Live theatre in England needs tender, loving care. My visit to Stag highlighted the obvious devotion and enthusiasm poured into this building, not only by its dedicated staff but also by its outstanding team of volunteers.

Margaret's persistence and determination over a period of 30 years has paid off and her strength of character has seen her through real-life traumas which would, I am sure, have defeated many.

A very human story of a truly remarkable woman.

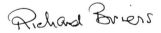

Life's Not a Rehearsal

The Overture

Wherever this adventure would take me, I had a deep feeling that it was all starting here – in Sevenoaks.

It was 1948 and England was beginning to breathe again after the war . . . and my family was moving house. Seven of us in total – my parents, Walter and Ivy Gavin, my aunt (sister to my mother) and four remaining children. Of the four I was the only girl.

There had been five siblings but my eldest brother Ronald had died in action in 1939. His tragic death at the age of 19 in Crete was a bitter loss to my parents and brought my first realisation that grown-ups could cry. I was five years old and can still remember the messenger's knock on the front door, the telegram, then my parents shutting themselves in our dining room for what seemed like eternity. Ronald was so young, had married the woman of his dreams, then had unexpectedly been sent abroad. At five years old I had for the first time been a bridesmaid. It was hard to understand that I would never see that handsome soldier again.

So, the four of us remained. Norman, the eldest, Laurence, me and Alan the baby of the family. Almost a five year gap between each of us, whether by accident or design I never discovered. Alan was born when my mother was just in her forties, a dangerous event in those days but happily not so in our case. I grew up surrounded by boys, sports-loving, very athletic, gregarious and not much like a young lady! The best female goal- and wicket-keeper for miles around!

The house my parents had chosen was beautiful – Sharsted in

Kippington Road. It was almost opposite a church, St Mary's Kippington, and next door to Churchill Court, an enchanting house which had been given to Winston Churchill and which was then a convalescent home for the British Legion.

Kippington Road was stunning – a private road with large houses in beautiful grounds – but despite the excitement of such wonderful surroundings, I was rather desolate at having left all my friends at the Ursuline Convent in Blackheath, the girls in my Girl Guide troop and my many friends with whom I had had such happy years. I had always been a very active child before we moved to Sevenoaks and it could only have been my inborn optimism and happy-go-lucky nature (of which I was entirely unaware) which stopped me being very fearful of not having friends for long though I knew no-one in Sevenoaks.

It was not too long before I made things happen. Having been attached to a church with my Girl Guide troop I went to St Mary's one Sunday for matins to find out what it was like and whether I would be welcome. The church was very pretty, not too large, had the most beautiful stained glass windows and an atmosphere which I can only describe as welcoming. I fell in love with the place from that first Sunday.

The incumbent was Archdeacon Grey, elderly, benign, quite delightful and with a great sense of humour. He had the bluest eyes and something I can only describe as an aura of real goodness. I have not been able to find the right words to this day, but he struck me forcibly as being holy without being pious. He welcomed me very warmly and I began to attend services regularly. It was so easy – fifty yards across the road in all weathers.

I noticed that the choir was not exactly large, often one boy and a man and sometimes two boys! I had sung in church ever since I could remember and I began to think about being in the choir and perhaps persuading some others to join when I made some new friends.

In the meantime I still had to attend school. I was fourteen and our house move had come at about the most awkward time in my schooling although in the late forties exams were not the

2

be-all and end-all of one's school career – rehabilitation after such an awful war took priority over all else. My father knew I had no ambition to attend university. I was fairly intelligent but in my heart there was only one thing I wanted to do – go on the stage.

Next door to Sharsted was a private school for girls called Farnaby. It catered mostly for boarders whose parents were overseas. The Headmistress and owner was one Mrs Le Poer Trench and she was not at all keen to take in a girl of 14. Her school educated pupils only up to that age and she was going to find it difficult to continue my education sufficiently. However, she had not before had dealings with my father! When he had a mind to, he could charm the birds out of the trees and he persuaded her to have me as a pupil. We all knew I was not an academic, the Convent had given me a wonderful grounding and Mrs Le Poer Trench knew she did not have to groom me for university entrance.

Farnaby was another very large house with large grounds and had perhaps fifty or sixty pupils. Mrs Le Poer Trench had one aim in life – to turn out caring, intelligent young ladies. Good manners were paramount and we learned a great deal about living as well as traditional school lessons.

The piano was another of my passions and I was allowed to continue my piano lessons at Farnaby. Practising was never a chore for me, even scales, and quite often my brothers would ask if I really had to play five finger exercises so early in the morning!

One day the school was introduced to a new member on the staff. Our future music master. He was an aesthetic, sensitive, charming Pole who played the violin like an angel. I developed my first adult crush. He and I used to spend hours playing duets out of school hours well after my piano lessons had finished and I loved every minute. The thrill of playing as a partnership was a new experience for me and I found it very stimulating – it gave me a great foundation.

Physical education was regarded as a high priority at Farnaby and during my time there a new PE teacher joined the staff, an ex military man by the name of Tom Shorrocks. He was used to drilling troops, not schoolgirls, and our 'serried ranks' must have broken his heart. He had a broad north country bellow (quite unheard of at Farnaby) that put the fear of God into us when doing our daily drill. One particular morning I almost had hysterics because we could hardly understand anything he was shouting and we kept getting his exercises all wrong. He became almost apoplectic and barked "Put yer 'ands on yer 'ips – don't yer oonderstand the King's English?!" How we all kept our faces straight I shall never know but he became a great friend to us all and our PE improved no end!

My three years at Farnaby were so happy. I was making new friends all the time, two or three of the day girls lived in Sevenoaks so I began through them to meet other young people in the town and to feel as though I might be starting to belong.

As a school we often attended matins at St Mary's and I started to think more about enlarging the choir and being allowed to sing in it. I asked the Archdeacon whether I might start a girls' choir. He hesitated and said he would let me know. I had not realised, but in the early fifties in the Church of England in the country it was fairly unusual to have a mixed choir and it created problems. What would the girls wear for instance? We could not arrive in mufti in the choir stalls with the two boys and one man in cassocks and surplices, it would look ridiculous. There was apparently no money for robes for girls but we were not to be deterred. I suggested that if my parents provided the fabric (my father owned a textile company) and some other kind soul made up the robes would we then be allowed to join the choir? Eventually the answer was yes and that was the start of some of my very happiest years. I persuaded one or two friends to join with me, we had our robes made and then some hats (how long did that decision take us!) and we were set.

The organ in St Mary's was a proper pipe organ and the organist a brilliant musician. His name was Claud Hunter and in 1950 he must have been in his eighties. He was very thin with the longest fingers I have ever seen on anyone. He had a droopy walrus moustache and his skin had that transluscent look that comes with old age. His rheumy eyes still sparkled with enthusiasm when he played, he was never seen without his old mac, his trilby, his brolly and his battered music case. He was delighted to have some more young voices in his choir and he introduced me to some of the most glorious and stirring music I have ever sung. We sang at all services every Sunday and often after Evensong we would all stay behind and sing through oratorios – the solos, the choruses, anything – we simply could not have enough. We performed anthems in the special services at Easter and Christmas and developed quite a reputation locally. More people began to join us.

During all this time my burning ambition to go on the stage was not diminishing. At home the usual discussions began to take place – "what are you going to do when you leave school?" I had only one answer – "please may I go to Drama College".

My father could not have been more opposed to the idea. My mother understood – mothers usually do – but my father was adamant. He had no intention of paying for his only daughter to study for a profession which he regarded as particularly precarious and which carried with it the label of promiscuity and free-living.

Looking back I realise I could not have been so desperate to enter the profession although I thought I was at the time. If I was so, so sure, why had I not just run away from home when I left school and joined a repertory company as a dogsbody? I could not bring myself to do it. I knew father would be heartbroken and after surviving such terrible times in the Blitz, family life was very precious.

I found it hard to understand Dad's absolute animosity towards the profession because our home was always filled with music. My father played the piano superbly by ear, using the tonic sol-fah, my mother had a glorious mezzo voice and my aunt played the piano from music, so we were always entertaining each other. To me it seemed the most natural thing in the world to perform – my aptitude for mimicry had been encouraged from a very early age – it was second nature. However there was no way father could be persuaded and no cajoling would change his mind. He must have felt very strongly because I could usually get round him even if it took a little time.

He decided that I should have a secretarial training (ugh!) – the best, of course – and I was enrolled into Pitman's Secretarial College in Southampton Row at the age of 16 for TWO WHOLE YEARS!

What an eye-opener that place was! Hundreds of students of all nationalities speaking many different languages and looking very different from my usual circle of friends. So many students in fact that each one was given a number – I was no longer called by my name. I thought that only happened in the services. I hated it.

Shorthand was a foreign language to me and typewriting something I had seen only on the silver screen. The noise of sixty students learning to touch type to a record on a gramophone in the same room on typewriters which would have scared the daylights out of any enemy will remain in my memory for ever. The voice on the record would announce "Carriage – RETURN!" at the supposed end of each line, and sixty dinging typewriter bells and clacking carriages would whizz back at different times making an unbelievable din. It nearly sent me mad. I could not wait for the end of each day in that first term, even standing all the way home in a carriage full of smoke was a joy after those appalling commercial lessons, but of course I was learning something which would forever stand me in good stead. I just didn't realise it at the time.

I decided that the only way I could bear two years of what seemed like purgatory was to work very hard and make the time pass quickly. I did just that.

Beginners Please

While all this was happening in London, life in Sevenoaks was absolute bliss. We still had a wonderful time with our music and I decided to form an amateur dramatic society for boys and girls of my own age. In the grounds at Sharsted we had a very high large room which we used as a playroom. This was where our first shows were mounted. It was very basic. We had no funds so we made or borrowed costumes, props and furniture, designed the sets (such as they were) and performed very simple revues or one-act plays. We could seat only ten in the audience, partly because of the size of the room and partly because ten chairs were the most I could borrow from the house. My mother always knew when we were rehearsing a new production because most of the furniture would go missing – it was always in the playroom.

Each member of the audience had to pay 2d to come in and friends and family were frequently dragged in to watch. The vast sum of ls.8d which we earned from a 'full house' always went on bits and bobs for the production, hiring of copies of plays and postage when there was no-one to hand-deliver our post.

We called ourselves The Sharsted Players. Our talents were diverse to say the least – pianists, singers, actors and those who preferred being backstage. Every one of us had to be prepared to share in all the jobs and we quickly learned to be versatile. We polished up our performances, became more ambitious and began to go on to proper full length plays. Sometimes we wrote our own revues and on those occasions four or five of us would play sometimes nine or ten different roles. It was a real learning curve.

Almost every week we spent an evening entertaining the men and women in Churchill Court who were there for a fortnight's convalescence. They seemed to revel in our visits. They joined in with community singing, laughed at our simple comedy and made us feel wonderful. It worked well both for them and for us and Mr Holland who managed the house was full of delight at the way we could lift their spirits for a few hours. As teenagers we were very aware of what these patients had been through, some terribly gassed, others with physical injuries. We felt that in our own small way we were saying thank you for our freedom.

We became more ambitious. A One Act Drama Festival was held in the Riverhead Memorial Hall – an enormous step up for us from performing in the playroom at home – and we entered a one-act play called *To Be Destroyed Unopened* by Morton Howard. The adjudicator was quite complimentary but said that I looked like Vogue's version of a charlady. We weren't quite sure how to take that but were much too excited to worry about it. To this day I don't know what she meant.

Performing in the Riverhead Memorial Hall was an experience in itself. In the early fifties many people used public transport and double decker buses went past the hall very regularly up until at least 10.30 in the evening. For most of us it was the only way to get about. The trouble was, the buses didn't just go past – the bus stop was right outside the hall, opposite what was then The Amherst Arms. On stage one could hear the bus coming round the slight bend – b-r-o-o-m – changing gear to get ready to stop – u-u-r-g-h – stopping –c-r-runch – then a pause till a loud 'ting ting' signalled the driver to move forward. Off into first gear – u-u-r-g-h – and away it went up the hill.

The first time it happened when I was performing on stage in Riverhead I simply lost my concentration. I had forgotten just how close and noisy those buses were, but we managed to deal with it and as the bus came round the bend whatever one was saying (and it was tough if you were speaking sotto voce!) you learned to increase the projection, breathe at exactly the right moment and either project over the 'ting ting' or wait for it to be over, all without spoiling the performance! It was a good training ground.

By now we were all beginning to grow up, members were going off to jobs, one or two to university, and The Sharsted Players finally disbanded. We had become quite a well-known group in Sevenoaks and had little realisation of the crucial lessons we had learned of teamwork, unselfishness and determination over hardship.

I was still very involved in the church choir as were my closest friends. One day I was introduced to a man called Andrew Hills. Andrew and his wife Vera lived in Kippington Road and I had seen them regularly in the congregation at St Mary's and heard his rich bass voice reaching the choir stalls. Andrew was the founder and conductor of a choir called The Sevenoaks Singers and I was very excited to be asked to join. Rehearsals took place once a week on Wednesday evening, usually in St Nicholas Church Hall (now no longer) in South Park. There were about forty or fifty singers, a wonderful accompanist by the name of Allan Pearce and I loved the experience of ensemble singing and learning new and exciting music. My mother despaired about the number of things I was doing. She used to tease me by saying "the only time you're available is between midnight and seven o'clock in the morning," but I knew that she was really a little concerned that I was never at home except to sleep. But I was young, bursting with energy and having real fun doing all those things which I loved so much.

I recall one of the first public concerts I sang with The Sevenoaks Singers. It was December, we had had nearly three feet of snow which had then frozen. The Concert happened to fall on the same night that the church choir had a vital rehearsal for a Christmas Anthem and I needed to be there. The church rehearsal was arranged for 6pm especially to accommodate me. I arranged for a taxi to collect me from St Mary's at 7.15pm to take me to St Nicholas Hall for an 8 o'clock start – plenty of time even in those weather conditions – the journey would normally take seven minutes maximum.

I went to the choir practice in my new white broderie anglais evening dress (complete with wellies) ready for the concert. The rehearsal went smoothly but the taxi arrived about fifteen minutes late which did not help my nerves. I got in and the driver decided he would continue right round the building instead of trying to turn on the treacherous surface.

Horror! The taxi slid on the icy ground, hit the seat at the rear of the church and was well and truly stuck. In evening dress and wellies I slithered back into the church to ask the men if they would come and help push the car. It took a lifetime. Once we had extricated ourselves we had to go so carefully – Kippington Road was a skating rink.

I was late. I felt sick with worry and anxiety and yet knew that I should go on to the concert if I possibly could. We eventually arrived at the hall about 8.30pm and I thought I would never again be asked to sing with The Singers. It simply was not done to be late for such an event – especially your first. My late arrival would appear unforgivable and I felt miserable.

I paid off the taxi and by this time was shivering with cold as well as sick to the stomach. I could hear the choir in full voice and realised I could not enter by the front doors. How could I sidle in? I slid round to the back of the hall and to my utmost relief found the kitchen door unlocked. I crept in and burst into tears. I couldn't stop shaking and wished the ground would swallow me up – I was convinced Andrew Hills would be livid. My concert position was right in the front row.

The door from the hall opened and a large, kindly man came in. It was Dr Edgar Archer who was our bass soloist in *The Three Kings.* He was extremely puzzled and surprised to see me. I blurted out what had happened and he promptly made me sit on a radiator to warm me up and promised he would explain to Mr Hills.

The first half of the concert was almost over, my face was a mess from crying but Dr Archer was kindness itself – I could have hugged him. The interval came and the choir spilled into the kitchen. Much sympathy, lots of leg-pulling about being in two places at once but to my relief Mr Hills said of course I could sing in the second half of the concert as long as I could do something about my face! I was so relieved I could have hugged him too, and our leading soprano, Rhona Archer, the aforesaid doctor's niece, repaired my face and restored my equilibrium. I never forgot that experience – it taught me a valuable lesson never to leave anything to chance and to allow more time than one suspects for things to go wrong.

All this time I was still at Pitmans. I worked exceptionally hard just to pass the time and became super proficient at shorthand and typewriting. My speeds were excellent and I won a Bronze Medal for shorthand even though I hated it.

The only lessons that made life bearable in that place were English and French. I was still hankering to go to Drama School. The Principal of Pitman's interviewed me during my last term to congratulate me on my achievements and to find out what type of work I would like to do. He listened very sympathetically when I explained that I wanted to go to Drama School and that I intended to try for a scholarship at The Royal Academy of Dramatic Art.

I had decided that I must have a try – if I was as good as I thought I was then surely I would get in? If I never tried how would I ever know?

My father did not like the idea, especially with all that secretarial training that he had paid for, but to give him credit he put no obstacles in my path. He knew that if I won a scholarship then I must have some talent – it was down to me.

To my surprise the Principal at Pitman's offered to give me some coaching. I had no professional coach at all, had never had a drama lesson or speech training in my life and I very much appreciated his offer. I was after all one of his star secretarial pupils who wanted to go down a path that had nothing to do with being a secretary.

I chose two contrasting audition pieces. One was from Shaw's Caesar and Cleopatra – 'You are a funny old gentleman' – and the other from Alice in Wonderland. I worked hard on them, mostly on my own with occasional help from the Principal when he could spare the time. My audition date was fixed for sometime during June and on the due date I arrived in plenty of time (!) quivering with anticipation and nerves, word perfect but naïve in every sense of the word. There seemed to be hundreds of hopefuls (I later learned that there were 250 applicants for 4 places), very few boys which did not surprise me and all these females.

I was eighteen at the time, unsophisticated, country fresh and totally unaware of what was expected of me. I noticed the girls disappearing into the cloakroom in groups and coming out made up to the nines, false eyelashes, mascara – the lot. I had nothing with me at all. In my innocence I thought you just went in there and gave your all – it hadn't occurred to me I might have needed a bit of help.

My turn came and I was ushered into this very large room, completely bare at one end with a number of spotlights and at the other a long table with about eight adults sitting at it. I did both my pieces – rather well I thought – and came out.

The following weeks were like being stretched on a rack. On August Bank Holiday Monday I received a letter which said I had not been accepted.

My world crumbled. I spent most of that day crying in my bedroom and foolishly did not want to speak to my father at all. I could not help feeling that if he had been prepared to pay for me to study at RADA I would have made it. The truth was I was not good enough. That hurt. It took me some time to get over it. Explaining to my friends that I had failed was not easy. I knew then that I had no choice but to become a secretary and continue with amateur dramatics.

By this time I had joined The Sevenoaks Players, the only Operatic and Dramatic Society in Sevenoaks. My first show with them was in the chorus of *The Mikado*, conductor Andrew Hills (yes, he was a busy man), producer Joan Lloyd.

Auditions for this were quite nerve-racking. Each individual had to sing alone in a fairly large room or small hall and I think on that occasion I was one of the only applicants for the chorus who could truthfully sing 'schoolgirls we eighteen and under'! To my delight I was accepted. I had a wonderful time in that show – my first full length musical – and that too was the beginning of some memorable experiences for me on the amateur stage and the foundation of some long-lasting friendships.

Competition to be in a musical was rife. There was always a waiting list of people (even men) to sing in the chorus and if you missed more than three rehearsals it was diplomatically suggested that someone else should have your place. Rehearsals were enormous fun but we made a lot of noise (nothing's changed) and I remember Joan Lloyd wearing a referee's whistle round her neck to shut us up.

Performances were held in the Drill Hall in Argyle Road and it was not until I had been involved for some time that I realised quite what a marathon task it was for The Players to turn the building into a 'theatre' for a week. The Drill Hall was rectangular with a good acoustic, constructed of brick with a glass roof. The land on which it stood had been given to the town by the Thompson family. Strange coincidence that the same family had played such a large part in the establishment of Kippington where I had been developing and nurturing my love of music and the theatre. There was no stage. It was just a large shoe box. A stage had to be erected each time The Players hired the hall. The Society owned a second hand boxing ring which they transported a fortnight before the show, assembled over two weekends, fitted up the set and lights and did all those things necessary to turn a flat floored hall into that magical place – a theatre.

On the Monday evening prior to opening the following night the orchestra had to be positioned, the technical rehearsal and dress rehearsal had to dovetail and cast and backstage personnel had their one and only opportunity to perform on stage. Quite a feat, but everyone just got on with it as it was the only place in the town of a size in which to mount a musical. Dressing room space was a joke – we had only two tiny rooms at the side of the stage, there was little wing space and looking

13

back I am astonished at the high quality of productions that were presented.

The amateur talent available was exceptional. Not only did we have singers and actors of very high quality but we had two, three or four extremely talented musicians queuing up to be musical directors. Local musicians often played for no fee and Joan Lloyd's talent for choosing a good show and then casting it was, and still is, legendary. I cut my teeth on *The Mikado* but more exciting things were to happen.

The Players chose to perform *The Heiress*, the dramatised version of *Washington Square* by Henry James. Joan Lloyd was to produce and she encouraged me to audition for the lead. I worked hard on my audition piece and to my delight was accepted.

The cast was excellent. My leading man was John Norman, son of the headmaster of The New Beacon School. He was perfect for the part of Maurice the philanderer. Tall, very good looking, with just enough arrogance to make the character believable. The only problem was he had great difficulty in learning lines. Often in the middle of rehearsals of our love scenes we would be embracing passionately and John would suddenly say – "Just a minute old dear, I have no idea what comes next!" He would then put his right arm right round my back into his left-hand jacket pocket and pull out his script and read it! Although this made embracing very difficult I simply could not help laughing at him.

The part of Dr Sloper, the stern father, was played by Dr Edgar Archer, the man who had sat me on a radiator at that fateful Singers Concert. He was ideal in the part. He was able to look so genial yet beneath that charming exterior he came over to the audience as a man of steel who despised me, his plain spinster daughter.

The show was obviously going to be a winner – you can somehow tell during the weeks leading up to performances. The Players decided to enter it for a Full Length Drama Festival (shades of 'Vogue's edition of a charlady' again in the Sharsted

Players). At least there were no buses to contend with this time.

The play required period costumes – its setting and dress were paramount to its credibility. The Society hired magnificent clothes. In those days when an amateur company hired costumes from the two or three theatrical costumiers in London the leading actors were treated with the greatest courtesy and attention. I remember travelling to Maurice Angel's and having personal fittings for each dress and at the same time seeing what the wig would look like with the costumes. Each dress was breathtaking, enormous crinolines in the most beautiful colours, and they fitted my small frame beautifully. Imagine my astonishment and delight when they told me that three of my dresses had been worn by Olivia de Havilland in the film of *The Heiress*. I felt I could not possibly put a foot wrong and I was thrilled to be acting in a proper play at last.

I could not have been happier. The performances sold extremely well and on the penultimate night (the Friday) we had our public adjudication for the Drama Festival. Nerves were jangling a little, John Norman was still paraphrasing his way through the script and getting away with it beautifully, entrances in a vast crinoline on the Drill Hall stage were almost impossible without various pairs of helping hands squeezing me onto the stage, but we all knew we had done our best and the audience was buzzing with excitement.

That evening's performance went extremely well. The tension in the hall at the end could almost be touched. That final curtain when Maurice is hammering on the door and Catherine refuses to answer and walks up the stairs with her head held high is a moment of high drama and somehow we captured it every night.

This performance was no exception. We took our curtain calls to thunderous applause and remained on stage to hear the public adjudication. The lady adjudicator slated my performance. She said I was far too young and had not had the experience of life to portray the underlying facets of Catherine's character. Apparently my diction had been excellent and she had heard every word – but for me that hardly counted. I sat there, in public, wanting to sink into my voluminous skirt. She said that John Norman (who did not know his words) had been outstandingly convincing – we swallowed hard – she obviously did not know the script but he was totally believable, the cad!

She then came to the performance of Dr Edgar Archer, a well-known and much-loved GP in Sevenoaks and the senior partner of a very large practice. She praised him for his characterisation and his appearance but said she had one major criticism. "It is so important," she said, "that when one is playing a professional man, particularly a doctor, one should really take advice as to the correct method of using the tools of that profession. What a pity no one showed you how to use a stethoscope properly!"

The Drill Hall erupted!

Here was one of our most popular doctors in the district being told he did not know how to use a stethoscope, however antique, and our audience on that night was made up mostly of his local patients!

I shall never forget that experience. It made me think and question the competence of adjudicators and not be too upset by what they have to say. However at the end of the evening I had to travel in the same car as the adjudicator because we were giving her a lift to the station. I have never been so silent in my life. I seriously doubted my abilities as an actress and worried very much about doing one more performance. Next morning however I had so many telephone calls from friends telling me that they had enjoyed the play greatly that I just got on with the job. I did not forget it, even so.

I was by this time working at my first paid job in London. The Principal of Pitmans was really delighted with my secretarial skills and had suggested that I see a personal friend of his who was looking for someone to work for him as a secretary and assistant. PA's were not known then, or if they were they were quite different from today.

The man in question was a Mr Martin Longman who owned

and ran a most beautiful florist shop in Fenchurch Street in the City of London. Remember, I had no experience and was fresh out of college so I felt quite special to have been given a personal introduction and recommendation. I attended an interview in Mr Longman's office situated at the rear of the florists, and my overriding impression was the perfume of all those magnificent flowers. The office was small, very smart and at the very heart of the operation. Mr Longman needed a secretary not only for the business but to help him organise his social life – he was an exceptionally busy Rotarian, the shop had been responsible for the wedding bouquets of the then Princess Elizabeth, and my boss-to-be had a high profile in the City.

I started my very first job and was given the most rigorous training by someone who was meticulous, did not suffer fools gladly and who expected 100% commitment all the time.

As I became increasingly confident more work was given to me. Mr Longman's favourite expression was 'look after the pennies and the pounds will look after themselves'. I dealt with the wages and letters, organised his diaries and was involved in all the aspects of running a very busy and up-market florists.

One delightful and unexpected daily event which I found quite endearing in this commercial world in which I now found myself was the appearance every morning of businessmen in their suits and bowlers who would purchase a rose or carnation for their buttonholes.

During my time at Longman's King George VI died. I thought I had seen that shop pushed to its limits on many occasions with City Dinners and famous weddings, but I was not in the least prepared for what was to come. As soon as the sad news was broadcast to the nation, the chief florist, Miss Connie, who had designed the famous wedding bouquets, began to plan for the deluge of orders from all over the world for wreaths and tributes to His Majesty. It was astonishing. Orders flooded in, extra staff were sought but were almost impossible to find because all the florists had the same problem. Everyone on our staff was told to be prepared to work non-stop and do anything that was

17

asked of them.

I had not realised this included me.

I have never seen such activity in a small shop. When the funeral arrangements were finally announced it was planned like a military operation – which wreaths could be made up when and with what flowers – how long the flowers would live, where everything was going to be stored and so on and so on – the organisation was complex to say the least. No-one stopped for food unless they felt faint, staff worked long and late and on the final run up things were so desperate they asked if I would mind helping with some wiring of flowers. I nervously agreed, never having wired a flower in my life, and hoping they would give me something simple which would not break easily. There was no time for replacements and everything had to be perfect.

They gave me an apron and brought into the office bunches of hyacinths.

Hyacinths?!

"What do I have to do?" I said, feeling anxious because hyacinth stems are rather fragile and prone to snap easily in the hands of a ham-fisted amateur.

"You just break off each floret from the stem and put this wire through it."

I turned green.

Each flower on a hyacinth is as fragile as can be and each flower on this occasion was precious – it had to be used ('look after the pennies . . .'). My heart sank and my stomach did a flip. This would mean the sack I was sure. I was about to wreck Longman's reputation for ever and everyone was so uptight and working so hard under pressure.

I had a go. My fingers felt like sausages and my hands were trembling – I was terrified. Luckily, no-one had time to notice me – they were all far too busy. I broke a few of those flower heads that morning but I did get better as time went on.

The atmosphere was electric and woe betide any ordinary customer who came into the shop for anything during those hectic forty-eight hours. They were served as quickly as possible but of course with the best possible manners!

When the time came to deliver those gorgeous floral tributes I am sure the sigh of relief could be heard all over the City. Everyone was drained but really pleased that they had managed to fulfil all the orders without mistakes even if they had to hide some of my rather sad-looking hyacinth bells.

I continued working for Longman's for about eighteen months. I made very good friends with the girls working there but I was itching to do something rather more creative and my role in the florist shop was limited. My workload increased every week. The more I coped with the more I was given to do and I began to realise that I was being taken advantage of. Also, being in the City every day had its disadvantages; there were no shops and whenever I needed to buy something or just window shop I had to forgo lunch in order to get over to the West End and back within the hour – time-keeping was very strict.

I began to look for another job and was very quickly offered one in an advertising agency called Coleman Prentis & Varley. It was in Grosvenor Street, Mayfair, and sounded exciting and quite, quite different.

I gave in my notice and was surprised and very flattered that Mr Longman did not want me to leave. He offered me much more money but it worried me that the rest of the staff would not take kindly to that. I also wanted a change so I declined his offer. I learned later that he then employed two people to do the work I had been doing single handed. At least I felt pleased that I had been successful in my very first job, doing something my heart was not in but making a fair go of it.

Life in the West End was a whole new world. Another eye-opener.

I was still very unsophisticated, very happy at home, still doing lots of amateur dramatics and hours of singing, going to weekly dances and generally enjoying myself with all my friends. We were involved with everything that went on – raising money for the church by helping out at bazaars, singing to the British Legion patients in Churchill Court and performing whenever the opportunity arose.

My best friend, Judy Dill, and I entered Arts Festivals in Sevenoaks and Tunbridge Wells and were often quite successful in the duet classes. Judy had a lovely soprano voice and her sister Jennifer sang alto, so musical evenings were a regular part of our lives – somehow everything was so uncomplicated then and we just seemed so carefree. Perhaps I imagined everyone else of my age had such a good time – I don't know.

My job at Coleman Prentis & Varley (CPV as it was known) was fascinating and stimulating. I was personal secretary to an account executive, Clifford Jackson, and dogsbody to the six young men in his Group. Mr Jackson was responsible for the advertising for a number of clients of national and international status and our Group was involved in all aspects. The offices were handsome and very large compared to my tiny space at Longmans and were situated not only in the heart of the West End but also in what had been one of the most handsome houses in Grosvenor Street.

I was working with men almost constantly but having been brought up surrounded by males I settled in very quickly and soon became absorbed in every part of the advertising business. Our Group handled Ryvita, Cadbury's Drinking Chocolate and Gossard Corsets among others and the days flew by. Window shopping at lunchtime was an especial treat!

The people working at CPV were from all walks of life. Artists, copywriters, finance experts, undergraduates training to become Account Executives, hard-drinking media men – all crossed my path on an almost daily basis and I loved it. I began to have a very busy social life in London as well as at home and at one time several undergrads and I started to write a musical in our spare time. The talent available straight out of university was a joy to behold. We never did produce that musical but we spent many happy hours in tiny flats writing the story, the dialogue and the music and my passion for the theatre was further fired by this creative activity which I so enjoyed.

My boss's group was awarded the Lines Brothers Account, the family company which owned Hamley's toy shop in Regent Street, and in 1953 a new man was appointed to our Group. His name was John Durdant-Hollamby. Little did I know that he would become my husband in 1956.

There were numerous handsome young men at CPV but John knocked spots off them. He was elegant, extremely good looking and frightfully sophisticated. This country bumpkin had never come across anyone quite like him. Unknown to me he had a reputation as a Mayfair playboy. His first words to me on the first morning he walked into my office were "Oh! I wouldn't kick *you* out of bed!"

If my father had heard that, he would have had John locked up. However I took it all very calmly but I discovered that he had the most wicked sense of humour. He was one of those people who had the ability to keep an absolutely straight face and tell you something quite outrageous and totally untrue. There was never any malice behind it, just mischief. It took me a little while to recognise a certain twitch about his mouth when he was fibbing and he caught us all out on several occasions.

I did not entirely like him at first, apart from admiring his appearance. I thought he had a certain arrogance of which I didn't approve and yet no-one could help liking him – he was such fun. He always wore a curled bowler, carried the most beautifully furled umbrella and was the receiver of admiring glances wherever he went; but I had my feet firmly on the ground and since everyone knew he adored glamorous, sophisticated women I treated him exactly the same as I treated everyone else – like a brother. I still had lots of friends in Sevenoaks, I had my own boyfriend and I was far too busy being busy to think about a relationship with someone much older than me.

Relationships were not so isolated as they seem today. We moved around in groups much more, couples certainly did not live together before marriage and although my boyfriend and I talked of marrying, it was not to be and the special relationship we had broke up.

So I remained unattached, extremely happy and enjoying London enormously. A group of us regularly travelled on the same trains from Sevenoaks to London and back. Often if the carriage was filled by all of us on the way home we would have a choir practice – church music, Gilbert and Sullivan – anything that took our fancy. The trains then had individual compartments so it was not too difficult to arrange to meet in the same one each evening and there were usually enough of us to fill it.

One particular morning when I arrived at work John D-H was late and my boss wanted to know where he was. No-one had any idea. There had been no message and the other men in the group guessed he had had a night on the tiles and was not yet awake. He strolled in about 10.30 and came into my office.

I was alone.

"Why are you late? Mr Jackson has been looking for you."

"My dear" he replied in his familiar drawl, doffing his bowler, "my wretched wife simply would not get up and make the tea."

"Why couldn't you make it yourself?" I asked somewhat surprised.

"Oh I had a late night, and anyway it's good for her to get up early even though she is pregnant."

I was stunned. None of us had known John was married let alone about to become a father.

"Is this your first baby?" I asked

"Good heavens, no, we already have two."

I was furious. If they had two children and his wife was pregnant with a third how dare he expect her to make his early morning tea.

"I suggest you make your own tea in future and take your wife a cup as well" and I ripped the paper out of my typewriter in anger. What a male chauvinist pig!

At that time I had not cottoned on to that telltale twitch around the mouth and later that day when the others were asking me why John had been late I related our conversation with absolute disgust. Their faces were a picture. I had been had! John was not even married, let alone the father of two children with another on the way. The Group thought it hilarious and even I had to admire the aplomb with which it had been delivered. I couldn't let him get away with it however and the Group helped me devise a way of getting my own back.

John occasionally had to work on the Gossard Corset account and the Public Relations chief there was a real dragon and well known in the advertising world for reducing grown men to pulp. She was extremely efficient and forceful. We devised our plot. Two days later we told John that she had asked to see him urgently as there was the most awful mistake in one of his advertisements in the national press.

It was a pleasure to see his discomfort all the morning waiting for this mythical explosive meeting in the afternoon. He stayed in with us at lunchtime trying to find this terrible error in the national press but all to no avail. Before he was about to leave for the meeting, looking immaculate, we owned up. He took it all in good part and from then on we called it quits. I learned when to recognise the twitch.

In the following months John and I spent a great deal of our leisure time together. He came down to Sevenoaks on a number of occasions, once walking all the way from Croydon when he had no money – carrying a basket of strawberries for me – it must have taken him hours. He met my parents and my mother and aunt fell for him. My father was not so easily pleased and he watched this budding liaison with trepidation. I am not sure whether he would have approved of anyone I really liked – fathers are so often of this view with regard to their daughters – and being the only girl of five children I suppose that made it worse. However, apart from dropping hints to me about his concerns regarding John, he did not in any way try to stop me seeing him. I really admired his tolerance as opposition at that time would no doubt have come between us.

My friends also were wary of this blossoming friendship –

they had met John on several occasions and were worried that I was being swept off my feet by someone I would be unable to handle. I was, but I just knew he was the man for me and nothing else mattered. We laughed together such a lot, played lots of sport (although he could beat me at any ball game) and learned everything we could about each other. We talked for hours on end and I discovered he had lost his mother when he was very young, his father was still alive and he had three other brothers – more men! He had been in the SAS for a while but only at the end of the war and he was indeed nine years my senior.

At CPV things were happening quite rapidly. John was responsible for the advertising and promotion of Hamley's in Regent Street, the largest toy shop in the world. He was very excited and delighted when he was approached by one of the Lines brothers to become the trainee buyer. What grown man could resist! A buyer of all those things which he secretly hankered after – train sets which covered half a floor, guns for boy cowboys, fancy dress for knights in armour and tricks and party games by the gross. He was in seventh heaven. He was also a very good choice because his attitude to customers was perfect and he had to deal with people from all walks of life. One of the highlights of his career was closing the shop to the public and helping the young Prince Charles to choose his Christmas presents.

He was to train under Miss Stewart who was elderly, excellent at her job and had been the buyer at Hamley's for as long as anyone could remember.

By now we were well and truly in love and financially the future seemed to hold a little promise. A trainee's salary was not high but the prospects were exciting. The work was very very hard but John was enthusiastic, very fit, and threw himself into the job wholeheartedly. We both possessed the same belief – if you are going to do something, do it well. The more I heard about Hamley's the more it reminded me of Longman's the florists. In the run-up to Christmas everyone on the staff was expected to do whatever was necessary to keep the shop stocked. When the lorries arrived in their droves John's immaculate suit was discarded, shirt sleeves were the order of the day and anyone who was fit helped to unload and unpack. The hours were exceptionally long, meals were a low priority and at the end of the day everyone was exhausted. Christmas to the staff at Hamley's meant sleep, sleep, sleep.

I was still working for Clifford Jackson of whom I was very fond. He had a great sense of humour, was a very kindly, jovial man and had completely taken me under his wing. He too watched this budding friendship which had started in his Group and I think he was quite relieved that JD-H was no longer at Grosvenor Street and perhaps not quite so available.

It was too late. It took John a long time to decide to give up his freedom and bachelorhood but when he proposed I accepted without a moment's hesitation. We were made for each other. My father's permission was sought. It was done properly then. Although I knew he had his doubts, to his great credit he kept them hidden. Our engagement was announced on 9th February 1955 and our wedding planned for 1956.

Not long after all this excitement in late 1955 my parents, aunt, younger brother Alan and I moved to Dulwich Village. My father had been finding it increasingly tiring to drive into London each day to his office in Soho Square and it was affecting his health. I hated the idea of leaving Sevenoaks but my wedding was in the offing so I was not nearly so unhappy about it as I would have been a few years before.

Our engagement period was the most deliriously happy time. Planning a wedding with a mother and an aunt and girlfriends was great, great fun and we spent hours talking and organising the great event.

We were married at my beloved St Mary's Kippington on 26th May 1956. The reception was held across the road in the grounds of Churchill Court where I had entertained the British Legion only a few years before. I had six bridesmaids all in different pastel shades and my aunt said they reminded her of a bouquet of sweet peas. The dear Archdeacon came out of retirement to marry us and Canon Thornhill, the then incumbent, assisted.

What a wedding that was! Glorious music provided by Andrew Hills and the Sevenoaks Singers plus the choir of St Mary's. The weather smiled on us.

Our honeymoon was spent in Monte Carlo and was unforgettable. On our first and only visit to the Casino John put some chips on no 13 and won enough to pay for one of our air fares. Magic! We left the Casino immediately!

John had taken the lease of a first floor flat in a very handsome house in Broadwater Down in Tunbridge Wells. He had spent many months redecorating the whole place (much to the surprise of my family and friends) and after our blissful honeymoon we returned to Tunbridge Wells to begin our married life. I realised I was married the first time I dropped some clothes on the floor in the bedroom and they were still there when I came back from the shopping. It was now my responsibility – not my mother's!

I took a part time job in Tunbridge Wells and John travelled each day to London.

Within a few weeks I was pregnant and very excited. I suppose in a way ignorance was bliss. There were no scans, no endless lectures about diet, I was extremely fit and we both agreed that I should have the baby at home. My doctor in Tunbridge Wells (a dear Scotsman) approved heartily, the local midwife was a lovely woman and I prepared for childbirth blissfully unaware of the problems or anxieties that seem to dog expectant mothers so often today.

I remember being what I thought was very large at about six months and walking down to the High Street in the Wells to do the shopping. It was very fashionable then to have wire shopping baskets, rather more fragile and prettier than the ones seen today in supermarkets. Whilst shopping, I tripped on the pavement and fell on top of my basket. No-one came to my aid. Perhaps they were afraid I might give birth. I eventually got myself up, looked at my basket and burst out laughing. It was squashed into the most deformed shape imaginable. Luckily the fall had done me no physical damage although I was terrified for the baby. My doctor reassured me that my child was so well cocooned it would take more than a little fall to harm it.

Our first son was late – ten days in fact – and I became very impatient. We had a very close friend, Alfred Kitchin, who lived above us at Tunbridge Wells. He took me out in his bright yellow Sunbeam Tourer over the bumpiest bits of unmade road he could find, but to no avail. Kim Graham John was born at 9.00pm on 26th March 1957 in our bedroom at Broadwater Down. He was beautiful. Weighing in at 9lbs (and didn't I know it – I wasn't much heavier myself!) he was blond and blue eyed just like his father.

Parenthood suited us both down to the ground but my entrepreneurial spirit had not been dampened and with my father's financial help we decided to take over the running of a small tea-rooms at the top of Sevenoaks High Street. Called Tinley House Cafe it was situated next to Raley's Bakers on the corner of Six Bells Lane. We leased the 16th century building and moved into the living accommodation over the shop. There were already two staff employed, Dorothy the cook and Winnie the waitress. John would continue to work in London but with shorter travelling hours and I would run the business and look after our son.

We served morning coffee, luncheon and afternoon tea. Mr Raley next door baked most of the cakes and scones for us and Dorothy cooked traditional meals for lunchtime. It was the greatest fun.

On Sundays John and I had no help so we used to do afternoon teas ourselves. The kitchen was situated one floor below the restaurant and we had a dumb waiter which we pulled up and down on a rope with the orders. My brother Alan often used to help us out on a Sunday and he would take Kim for a walk in the pram or play with him upstairs whilst we dealt with our customers.

What hard work those Sundays were! One particular Sunday we did 96 teas – a record for us and not bad going for two people – and the cafe was teeming with visitors from all over the place. Knole House in those days had no restaurant and no public lavatories, so Sunday visitors would pile out of the house and fall into Tinley's, desperate for both a loo and a cup of tea.

Orders were whizzing up and down in the dumb waiter and I was flying from table to table trying to remember everybody, serving, clearing tables, taking the money and generally being polite. Suddenly a loud American voice came across the room: "Hey, miss, miss" (and me a married mother!) "could you explain something please? Do you usually serve only hot water in tea pots in England?"

She demonstrated. I was covered in embarrassment. In the rush downstairs John had forgotten to put any tea in her pot. The other customers joined in the laughter and a rude note went down on the dumb waiter complete with a teapot of boiling water. I heard the voice downstairs say "Oh, ******" and all was put right.

We had no dishwasher and when everyone had gone one of us would feed and entertain Kim and the other two would wash up for what seemed hours on end. Once Kim had been put to bed the three of us sat down and had a well-earned tea if there was anything left. Our training had stood us in good stead and we felt able to cope with almost anything.

Some months later I discovered I was pregnant again and our second son Noel Ian Drummond was born in our bedroom upstairs at Tinley's during the lunchtime session on Saturday 5th July 1958.

Many of our regulars were in for lunch, most knew of the impending birth and there were loud cheers from downstairs once the arrival of our second son was made known. I cannot imagine what a health inspector would say today with lunchtime customers on one floor and the proprietor having to take the waste discreetly through the back of the restaurant.

Noel very sweetly was not ten days late, did not take more than a couple of hours to arrive into the world and had allowed me to do the wages that morning! Once more we had a perfectly healthy son, weighing in at less than his brother, 6lb 12oz, blond, blue eyed and beautiful.

I was soon back to running the business. The building however did not lend itself to tiny children and it became obvious that I could not manage two babies in a 16th century building where everything was on a different level. We began to look around for something else and again with my father's help we purchased a house called The Moorings in Hitchen Hatch Lane. It was owned by Mr and Mrs Bertie Packman, who also owned and ran the two wet fish shops in Sevenoaks.

For us it was perfect. It was Edwardian, all the rooms had high ceilings which we loved and had missed so much at Tinley's, and it had a wonderful garden for the children to grow up in. I became pregnant for the third time. I decided that this time it might just be a girl – I felt slightly different and the kicks seemed not quite so severe. I knitted the first ever pink baby jacket just to help things along a little!

Six weeks before the birth my father died. A dreadful shock – the loss of a parent. No time to think or wonder during the following days, the two little boys seemed never to stop talking, asking questions and simply needing attention for their enormous energies. It was only much later that I realised how grateful I was for their constant prattle. In 1960, two years after we had moved into the house which my father had helped us buy, our third son, Barry, was born in the front bedroom. He weighed in at 7lb 4oz, was beautiful but once again blond and blue-eyed. I wondered why I had bothered. I was very very dark with hazel eyes and all the boys had John's colouring.

We now had three children under three and a half and life was busy. I was in my element. The main disappointment for us was that John's work was keeping him away from home more and more, particularly at holiday periods when Hamley's was at its busiest, and he was missing so much of the children's development. Not only that but financially we were very stretched and we were very keen to give our sons a private education.

Four years later we decided to open The Moorings as a guest house. It was to be very simple, just bed and breakfast, which with the three boys at school at Winchester House in Hitchen Hatch Lane (about a hundred yards from our home) was perfectly feasible. It would earn us the much needed extra money but I would still be at home for the children and for us that was the most important aspect.

We started with one bedroom on my birthday 8th April in 1964 and had our first guest. John had decorated the house over the years and although we had had neither the cash nor the time to start on the attic floor (which had four large rooms) the rest of the house looked delightful and we were very excited to be in such a lovely building with the prospect of a good future. Even getting to the station for John took only two and a half minutes – he had it down to a fine art.

I had been in only two shows for the Players in five years. I took the lead in *Rebecca* and the part of Mad Margaret in *Ruddigore*. Many of my friends said the part was written for me! John and the children always came first and if I was in a show one year then I did nothing for the next twelve months.

John was equally unselfish. He had always adored his golf, had played a great deal before we were married and even occasionally after Kim was born, but although he remained a member of Knole Park Golf Club he gave up playing when the children were small. We were of one mind about each other's hobbies. We agreed that neither one of us should drop our interests, but neither of us ever abused our free time to the discomfort of the other and the children always came first. We could not give them material things but we gave our time willingly and it paid off. It was often tough, but we were both very fit, exceptionally happy and we had our values firmly established.

30

I was still passionate about acting and when it was possible I revelled in performing. I remained in The Sevenoaks Singers and sang whenever possible. I found the breathing disciplines required for singing very helpful during my pregnancies and used to sing in the Singers till the last possible week before a birth except when my bump would have been an embarrassment to an audience.

The bed and breakfast business increased gradually through word of mouth and we were astonished to discover how many foreigners came to visit Sevenoaks. They were delighted to stay in an English home, visit the famous historic houses which proliferated around Sevenoaks and still manage to do their sightseeing in London.

John decided to leave Hamley's. He was spending more and more hours there for no more pay, the B & B business was getting too big for me to handle on my own and we had three growing sons who needed a father around.

We ran the business together. It was always a financial struggle, exceptionally hard work, often an eighteen hour day in the height of the season, but we loved working together and we were always there for the boys. Holidays were unimportant. We were in the tourist business which demanded our attendance at peak holiday periods. Between us we still had lots of fun and we managed to pay for the boys' prep school education and that meant a great deal to us.

Curtain Up

In 1966 I was asked by the Players if I would produce the annual musical. I was thrilled. I had played two lovely roles over the previous years – *The Prime of Miss Jean Brody* and *The Queen and the Welshman*, both under the direction of Joan Lloyd. I was ready to spread my wings a little.

In those days in the Players we had an annual event called a 'Conversatione'. This was an evening when new producers were given the opportunity to try their hand at directing and I had cut my teeth on a one-act musical. I felt therefore that I had 'passed the test' and approached the chance to direct with enthusiasm. I was introduced to the man who was to be the musical director, a Dr Douglas Gibbs, and we hit it off from the start. Douglas was an exceptional musician and a perfectionist. Our ideas for the show were in tune from the start. It was quite a step for The Players – an unknown new team for their annual musical – and we both felt privileged to be asked.

Once again we were using the Drill Hall and I decided to try to make the experience more pleasant for our audience by raising the rows of seats after the fourth or fifth row so that people could see and hear better. It had been widely known for some years (and moaned about) that if you were not tall and had seats anywhere further back than the fourth or fifth row you spent the whole evening trying to hear and what was worse trying to see. Douglas fully approved of my attempts and I spent a great deal of time begging and borrowing platforming from Sevenoaks School to place on the floor of the Drill Hall. In fact, I spent so much time on this that I began to wonder why on earth Sevenoaks did not have a proper theatre in which to perform. The town had quite wealthy residents, there was an abundance of artistic amateur talent and I felt that it ought to be perfectly possible to establish a small but purpose-built theatre for the numerous societies to use.

Little did I know that that germ of thought was to be the beginning of a campaign which would absorb most of my spare time over the next 25 years.

Douglas Gibbs and I produced *Patience* by Gilbert and Sullivan – the most significant title if I had only known. It was very successful and we enjoyed our collaboration greatly. When it was all over I happened to mention to a fellow Sevenoaks Player, Hugh Barty-King, my idea for a theatre in Sevenoaks. Perhaps he would think it was stupid, but to my delight he was very enthusiastic and said that he would help with the paper work if I would do the setting up and get it going.

So, the two of us, full of enthusiasm and bright ideas, began our campaign to try to find a suitable site in Sevenoaks on which to have a small theatre.

Our first idea was the Drill Hall itself.

The Drill Hall was the only building of any size in Sevenoaks which could possibly be converted into a small theatre. Parking was not good but very few theatres had car parks anyway and audiences had managed up to then. Drivers parked wherever they could and walked the remainder of the way.

There was a Conservative Government in power but a general election looming. Rumour had it that when Labour was returned to govern (and it was generally agreed that they would win the election) they would disband the Territorial Army and the Drill Hall would then become redundant. Hugh and I thought this an ideal opportunity to stake our claim and we had our first serious discussion about our plan of action.

There was no possible way we could deal with this idea on our own so we approached the Sevenoaks Urban District Council. (In 1967 there was an Urban and a Rural Council). The Clerk to the Council, Mr Arthur Davies, received our idea with some sympathy but a little scepticism. We explained what we had in mind and said that before anything could happen, we needed to know whether the idea of converting the Drill Hall into a theatre was a practical one. Perhaps the building itself would not be suitable, maybe its size would be a problem, perhaps the glass roof would be expensive to replace and so on and so on. After much negotiation, discussion and numerous meetings when we were questioned closely about our commitment to this project, it was agreed that the Urban District Council would employ a professional theatre consultant to do a feasibility study on the whole building.

During the ensuing months Hugh and I carried out exhaustive research. We drove to anywhere accessible which had a small theatre that was thriving. The Questors Theatre, Ealing, was a prime example and with The Stables Theatre, Hastings, was among our ports of call. We pumped people unmercifully for information about running theatres. We listened to their stories, watched performances in their theatres, learned by their mistakes and picked out all the things which they had got right and which were working. All of this was noted down by Hugh and the documentation began to pile up. Hugh was superb at keeping precise records.

At that time Sevenoaks had two local papers, the *Sevenoaks News* and the *Sevenoaks Chronicle*. The *Kent Messenger* which had a wider circulation had an office in Sevenoaks but was in fact based in Maidstone. Basil Copper was the representative in the town for this paper. We visited both local editors and told them of our plans. They listened but we could tell at once that they did not believe in what we were going to do. We badly needed publicity but they explained that in order to have any credibility in the eyes of the press we had to have a name. What were we called?

It was de rigueur in 1967 to have an acronym and we had to think of something fast. Hugh came up with the idea of "T.H.I.S." – Theatre in Sevenoaks. We both thought it terrible but it was the only thing he could come up with in a hurry. Our campaign locally began in real earnest. We were both wildly enthusiastic, absolutely convinced of what we were doing and sure that we would achieve our goal. What optimism!

In the meantime John and I continued to run The Moorings and it all fitted in beautifully. I was still always at home for the boys and as parents we supported them in all their activities. They in their turn encouraged me in my campaign for a theatre. There was no friction but there was a lot of activity.

The Urban District Council appointed Martin Carr, a professional theatre consultant, to carry out a feasibility study on the possibility of converting the Drill Hall into a small theatre. Hugh and I met Mr Carr, explained what we were trying to do and waited patiently over the ensuing months for his conclusions.

During this waiting period we attended committee meetings

of as many local societies as we were able, telling them of our proposed idea, trying to persuade them to commit themselves to our project and have a better home in which to perform to their audiences. What an uphill task that was. Almost every organisation agreed that they needed such a theatre but whilst they were happy to complain about current conditions, when asked to commit their support to us on paper, in the majority of cases such commitment was not forthcoming. They would love to have somewhere nice to perform but would rather wait and see before attempting to help! I found that very frustrating and disappointing and it did not give us any Brownie points in the eyes of the Council. Were Hugh and I perhaps the only ones who wanted a theatre?

The Feasibility Study was finally presented in July 1967 and it was encouraging. The Drill Hall would make a more than adequate small theatre providing certain works were carried out and, after even more meetings not only locally but in London too, it seemed as though the Urban District Council might really be persuaded to pay for the transformation to take place.

Now to wait for the new government. As soon as the Election was over we would be able to go ahead and it was hard to curb the impatience during the following months.

The General Election brought its own surprise. Labour did not win, the Tories were re-elected, the Territorial Army was not disbanded and all our hopes and dreams of converting the Drill Hall immediately went down the drain.

All that work. We were completely deflated. All that time we had been concentrating solely on the Drill Hall – it was without doubt the best bet – and there was absolutely no other site available or suitable in the town. We gathered our wits, licked our wounds, collected up all our paper work which I kept at The Moorings and vowed to keep our eyes and ears open for any other possible site which might become available. However, our hopes were not high. The Drill Hall had existed as a building – four walls and a roof – and the local authority thought it a strong possibility. It would not be so easy to convince them about any other building and we knew they could not go on paying for feasibility studies ad infinitum.

Meanwhile, our boys were growing up, the business was increasing all the time and we obtained our first star from the AA. We felt quite proud. Our reputation in Sevenoaks was second to none, accommodation was sorely lacking in such a vital tourist spot (although John and I were certain few people in Sevenoaks recognised it as such) and we knew that if we were prepared to give 100% service to our guests we would succeed.

We loved working together. Our time at CPV had prepared us for each other's attitudes to work, John's retail training at Hamley's could not have been put to better use and we both took delight in making our guests happy and welcome. Our maxim was 'Mayfair service at country prices' and that is what we always tried to achieve. Nothing was too much trouble and our efforts in the business were rewarded by being able to pay for our three boys to have a private education. We did not begrudge one penny of it – they were so happy and fulfilled and the house rang with laughter more often than not. Our guests enjoyed the happy atmosphere which we all created, we encouraged the boys to bring their friends home, they had a large garden in which to play and anyway we just loved children.

Running the guest house was all we had hoped it to be. Rewarding and exhausting at one and the same time we had the opportunity to meet people from all over the world. In the early days although we did not serve meals in the evening there was still the family to feed, there were the usual debates about homework(!) and from April to the end of September the doorbell rang constantly. Often we would fall into bed quite late only to be woken at 2 or 3 in the morning by some foreign visitors desperate for a bed for the night. John was always the one to answer the middle of the night bells! He also served the early morning tea (no machines in the bedrooms) so quite often he had only four or five hours' sleep before he was on duty once more.

During 1967 we had a small claim to fame. We were approached by the BBC to accommodate a team of actors who were coming to Ightham Mote to film parts of Sir Walter Scott's *Ivanhoe*. At the time of the booking we knew only that we would have two actors and some technical staff. Imagine our delight (especially mine) when we heard that we would be looking after Jeremy Brett and Prunella Ransome. Jeremy Brett was already a firm favourite of mine and the excitement of having a professional actor in the house was catching – even the children were keyed up.

The team arrived (late of course) and Jeremy Brett was all that I had imagined and more. He had a voice that could melt icicles and he really enjoyed being part of our family. He was very warm with the boys, very un-luvvy and surprised me greatly on the first morning by coming into the kitchen, sitting on the draining board whilst we cooked and served breakfasts. He wanted only freshly squeezed oranges. The morning visits became a habit and he talked quite freely about his family. I told him of my idea for a theatre in Sevenoaks and he was very enthusiastic. He even offered to appear in a performance of *A Midsummer Night's Dream* in the open air if the dream of a theatre became a reality.

He posed with Kim, Noel and Barry for photographs as a memento and was thoughtful enough to wear his costume for the TV series which matched so well with the boys' suits of armour in which they conducted various battles! Once news got around that he was staying at The Moorings, it was quite funny to look down the drive and see a little queue of schoolgirls waiting for a glimpse of one of their idols. He never appeared for them and managed a neat scheme of dodging them every day.

I wrote to him in later years to tell him about the theatre, but he was spending a great deal of time in the United States so I think my letters were not received.

Ironically I did meet up with Jeremy Brett once more before his death. In 1992 we were holding a family celebration in a little

D'Artagnan Crosses Swords with Sevenoaks

JEREMY BRETT, star of the B.B.C.1 serial "The Three Musketeers," has pledged his support to the setting up of a theatre in Sevenoaks.

In a recent interview with our reporter, Jeremy said that he had hoped to see the local repertory company in action while he was staying in Sevenoaks last week.

"I was astounded when I heard that no such thing existed," he said. "For a town of this size and character it is amazing."

He and other members of the cast stayed at the Moorings Guest House during the filming at Ightham Mote of the future BBC 2 serial "Kenilworth," by Sir Walter Scott. The serial will begin at the end of July.

Open-Air Protest

During his stay at the Moorings, Jeremy suggested to Mrs. D. G. J. Durdant-Hollamby, wife of the proprietor and member of the "Theatre in Sevenoaks" Committee, that she should stage a performance of Shakespeare's "A Midsummer Night's Dream" in her garden as a protest.

He feels that Sevenoaks lacks "a sense of identity."

"There is very little to offer in this town for teenagers," he said, "and a theatre would be a chance for the people of Sevenoaks to meet on a genuine social basis.

"It could be used by all members of the public and perhaps be used as a discotheque for teenagers, when not in use as a theatre."

Italian restaurant in Fulham. Jeremy was at a table in the corner. He realised this was a special occasion and raised his glass publicly to Kim whose birthday it was. It gave me the opportunity to re-introduce those three little boys who had been in awe of him at The Moorings. He was astonished and very delighted to learn that the theatre about which I had talked so much had by now become a reality.

The guest house became busier and busier. I performed occasionally for The Players – life cannot be all work – but I was very careful to make sure neither the family nor the business suffered. John's relaxation would be games of squash with the children and then a pint in the local. He occasionally tried to have a round of golf, but the busier we were, the more impossible that became. Our first real summer holiday was in 1970 when we took the boys to the Algarve and paid a friend to run The Moorings for us. What bliss that was! We had a self-catering apartment at Armacao de Pera with a maid who made the beds and washed up. I thought I was in heaven. Glorious weather, beautiful beaches and delightful people. We were all so happy and came home tanned and very fit. We settled back into our routine of working hard but I felt very disheartened when I learned that Hugh Barty-King and his wife Jennie were going to move to Ticehurst – I would be losing my document expert and the other enthusiastic half of T.H.I.S.

An Alternative to the Drill Hall?

One day Mr Davies, the Clerk to the Council, rang me to ask if I would attend a meeting in the Council Offices to discuss the relocation of Bradbourne Girls' School which was to have a drama studio attached.

At the meeting it was explained that Kent County Council intended to relocate the school to the Bradbourne Vale Road from Bradbourne Park Road. Drama and its performance was the new important factor in the Education system and it was very likely that the school would have its own drama studio to be used as a theatre for its pupils. Mr Davies's question was could I categorise the extra facilities which would be needed if this drama space was to serve the needs of the town and provide a small theatre for amateurs?

It seemed to me an eminently sensible suggestion. Not only would it give the new school a real performing space but, by planning it properly in the initial stages, it would save the Local Authority money, give the County a wonderful facility and at the same time provide Sevenoaks with just what it needed – a purpose-built theatre within the boundaries of a public building with ample car parking on site. I looked critically at all the things we had been trying to achieve in the Drill Hall and came up with a practical list of the necessary requirements if such a building was to work.

Many, many months later it was arranged that Mr Davies and I would attend a meeting in Maidstone with members of the KCC to discuss the details of what I deemed necessary to make a theatre work for the community in the new school. I was really quite optimistic. I had been through all my recommendations in great detail with the Urban District Council, we had thrashed out this and that and knew that our case was well prepared and quite watertight. Also, all the signs from KCC via Mr Davies were that the scheme was a sensible one and an excellent solution to a number of problems.

The meeting in Maidstone was well attended, Mr Davies and I being the only non-County or educational members. After various discussions on other aspects of the school building, Mr Davies was asked to outline the proposal we had prepared and it was listened to attentively with the odd murmur or two of approval. Discussion took place on various details of the requirements and there was not a voice of dissent.

I could hardly contain myself. Was no-one going to object or put some spanner in the works? It seemed not, and hardly daring to breathe I realised that everyone thought it an excellent idea. We were actually going to get our theatre and the County and local Council were going to pay for it! Unbelievable!

Suddenly, one man asked permission to speak and this was granted. He said that before a final decision was taken at County level he would like to make clear when this new theatre would be available for local use outside the school's requirements. I thought all this would have been discussed before the meeting and as Mr Davies and I listened carefully to the oration my stomach began to churn once more. Apparently, the new theatre would be available only after 5.00pm Mondays to Fridays, at weekends during term time, rarely in the half-terms because of caretaking and cleaning difficulties but often in the school holidays although all maintenance would have to be specially arranged.

This was USELESS.

Anyone who has put on a show or a concert, however small, knows that there are vital and numerous tasks to be done before the event. To mount a show there was scenery to be set, lighting to be rigged, costumes to be hung, props to be delivered etc etc – the time available would make it impossible for local societies to mount anything. As for making the holidays available, that was hopeless. All amateurs had the same problem – the holiday periods were often the most impossible time to produce shows.

I left that meeting thanking everyone for their courtesy, refusing to show my disbelief but inwardly seething and once again bitterly disappointed. On the way home Mr Davies asked me if I thought it was worth going ahead despite the restrictions. I said no. My view was that both the County and the Local Authority would be wasting money. The time restrictions would make it a white elephant and the school would have a space which would be perfect for the pupils but which would sit idle for many hours in the year.

So that was the end of that – another couple of years' work – and for nothing.

We had our little adventures at The Moorings.

One young couple who booked in advance had told us

proudly that they were spending their wedding night at our guest house and we were rather excited to have our first honeymoon couple. We gave them the very best room, a pretty double at the front of the house, and when we served early morning tea (or rather when John did) the next day I put a single rose in a vase on their tray and made it look very special with white linen traycloth and our prettiest china.

John duly knocked on the door at the bidden time and was asked to come in.

He tried but the door handle appeared to be stuck.

He tried again but to no avail.

"I'm frightfully sorry, sir, but I cannot open the door."

Mumblings from inside the room and then the husband said "Oh it's my fault, I locked the door, hang on a moment."

John could hear our very old fashioned and unused bolt being grappled with. It would not budge. Both men on both sides of the door tried their hardest but with no result. Our first honeymoon couple and they were locked in the bedroom!

There was no one better than John in a crisis. He told the bride and groom that he would have to get a ladder up to the window and get the bolt off from the inside. In those days we had no keys to the rooms and the bolts on the doors had never been used. There was only one solution – remove the bolt from the inside. John gave me the tea tray, went outside, fetched the ladder and duly climbed up to the first floor of The Moorings. At least they were expecting him by this time and amid much laughter he climbed through the window with his tools and removed the offending bolt.

We don't think they ever forgot their first married morning – we certainly did not and as soon as our first honeymoon couple left all remaining doors were checked.

About two years after Hugh Barty-King and I had started T.H.I.S. a Sevenoaks resident by the name of Reg Quinnell had begun a campaign for a community centre in the St John's area of the town.

Reg was as passionate about the centre as I was about the theatre and we met and talked over each other's projects. Reg was adamant that the residents in the northern end of Sevenoaks, many of whom were less affluent and therefore less mobile than others, needed a decent hall with small rooms for meetings etc. The community centre project ran almost parallel to ours but community centres had at that time a national body with all the influence and experience that that brings. After our disappointment over the Drill Hall and the further blow about the drama studio in the school, Reg and I agreed that if either one of us found a piece of land the two groups would discuss it to see whether an advantage could be obtained by sharing a site.

Life remained hectic, various sites were suggested over the years but each was turned down for very practical reasons although I spent years on research, seeking planning permission, building permission etc but all in vain. I continued to hold meetings to 'rally the troops' every time somewhere possible was suggested but for very sound reasons no site was appropriate. Everyone thought I had a bee in my bonnet and very very few believed my vision would ever become reality.

I had great highs and great lows. How I would have loved to discuss all this with my father – he would have so enjoyed the continuous tussle.

By this time (1973) we had extended our guest house, turned it into a proper but small hotel and added more bedrooms. Accommodation was still at a premium in Sevenoaks and friends of ours who had a very successful hotel in North London had warned us that our worst problem would be staff.

How right they were.

We decided that as we now provided dinner in the evenings we would have to have a cook – not a chef, a cook. We neither wanted nor could afford ostentation – we just needed an excellent cook for a small family hotel.

Having been warned about the vagaries of catering staff, I decided to take a crash course at the Cordon Bleu School in Marylebone. It was for only one term, once a week in the afternoon. I was quite a reasonable amateur cook, I loved preparing food and entertaining but I had no professional expertise and needed to learn a few tricks of the trade if things went wrong.

The course was wonderful. One teacher to four pupils and each week we cooked a four-course meal – one course per pupil. At the end of each session we each took home our cooked course and the day I carried home Pheasant Cordon Bleu in the train it was exquisite watching the natural British reserve crumbling as noses began to twitch with the delicious smells emanating from the bag on the luggage rack. Our particular tutor was superb and, as I was the only one of our four who genuinely needed the lessons and was not just trying to fill in my boring day, we built a very good rapport between us and she took a great deal of trouble to give me as many tips as she could. I loved every minute. It cheered us no end the day she had a failure with a chocolate mousse and showed us what to do to retrieve it! I learned a great deal and felt more confident should anything ever go wrong.

In 1973 my mother died. She had been ill for some time and spent the last few months of her life in Bradbourne Park Nursing Home. She adored the children, loved the excitement of the hotel and every day I used to collect her around 3pm and bring her home until the middle of the evening.

I sat with her that last evening. When I walked into her room that day she smiled, said my name then dropped off to sleep. The Sister explained that she no longer knew I was there but she kept moving and half speaking and I just could not bring myself to leave her. What if she suddenly realised I had gone? I sat with her for about five hours until she died and did not for one moment regret staying although she had no idea I was there. It was the first time I had seen anyone die.

There was little sleep that night. However prepared you are for your mother's death, it leaves a great, gaping hole.

In 1974 John and I applied for and won a grant from the

Government which helped a little towards extending and improving the hotel. The process was mind boggling. I am sure if we had had any idea how difficult it would be to apply and then succeed, we would never have tried.

The rules and regulations were complicated to say the least. In our innocence and enthusiasm we simply applied, put ourselves through the hoop to achieve what was required by a midnight deadline date of 31st March and breathed a huge sigh of relief when it was all over. It was frightening and, just like show business, the finishing touches of paint and door handles were being put in place as the clock crept towards that midnight deadline. The hotel was completely refurbished and we decided to have an official opening. The new evening cook, who had been with us for some weeks, worked almost all night with me in the kitchen and we prepared a lavish feast for about 300 guests. It was huge fun and very exciting.

Our opening day was an enormous success. Sevenoaks had a new hotel.

About three weeks after the opening I decided that I must have my hair permed. In the 70's a perm for my type of hair took almost three and a half hours and it had not been possible to fit one in whilst running the business. Now we had a cook who was familiar with our new kitchen I felt I could go out quite happily from about 3 o'clock and not be back until the dinners were well under way. The day before the perm we had discussed the menus in detail, I made sure that cook knew where everything was and trotted off happily for my hair appointment.

Bliss to have a few hours to myself – perm or no perm – and I relaxed happily. It was a real treat. John would be at home when the boys came in, he would open the bar for our guests and take the orders for dinner – nine were already booked from that morning. I arrived home around 6.15, noticed that John had a bar full of people, checked that everything was alright with the boys and went straight to the kitchen.

Not a soul in sight . . .

The menu was still sitting in the middle of the kitchen table, nothing had been touched, nothing was switched on. My stomach did another of its, by now, customary flips! Where was she? Where was my cook who had told me to enjoy my hairdo and not worry about a thing? I turned everything on then tried to extricate John from the bar. We had a number of men from a management course at The Marley Tile Company staying with us and a sprinkling of tourists. John pretended he was bringing me a 'consolonte' (a drink for the kitchen staff) and said that by the time he had realised cook had not shown up he was busy serving drinks, doing reception and had not been able to get to the phone. He did not want to let our guests know there was a problem and he had just been praying I would not be too late.

There was no time to lose and definitely no time to find out what was the matter with cook. I had never worked so hard and so fast in my life.

The menu had to be changed slightly as there was no time to prepare our 'special'. I settled for dover soles, fillet steaks, scampi, omelettes – all food which could be cooked to order. By now 16 people had ordered dinner.

There was no time to be frightened and anyway we needed all the business we could get. Kim, aged 16, often waited at table for us and he was warned of the problem. Noel, 15, was enlisted to make the prawn cocktails (the boys were mean prawn cock-tail makers!). The boys were angels and as soon as John had an empty bar he set to as well.

That was one of the most hair-raising experiences in my life (and me with a new perm!). I had had no conception of the mental strain involved when you are being paid for what you have cooked, but from that evening I understood why chefs are so often uptight and temperamental.

By 10 o'clock that evening I felt as though I had been put through a mangle. Totally exhausted, unable to eat, I suddenly realised that I had done it with only the family's help. No-one had complained or even realised there was a problem. Three cheers for the crash course!

From that day we did not hear one word from the cook. We telephoned her house (I was convinced something terrible must have happened) and were told that she had gone to the doctor with pains in her fingers. I would like to have given her pains somewhere else! She did not write or telephone to apologise and from that moment I did all the cooking myself. Our friends had been right – staff would be the greatest problem.

For the next two years we walked a financial tightrope. Business was excellent most of the time but our prices were low and the boys were growing up with all the expense that that entails. There was never enough time and the theatre campaign slipped well into the background.

Reg Quinnell was still beavering away for his dream community centre. He worked desperately hard but had great difficulty in persuading anyone in authority that his was a serious effort. He needed credibility and a bit more bite to his fundraising. I offered help in whatever way I could and we had quite some success in raising small amounts of cash towards the centre when it was eventually built. According to Reg the fact that I was helping in some small way gave their group more clout and I was delighted to be able to assist.

At last a site became available for the community centre and it was exactly where they wanted it. At Bat and Ball, right in the heart of the community and within walking distance of so much housing. The National Association of Community Centres was able to help and Reg was delighted that all that hard work and patience had paid off.

The site was very large, almost two acres, far more than the centre would occupy, and Reg kept his promise and suggested that if the theatre could use part of it he would be more than happy.

OFF I GO AGAIN . . . Everything went into gear once more. The documents were raked out, societies were urged to commit themselves to using a theatre on that site if it became available, meetings were once again arranged in our newly built conference room in the garden at The Moorings and plans were drawn up for a purpose-built theatre.

The excitement was intense but there were still hurdles to overcome – namely planning consent. This time however that did not seem insurmountable – there was already planning permission for a community centre with ample parking. I wrote to HRH Prince Charles to ask for his support. The reply from his aide was polite but not quite what I would liked to have heard. The Prince wished me every success with my quest for a theatre but explained that it was not possible for him to help as I was still seeking planning permission.

We went through the usual routine – endless discussions about finance, planning the building, the exterior design, public lavatories, public kitchens. I really believed that this time we were in with a really good chance. I knew from my research that many local people thought a theatre at Bat and Ball would be a bad idea (not the right location) but my instinct was that once it was there, with adequate parking and an attractive building, the inclination to be snobbish about its position would disappear.

Once again I was to be bitterly disappointed.

The Kent County Council refused planning consent for a theatre on the grounds of the public danger on the main road from a large number of cars leaving the car park. Although they had granted permission for the community centre and even though the local police had not been consulted (I know because I checked) it was turned down on grounds of traffic danger. I could not believe it – all the work and time – and again for what? Reg Quinnell was disappointed for me too but I could not help but be delighted for him and all his helpers. They had achieved their goal – wonderful.

It took me a few more months to bounce back and once again I decided to continue with my campaign for a theatre. This meant that I would have to leave my friends at the community centre to carry on by themselves. Reg understood completely. He knew my passion was still a theatre for Sevenoaks and with my family and business commitments it was quite impossible

The Family

Right
Taking the air at Folkestone: Father, Mother, me and baby brother Alan.

Far right and clockwise
Posing for the camera: Mother's sister Ellen (nicknamed Bubby).

My handsome soldier brothers: Ronald, Norman and Laurence.

Below
Our beloved home: Sharsted, Kippington Road, Sevenoaks 1948.

The Glamour of it all!

Right
The Sharsted Players in its entirety: Christine Reidemeister, Geoffrey Blackwood, Jenny Evans, Laurie Gavin, Jill Davies, Tony Durrant, Jim Holmes-Higgins, Rodney Crouch, Alison Reidemeister, Leslie Sayers, me, Paul Clark and Judy Dill.

Left, centre
Me and Rodney Crouch – Looks scared, don't he?

Right, top centre
Freezing fairies at an outdoor performance of *A Midsummer Night's Dream* at St Hilary's School.

Right, lower centre
Me and John Norman in *The Heiress* – wasn't he gorgeous?

Below
Glamorous nights with The Sevenoaks Singers: Andrew Hills, far left, and me, fourth from left holding our mascot.

Fond Memories

Sevenoaks Players in *HMS Pinafore* at the Drill Hall – is the orchestra being sea sick?

That fateful show – *Patience,* of all things. Drill Hall, 1966.

There was no-one madder! Sir Despard and Mad Margaret (Tony Branson and me) in Sevenoaks Players' *Ruddigore.*

Where did you get that hat? Richard House and myself in *Angels in Love* by Sevenoaks Players in the Cornwall Hall, Sevenoaks.

Marriage Of Mr. D. G. J. Durdant-Hollamby and Miss M. A. Gavin

At St. Mary's Church, Kippington, on Saturday, the marriage took place between Mr. Dudley Graham John Durdant-Hollamby, second son of the late Mr. and Mrs. R. C. Durdant-Hollamby, formerly of Tunbridge Wells and Richmond, Surrey, and Miss Margaret Anne Gavin, only daughter of Mr. and Mrs. W. H. Gavin, "Eastlands." 91, Court Lane, Dulwich Village, S.E., and formerly of Sevenoaks.

The bride was in a classical bag and shoes.

The best man was Mr. B. Scott.

Officiating at the choral service were the Venerable Archdeacon William J. Gray (retired), formerly Vicar of Kippington, and Canon J. F. Thornhill. The organist was Mr. E. Hudson and the hymns were "O Worship The King" and "Lord Of All Hopefulness." The singing was led by the Kippington church choir and members of the Sevenoaks Singers.

After the service the bridal party and their 100 guests

Our Wedding Day

The Bridal Party walk from the church to the reception – mine is the best looking!

St Mary's Church, Kippington, Sevenoaks 1956.

style gown of ivory duchesse satin, gathered on the hips and falling into a full train. Her head-dress was a small coronet of artificial orange-blossom with a full length tulle veil, and her bouquet was of lilies of the valley and white rosebuds, interspersed with tiny loops of white ribbon. She wore a single row of pearls.

Miss Gavin was given away by her father and attended by six bridesmaids: Miss Judy Dill (chief bridesmaid), Miss Brenda Vokins, Miss Patricia Davies, Miss Muriel Stanton, Miss Jennifer Dill and Miss Jane Thornhill. They wore full length dresses each in a different pastel shade of nylon organza over taffeta, with head-dresses, gloves and shoes to match. Each carried a spray of sweet peas.

The bride's mother was in a deep blue two-piece, with white fleck and French blue hat and gloves, navy blue walked across the road from the church to the grounds of Churchill Court, where the reception was held in a lovely setting, with the church towering in the background. The guests were received near the marquee which had been erected.

Later Mr. and Mrs. Durdant-Hollamby left for their honeymoon which is being spent in Monte Carlo, the bride travelling in a buff silk dress, matching fitted coat, and a lilac and mauve hat with matching gloves and buff shoes. Their future home will be at 11, Broadwater Down, Tunbridge Wells.

The bride has many social connections in Sevenoaks. She is a founder member of the female section of St. Mary's Church choir, and of the Sharsted players. She is also a member of the Sevenoaks Singers and the Sevenoaks Players. The bridegroom is a member of Knole Park Golf Club.

Family Business

Noel's birthplace –
opposite Knole.
Tinley House Cafe,
Upper High Street,
Sevenoaks.

I'll tell you a story –
our three sons, Barry,
Kim and Noel.

'In which we
served. . .'
The Moorings,
Hitchen Hatch Lane,
Sevenoaks.

Three henchmen
stand guard – Jeremy
Brett with the boys at
The Moorings.

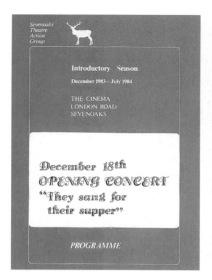

Sevenoaks
Theatre
Action
Group

Introductory Season

December 1983—July 1984

THE CINEMA
LONDON ROAD
SEVENOAKS

December 18th
OPENING CONCERT
"They sang for
their supper"

PROGRAMME

Opening Night

Above: The programme cover of the opening show, 18 December 1983.

'Oh dear, can't have *that*' with Ian Wood two hours before the opening.

Right: Our first logo.

Below: The Ace Film Centre as it was when we opened – soon to become The Stag Theatre.

Sitting in the front row trying to look warm – some familiar faces on Opening Night.

*Sevenoaks
Theatre
Action
Group*

Sevenoaks Theatre
Action Group Ltd (STAG)
The Cinema
London Road
Sevenoaks
Kent

Fund Raising

We've struck oil! – presentation of a cheque from Mobil, 1984.

Oh boy, another cheque – Peter Othick, the man from TVS, me, Maria Strother Smith, Ian Wood and Rod Nipper, 1984.

Fun-loving fund raisers: Heather Brown with some of those who raised £30 each.

Fund-Raising – continued

Christmas Fairs raised much needed funds – and our Santa is having a *very* Happy Christmas! (Gloria Hunniford, Patrick Harper and happy songsters).

We 'doubled' our money – the presentation of the ABSA Award. Patrick Pascall, the man from Mazda, Richard Luce and me.

We did it all for this – the auditorium seen from the stage – but we didn't own the piano.

for me to be involved in what would now become a very active and large organisation.

I was truly thrilled for Reg, I guessed how euphoric he must feel and it gave me more encouragement to carry on with my little cause.

My disappointment over this latest set-back went much deeper than I realised. It really began to seem that Sevenoaks did not want or need a theatre, and yet the feeling of not giving up stayed with me – why I don't really know. I did have a passionate outburst. At home in the garden one autumn day I collected up almost all the paperwork Hugh and I had amassed, plus all that which had followed, and had a giant bonfire.

The three boys thought I had gone mad because I danced round that fire shouting that I would never again do anything for Sevenoaks. I really enjoyed watching those papers burn. I did keep one or two so I obviously had a sneaky feeling that I might need them at some time and I have them to this day.

It gave me the opportunity to get the frustration out of my system and I felt much better for it.

The Big C

John and I decided that in 1975 we could afford a fortnight's holiday. The boys were then 18, 17 and 15 and we knew we were reaching the time when family holidays would cease to appeal. We chose Jamaica, but in August when it was at its cheapest (and hottest). To our disappointment Kim decided that he did not really want to come away with us – the delights of independence beckoned for him and we were not altogether surprised. My younger brother Alan joined us and good friends of ours, John and Vera Edwards, agreed with pleasure to run the hotel for us.

In March of that year I had a medical for an insurance policy which was essential to our mortgage. I passed with flying colours. No surprise to me.

We booked our holiday in Jamaica and got on with the business of running a very small but busy hotel.

Shopping for some holiday clothes in June I noticed a small bump. Right at the cleavage point but nearer my left breast than my right it looked as though it was going to become a boil.

Life continued to be extremely busy, the lump did not appear to be doing anything, certainly not coming to a head as I had expected and I was a little puzzled but not alarmed.

We had a wonderful, wonderful holiday. Our villa was at the edge of the Caribbean, there were three staff on duty, we had a private pool and apart from Noel and Barry both being stung badly on the foot by sea urchins Jamaica was everything we had imagined and much, much more. The gardener's friend had worked for Noel Coward and towards the end of our holiday we were taken up to the Master's magnificent villa overlooking the bay. It was very thrilling to be in the great man's house.

We returned after our fortnight very tanned, very fit and very happy. There was no time for jet-lag. Our friends had to leave as soon as we arrived back so even after a nine-hour flight we had to get straight back into work and start looking after our guests once again.

My little lump, though beautifully tanned, had grown slightly larger and one night in November John said he thought I ought to have it checked out. At that time the national press was filled with articles urging women to check their breasts and stories of breast cancer were everywhere. I knew it did not apply to me but decided it would be sensible to see my doctor.

I had been a patient of Dr Jennifer Daniel since before Barry was born and we had an excellent rapport. She had watched us bring up the children, seen them and me through chicken pox and mumps and was a real family friend. She suggested that I see a consultant as soon as possible although she was very optimistic because my lump was very visible and had not been there when I had my medical in March.

I was referred to a Mr Walker-Brash about whom I knew nothing. I visited him in his consulting room and he too was optimistic. I remember lying on the narrow white bed whilst he stood at the far end.

"Oh, yes" he said "I can see it from here." My stomach churned.

"What does that mean?" I asked terrified of what his answer might be.

"That's a good sign" he replied. "If it's something more serious it's often not so visible as that."

He drained the fluid from the cyst, explained it might well fill up again as they often do and said that if that happened he would see me in six weeks' time (early February). I felt quite euphoric. My lump had disappeared, the prognosis was very optimistic and arriving home at 4 o'clock in the afternoon I had a large brandy with John – I was so relieved.

The ensuing weeks were like being on a roller coaster. Guests to look after, Christmas to prepare for and a determination to avoid thinking the worst and certainly not worrying the family. All the time a small part of my brain would keep asking "what if?"

The cyst did fill up again. A second appointment was kept with Mr Walker-Brash and a time arranged for me to spend the day at Sevenoaks Hospital to have the offending lump removed.

It was like living with a time-bomb. One minute I was convinced everything would be fine, the next I was secretly planning how on earth we could run the hotel with its busy schedule and how the family would cope. The days passed like a bad dream but I was still very optimistic. I had never smoked, I drank very little and I felt as fit as a flea. It simply could not be possible.

The removal of the cyst was on a Friday. By 5 o'clock I was home, very relieved, a little wobbly and very slightly sore. We all sort of celebrated. That was that and thank goodness it was all over. The telephone was hot that evening with family and close friends ringing to see that all had gone well. It had and I put it out of my mind.

The next morning, Saturday, I was back on duty, feeling fine and so relieved it was all behind me. At about ll o'clock the telephone rang at reception and I answered it.

"Mrs Durdant-Hollamby?"

"Yes" I replied.

"It's Monro Walker-Brash".

I reached rapidly for the hotel diary. The name did not mean anything to me and I scanned the pages quickly to find the booking. I simply could not recall a guest of that name – perhaps John had made the reservation whilst I was at the hospital.

"Mrs Durdant-Hollamby, it's Monro Walker-Brash. I'm really so sorry to tell you but your biopsy has shown a malignant tumour and I want you to come into Orpington Hospital tomorrow for surgery."

I still did not grasp what he was saying and was sure that we had not booked in this Mr Walker-Brash – oh dear, I hoped we had not made a double booking.

He repeated what he had said and I suddenly understood. I called John and asked him to take the details – I was no longer capable.

Poor John. He was devastated. When he came off the phone and found me the floodgates had opened and I was inconsolable. Cancer. That most terrifying of illnesses and I had it. I don't remember how the three boys spent that day. I know they kept coming in to see me but I could hardly stop crying.

Our very dear friend Joyce Haslehurst was called and rapid arrangements were made for her to help John run the hotel. In one tiny compartment of my mind I had actually thought about the bookings and arrangements and had looked in the diary to see how best things might be covered should the worst happen, and we managed to arrange adequate help. I was expected to be in hospital for about ten days and would then need convalescence. I decided to convalesce at home where I would be happiest.

The next forty-eight hours were ghastly. I was frightened but 'being brave' for the family. I really had no idea about the operation. I only knew it was called a mastectomy and meant the complete removal of my left breast.

John and I slept little on that Saturday night. John was wonderfully positive, at least on the surface, and kept assuring me that everything would be fine. He made a good job of not letting me see how scared he was.

The boys were very quiet the next morning but also very optimistic.

Dorothy Parrott, very well known in Sevenoaks for her marvellous work in the community and secretary of The Sevenoaks Players, delivered the prettiest pink bed cape for me and that sent me off into more floods of tears. Dorothy was a very good friend of the family and had telephoned on the Saturday evening to find out how my little op had gone on the Friday. She was extremely distressed when John told her the news.

We had tried not to tell all and sundry – after all we had a business to run and could not afford to lose bookings – but news travels fast, particularly bad news, and the telephone was soon red hot. I simply could not speak to anyone. I was so upset and sympathy merely opened the floodgates.

John delivered me to Orpington Hospital and with stiff upper lips we parted, John giving me a huge wink and a thumbs up at the door of the ward. I had never felt so alone or so frightened. I hated hospitals. I unpacked, undressed and took out my book.

I tried to read but it was useless. I went down to the loo at the far end of the ward and inside were two patients who hurriedly hid their hands behind their backs as I entered.

"Thank Gawd for that, we thought you was the nurse."

Two cigarettes came out from behind two backs and they puffed away.

"You're new aren't you. Whatch'you in for, love?"

For some reason I couldn't help thinking of the tales my aunt used to tell me about bodysnatchers and I felt the goose-bumps rising. It nearly choked me to say "a mastectomy" because it was the first time I had said it aloud to anyone. To make matters worse they did not know what it was and I had to explain, my voice getting quieter and quieter.

"Oh bad luck dear and you're not that old are you?"

I went back to my bed and started on the hospital routine. I was told that my operation was to be at 8.30 next morning. I lay awake most of the night just waiting for it to be over.

The National Health Service was going through a very difficult time in 1976 and with the backlog of patients it was quite common to be kept waiting for one's operation long after the appointed time. I was fortunate. Mr Walker-Brash was to operate and I went down to theatre on cue. The operation was successfully carried out and I was back in the ward as expected.

It was then that everything started to go wrong.

Blissfully unaware of what was happening, I haemorrhaged violently and almost lost my life. I was readmitted to theatre where the wound was reopened, padded and then restitched. A blood transfusion was essential and had to be rapid. Intensive care was the next port of call and I was there for 24 hours.

I remained oblivious to all of this and so, by a freak, did John for a period of that day. He had been told to call the hospital around noon to find out how I was. This he did. When he gave his name they said "Mrs Durdant-Hollamby is still down in the theatre. Please ring in about two hours." It never crossed his mind that anything was wrong as everyone was aware that operations were getting delayed and he quite naturally assumed that I had been kept waiting.

In the meantime his brother Nigel and wife Brenda had phoned him to ask about me and he relayed the hospital's explanation to them. They agreed to speak again as soon as John had some news. However my sister-in-law became very concerned as time went on and asked Nigel to ring the hospital himself – they did not want to scare John unnecessarily but Brenda felt uncomfortable.

Nigel telephoned, introduced himself as Mr Durdant-Hollamby and the nurse at once explained that there was a crisis and could he please come to the hospital as soon as possible. The hospital thought he was John.

My first coherent thought after the operation was that I was definitely dead. I awoke in a pale green room, totally silent. Opposite me, propped up in a bed with bandages round his chest and one arm, was a black man.

Even in 1976 mixed wards were only being whispered about and I was utterly convinced that I had left the world. I was blissfully ignorant of the fact that I was in Intensive Care.

My next bout of consciousness showed me John, holding my hand very tightly and telling me that everything was fine and it was time I came round.

I did as I was bid.

The next day I was returned to my ward. What a difference. I had been in a very big room with total strangers on the Sunday and suddenly I was swamped with affection, little visits from mobile patients who were complete strangers, all telling the same story. They were so pleased I had made it.

At one point I awoke to find a large, wonderful black nurse standing at the end of my bed.

"Ah honey, ah sho' am glad to see you alive today. We pumped so much blood into you yesterday but ah thought you was a goner."

I could hardly believe my ears and my brain began to tell me that all was not nearly as well as I had thought. My blood pressure was taken every ten minutes for the next 24 hours so sleep was out of the question. I was not in pain but very uncomfortable and very thirsty and allowed only sips of water. How I longed for a cup of tea.

John visited me that evening and we just held hands – I couldn't bear to let go of him. He was cheerful, positive as ever, said that the boys were fine and the hotel was running like clockwork. All I had to do was get well and come home. He must have been in turmoil. He loathed hospitals, hated tubes and drips and I had it all, but he did not give a hint of his horror of the situation or the agony he had been through the day before.

When I look back and remember the attention I had from

every member of staff on the National Health Service I realise that in an emergency they are specially wonderful.

Early next morning I was seen by Mr Walker-Brash. He spent a long time with me explaining exactly what had happened, how successful and complete the operation had been so far as the malignant tumour was concerned and how very sorry he was that there had been problems after the operation. He told me everything. It hit me in one great wave – how lucky I was still to be alive. The cancer suddenly did not seem nearly so important – I had almost died but I was alive – that was what was important! Mr Walker-Brash was very kind and promised to visit me next day when he knew I would have many more questions to ask.

Two beds away from me was a very elderly lady, very very thin but very bright and chatty. Everyone called her 'gran' which she hated and she kept shouting questions to me and anyone else who appeared in the ward. The next day the flowers, cards and letters started arriving in their dozens and I was overwhelmed by messages of love and goodwill from relations and friends.

'Gran' was moved a bed nearer.

" 'Ere" she shouted," you royalty or somefin? I never seen so many bloody flowers!"

I felt royal, or at least very special – it was impossible not to with all the good wishes that came pouring in.

I made slow but steady progress. I was so happy to be alive that I did not worry about the agonisingly painful trips to the bathroom holding a bottle or the first venture in a bath of blissful warm water where I was terrified I would slip. None of it mattered. Mr Walker-Brash eventually convinced me that he had removed all the malignant tumour and that was all I cared about for the moment.

The Sister in charge of our ward was wonderful – a proper hospital Sister. Very precise, calm, ordered and efficient. Most of her staff were in complete awe of her. I loved her. She always made time to explain things to me. The evening before I was due to have my forty-two stitches removed she sat by my bed and asked me what was wrong. I had to admit to her that I was sick with fright. The thought of a young nurse pulling away at those stitches gave me nightmares. I was sure I would haemorrhage again and could think of nothing else.

My other bogey was that I had not yet seen what had been done to me and had no inclination whatsoever to look. She understood this fear but was surprised how scared I was about the stitches. I had to admit that my imagination was running riot after all the panic. I was terrified I would rip open again and end up back in the theatre.

Sister was wonderful. She realised my absolute terror and asked if it would make any difference if she removed the stitches. I was so relieved. The job was done next morning with the utmost skill and care and although some really pulled I trusted her completely. When it was over she said "How about taking a look?"

"Do I have to?"

"My dear, you'll have to sometime. You may as well get it over now, while I'm here."

I took my very first look. For the first time I forgot how fortunate I was to be alive.

Sister brought me a very strong, sweet cup of tea.

My progress from then on was rapid. I was eventually transferred to Sevenoaks Hospital (so much easier for family visiting) and I spent most of my time laughing with the sheer relief of it all being over. Mr Walker-Brash continued to be supportive and very understanding.

I had no idea how anyone could ever look normal again after such an operation and during one visit Mr Walker-Brash explained that the fitter would come to see me and arrange an appointment at Outpatients when I had left the hospital. He said very firmly that he wanted me to continue to wear the style of clothes I had always worn and that he would do everything in his power to ensure that my shape and size would not be any different. I listened to all this without any real understanding but at least with hope. I secretly felt deformed – but I was in his hands.

Maybe I'm odd, but in a ward with a number of other ladies, many of whose visitors I recognised as they were Sevenoaks residents, I didn't actually go out of my way to broadcast what operation I had had. Many of the patients were elderly and cancer was still one of those things you didn't say out loud; there were also two other patients who had had mastectomies by other surgeons and when the place was full of visitors I tried to keep my medical condition to myself. I don't know why I bothered. One afternoon when our friend David visited me with an armful of flowers a man walked down the ward calling out "Mrs Durdant-Hollamby? Mastectomy?"

I wished I could hide. David excused himself rapidly and left. It was the surgical fitter come to make an appointment for me in a few weeks time. Hospital is no place to be bashful.

My recovery was remarkable. I convalesced at home and was so very fortunate to need no further treatment of any kind. Of the three breast cancer patients in Sevenoaks Hospital I was the only one to survive – there but for the grace of God . . .

For my first appointment with the fitter I was very nervous. My scar was healing well and I was rather anxious to get back into some nice clothes and wear a bra once more. My turn arrived and I went into the fitting room. He greeted me cheerfully, opened a small box and threw something soft and squidgy across the room to me. I gasped but caught it (all those years behind the wicket had not been in vain) and found myself holding my new left breast.

What a shock. To this day I have not been able to decide whether this was done deliberately or whether he really was an insensitive man – I hope it was the former.

My next visit to Mr Walker-Brash was very reassuring. He carried out his medical examination and was delighted with my progress. Then we had the modelling bit.

He made me stand wearing my close fitting jumper and my

new prosthesis (the new breast) and walked all round me studying me from all angles. Not quite the casting couch but I couldn't help imagining the similarities! He expressed complete satisfaction and I will never forget what comfort that gave me. He had said he would be really critical and he was. He said I looked NORMAL. Heaven. I walked out from his room that day feeling very tall and grinning inanely at everyone.

It is of no use whatsoever to pretend that then it is all over, because it never is. The first cold, the first pain, all the fear comes back, but it fades as the years pass. My main trouble was that I felt like a leper. I felt unclean, as though I shouldn't kiss or hug people in case they were afraid they would catch something. For a long time I felt that everyone looked at my left breast at the moment of meeting. Ridiculous, I know, but I couldn't help it.

I was soon back into running the hotel with John and although I felt extremely fit and well John was very frightened that I would overdo it, the cancer would recur and he would get all the blame for letting me work.

We had in the last three years acquired two semi-detached cottages next to The Moorings and had let them as self-catering units. They were extremely successful and in our minds we had both thought that we would be leaving each son a piece of property. It was no good. Although I needed to be active there was no doubt that for me the pleasure had gone out of receiving strangers at the front door. In a business where you must want to see new people the sparkle for me had gone.

We did not rush into a decision but there was no doubt that we had only one route to follow – sell The Moorings and the two cottages.

During all this time the theatre project had been very much on the back burner. The most important thing I learned from being so ill was to get my priorities right – about the greatest lesson in life one can be taught – and for that I was very grateful.

59

We eventually sold the business, the house in which Barry had been born and which held so many happy memories for us despite the exceptionally hard work. We could hardly have picked a worse time. Property was almost at rock bottom in the second half of the seventies and we were left with virtually nothing after settling our mortgage. Never mind. I was continuing to remain very well and that was all we cared about. The boys were happy and we decided to rent a house until we made up our minds about the future. For a few months I went back to being a temporary secretary in London and John took a local retail job.

Two of my brothers, Norman and Laurie, were still running The Marlborough Textile Co (by now moved to Riverhead) and at their suggestion and with their encouragement we opened a small curtain business attached to their company. The Unique Curtain Service.

About two years after our move in 1977 I was shopping in Tesco's one day when I met Rosemary Tammidge, wife of the then headmaster at Sevenoaks School.

"Oh Maggie, I'm glad I've met you. Do you know a man called John Marsh? He is an architect, passionate about the theatre, and wants to know why on earth Sevenoaks doesn't have one of its own!"

I told Rosemary I would be very happy to tell him. We were introduced and John Marsh said he would help me campaign for a theatre in Sevenoaks. He had recently moved into the Weald and could not believe the dearth of performing space in such a town.

So I was off again.

Curtain Up on S.T.A.G.

Through a business contact, John Marsh met Ian Wood of Fraser Wood Properties. Ian was a long-standing acquaintance of mine and had known about my campaign for a theatre. He had even helped me raise money for the Community Centre. He was a stalwart of the Sevenoaks Rugby Club and very supportive of my idea for a theatre.

In 1981 the Sevenoaks District Council announced that Old Post Office Yard, a large piece of land behind the Sevenoaks Chronicle in the High Street, was to become available. The brief was for a supermarket and community use. John Marsh was to be the architect for Fraser Wood's submission to the Council and it was suggested by John and Ian Wood that the theatre project should be the community use.

Was I interested? Need they ask? We had by this time formed a small group of seven very committed people, one of whom was my youngest son Barry. He had suggested our new name – Sevenoaks Theatre Action Group – S.T.A.G. Clever – with our proximity to Knole Park and its herds, and cheap – only four letters to print.

We formed a Board of Directors, registered as a charity, and threw ourselves wholeheartedly into preparing our part of the brief. This opportunity was a real one. We still had no cash – we would worry about that later. Competition for the site was fierce but we were the ones with the community use sitting there all ready to go, well nearly all ready.

Fraser Wood were acting for the Waitrose Supermarket and suddenly we were catapulted into dealing with big business. The John Lewis partnership had an excellent reputation and although a large number of local residents felt that one supermarket (Tesco) in the town was quite enough, the Waitrose group had obviously done their research and were keen to be in the High Street.

The months of preparation were both agonising and exciting. This really was the chance of a lifetime. In all the preceding years it had seemed beyond my wildest dreams that we would ever have a building near the town centre. The possibility of being just off the High Street was almost unbelievable.

The Sevenoaks Theatre Action Group still had no money. I had not budged about refusing to collect funds when there was no definite site, so we relied completely on Fraser Wood Properties and John Marsh for all the work which had to go into preparing detailed plans for the theatre. Fraser Wood, with Ian at its head and another partner John Morrison, were exceptionally generous. We all knew Waitrose would not get the site without a community use, but even so the expenditure on fees of all kinds was enormous. We simply could not have been part of that submission without a lot of help.

Our plans were straightforward. We wanted a purpose-built theatre seating about 300 with a proper stage, dressing rooms, bar and foyer. Nothing over-elaborate but a building that would work as a theatre – not a multi-purpose hall. Somewhere that would be available for all amateurs with facilities that would encourage them to improve their standards and thereby increase their audiences. How it was to be run had not crossed our minds except that we probably thought we would need to employ a person to take bookings. Huh! How naïve can one be!

As we neared the date of Presentation to the Council the excitement mounted. On 5th January 1982 we gathered at the Council Offices for the Meeting. I was the S.T.A.G. representative, John Marsh the architect for the whole project, Ian Wood and John Morrison represented Fraser Wood Properties and there were various personnel from the John Lewis Partnership.

The Presentation went well. The scheme looked superb and plans were displayed in the Council Chamber. We had all played our part. As the meeting went on it was clear that not every Councillor was in favour. One or two expressed strong misgivings about a second supermarket but the theatre itself came in for little criticism. I had to put our case, the same old story for the umpteenth time – how it was now seventeen years from the beginning of my campaign and what a wonderful opportun-ity this presented to the district of Sevenoaks.

The vote was taken – we held our breath – planning permission was GRANTED! *After seventeen years and I don't know how many sites!*

I couldn't take it in. I rang my husband who was sitting waiting at the end of the phone and told him the great news – he was delighted.

"We're going out to celebrate, is that alright?" I asked.

"Of course. Have one for me."

Ian, John Morrison, John Marsh and I went to the Prince of Wales in the Weald where Ian knew the proprietor very well. We had the most glorious steaks and champagne. What excitement. Euphoria had taken over although the others warned me that the problems were only just beginning. I didn't care. We had planning permission for a theatre. Whatever cloud is above nine I was on it!

Ian allowed me to drive him home in his Porsche and that car felt as though it had wings. Hubbards Hill had never felt so flat!

We made the headlines. The local press was full of the news that week.

Not everyone was pleased of course. Within a matter of weeks we learned that a local businessman and a traffic expert, Mr Terry and Mr Ogilvie respectively, were to take the Sevenoaks District Council to the High Court over its planning decision. More nail biting and more waiting but not for too long.

On Saturday 17th July 1982 the front page of the *Sevenoaks Chronicle* carried the result we had been longing for. Nothing stood in our way now, except that S.T.A.G. had to do a precise exercise on finance and get its skates on about practically every detail.

John Marsh and I headed our small group of supporters (Barry, Jill Hargreaves-Browne, Peter Strother Smith, Peter Scoble and Sally). We got down to the serious business of money

– how much we would need, how we would raise it and by when. These questions had lurked in the background before – we had had no site – but suddenly they were real and serious. Economics compelled the developers into urgent action to build the supermarket and Waitrose announced that it would be open for Christmas – that was only five months away! The bulldozers were to move in on site at the beginning of August. When you had money you could move fast.

S.T.A.G. decided, after much heart-searching, to employ a professional fund-raiser. None of us had either the expertise or the time to do the job properly and, although we had very conflicting thoughts about fund-raisers in general, we felt we had no choice.

We spent a long time conducting interviews and finally settled on a man called Red Mullen. He knew we were starting from a cashless base but was prepared to start research into whether or not Sevenoaks would be interested in funding a theatre. It was a mistake. He employed a Dutch girl to do the initial probing, and I well remember a telephone call one day from my valued friend, Sir Desmond Heap.

"My dear Margaret, I don't know quite what you have in mind, but if you are trying to encourage people to donate towards a theatre in Sevenoaks, I do think it would be a very sound idea if you used someone who could speak the Queen's English!" He was absolutely right. We knew instantly that that reaction would not help us at all. Various other aspects of the fund-raising probe were also worrying us. Before we went in too deep with Mr Mullen we decided not to use him any more.

By now it was August – a difficult month to achieve anything. Most of my colleagues were away for longish periods so it was hard to get opinions on decisions. To my surprise the front page of the *Sevenoaks Chronicle* on 7th August carried the headline 'CINEMA SHOCK'. This was not totally unexpected as cinemas generally were going through a very bad period. Films were not good, video mania was sweeping the country and our local cinema had been run on a shoe-string for some time and was quite run down. It was not a place that people looked forward to visiting. The press announcement stated that it would close in October and the cinema staff launched a petition to save it and their jobs. The response was good with over 3000 signatures.

One Friday, later that month, I received a telephone call asking me if S.T.A.G. would be interested in taking over the lease of the cinema building from The Rank Organisation. You could have knocked me down with the proverbial feather. Years before I had written to the chairman of Rank asking him to let me know if the cinema site would ever become available and had received a very firm reply in the negative. Here was I, in August 1982, having taken seventeen years to get planning permission for a theatre, and now, like the London bus, two sites came along almost at once. It was extraordinary.

A decision could not be delayed. If I did not give at least an indication of my interest within two or three days the site would be offered on the open market (it would very probably be bought by a competitive supermarket!). Added to that, Waitrose would have to be informed rapidly of any sudden decision not to build a theatre on the Old Post Office Yard site and the Council would have to be consulted about the 'community use' which had been such an integral part of the planning brief.

The dilemma was not helped by the fact that S.T.A.G. had no money – what on earth were we to do? I spent the whole weekend weighing up the pros and cons and trying to seek help from my colleagues – those who were not away were very happy to leave the decision to me.

The pros semed quite clear:

1. The cinema building existed and had four walls and a roof neither of which was in immediate danger of parting company with the other.
2. The public was used to going to that building for its entertainment in Sevenoaks.
3. We would not have to start from scratch.
4. The cinema had a very large car park (South Park) which

was leased to the District Council and maintained by them.

5. Expecting members of the same household on the same night to go to two different buildings for their entertainment with the complications of where to leave the car etc

seemed to me to be asking for trouble.

6. We would have somewhere to perform much sooner than anticipated.

So did the cons:

1. We had no money to purchase the lease – not a penny.
2. I couldn't think of another!

The pros won. I decided that, if it was possible, we would change horses mid stream. That decision had to be communicated very rapidly to everyone concerned. Any hesitation and the wheels would have been set in motion to market the lease of the cinema commercially. On the following Tuesday, my heart in my mouth, I expressed a serious interest in the lease of the cinema.

During the spring and summer months of 1982 the main item of news in the local paper had been the public's disquiet over the lack of parking in the town. The District Council was under enormous pressure to do something about it and I was very aware of this. I felt convinced the Council would wish to retain the South Park car park. If S.T.A.G. did not take the lease of the cinema building it was more than likely that the site would go on the open market and the public car park would be lost for ever.

I began negotiations with the then Chief Executive of the District Council. John Marsh and Ian Wood by this time knew and agreed with my decision to relinquish our piece of land next to Waitrose. Ian explained that it would have to be done legally and to the complete satisfaction of all concerned.

I fully agreed and held urgent meetings with the District Council's Chief Executive. To my delight within two or three weeks the Council agreed that S.T.A.G. could relinquish its planning permission on the Waitrose site with no penalty to the supermarket as the community user was to be housed elsewhere. Since the Rank Organisation had offered the lease to S.T.A.G. and not the Council, it was agreed that we would conduct the negotiations. The District Council would provide the money for the purchase on condition that the South Park car park remained in their hands. It was all moving so fast.

By now the contractors were already busy on the Old Post Office Yard site and legal documents were prepared rapidly for us to relinquish all rights to our piece of land next to Waitrose. Our S.T.A.G. member, Peter Scoble, one of our seven volunteers, was our solicitor and he had a very hard time for a few weeks.

Ian Wood, John Marsh and I did all the negotiating. The Rank negotiators were experienced, hard-nosed business men who nonetheless seemed to empathise with this mad woman who had taken seventeen years to get planning permission for a theatre. The dynamics of the team worked well and we successfully negotiated an excellent price – £250,000 for a fifty year lease of the whole site including the car park. We were exalted. Ian's personal property expertise and the soundings which he had taken all underlined that we had done a very good deal.

The District Council was delighted with the outcome and after many more rapid meetings it was agreed that, whilst they would advance the whole sum in order for the purchase to go ahead, S.T.A.G. must promise to repay £100,000 within a year as its part of the bargain.

For us, an enormous sum of money – we still had nothing but optimism – but it seemed well within our reach, bearing in mind that we would have a building and that we would be able to raise funds from the public and societies once they realised there really was a site with a future. Compared to the figures we had been 'guessing' to start from scratch on the Waitrose site, £100,000 seemed very attainable.

The Chief Executive of the Council, a very positive man called Peter Hodgson, with his Council's authority, recommended that the lease should be purchased by the District Council on S.T.A.G.'s behalf, instead of giving S.T.A.G. the money to make the purchase. Mr Hodgson explained to me that it would cause great complications and delay if the Council loaned the money to S.T.A.G., and he also questioned me about whether we wanted to 'run a car park'. I had no idea, I knew nothing about public car parks. When he explained just how much they cost to run and maintain I decided that the last thing S.T.A.G. wanted was the responsibility of the car park. It seemed to me completely logical for the Council to purchase the lease, retain their hold on the car park and grant S.T.A.G. a sub-lease.

We had by now given up all rights to the site next to Waitrose. That decision had had to be made final because the contractors would be able to modify the car park for the supermarket if the theatre was not to occupy part of the land. I had no doubts in my mind that we had made the correct decision but I felt very slightly in limbo. I immediately informed Rank that the purchase of the lease could go ahead as the District Council had agreed to fund it on our behalf. On a Friday in late August of that year I received a call from a senior executive of Rank informing me that the company had changed their mind about the sale.

I could not believe my ears.

According to one of the negotiators with whom we had had dealings, Rank were convinced that once the District Council had purchased the lease at the very reasonable price S.T.A.G. had negotiated, it would give S.T.A.G. the boot, do what it wanted with the site and the theatre project would be lost. That thought had never crossed our minds.

No amount of disbelief on my part made any difference – Rank had made up their mind. They were determined that a Local Authority was not going to reap the benefit of such a purchase which the organisation would then have to explain away to their shareholders. Neither were they keen to see our long haul completely scuppered.

Very noble – but what was I meant to do now? My feelings as

I put down the telephone that Friday morning were indescrib-able. Seventeen years, then planning permission on one site, then two sites in the offing and now – nothing.

It was August still and my nearest colleagues were away. Again everything had gone horribly wrong. I telephoned Mr Hodgson and told him of Rank's decision. He was very upset, extremely taken aback and assured me with real conviction that the Council had no such evil intentions. He tried to speak to Rank that afternoon but of course the person he wanted had left for the weekend. There was nothing more to be done before Monday – except THINK. And think I did – about nothing else practically the whole weekend.

The Council could not change its decision and, even if it did, Rank would still suspect that it would kick S.T.A.G. out once the lease had been purchased. S.T.A.G. had no access to that kind of money at all and I genuinely believed that we were completely safe with the Council. We had built a good trust between our-selves, the Officers and Members of the Council. I could not be persuaded that it had all come about simply to give the Council the power and the desire to see our project completely under-mined.

My conviction did not waver. Somehow I had to persuade Rank to complete the sale of the lease. There was only one card left up my sleeve and many times over that weekend I veered between using it – or doing nothing. If I did nothing I would wonder for the rest of my life whether I could have saved the project. After all this time and effort I would never forgive myself if I looked back and said "if only . . . "

I was not very used to dealing with big business people, but I decided that my last course of action would be to present myself at the Rank Organisation's Head Office by 8 o'clock on the Monday morning and ask to see Mr Ron Hunter the Managing Director. Only my husband John knew of my plan – I hadn't the courage to tell anyone else.

I drove to Whyteleafe and arrived just after 7.45am. I hoped to take Mr Hunter by surprise. I was slightly startled to find the car park quite full and the whole building looking busy. I didn't care how long I had to wait but I was determined not to leave the building until I had seen him. I announced myself to the receptionist who informed me he was already at his desk.

Much to my surprise he saw me at once, and was courtesy itself. For forty-five minutes I gave him the full history of the theatre campaign, what it meant to us to get within striking distance of having a building at last and how convinced I was that the Council had no intention of pulling the rug from under our feet. I could after all tell only the truth and I believed with all my heart and instincts that this was the case. He listened, asked questions, shook his head occasionally and the interview came to an end. I was completely drained.

He promised he would come to a decision by the Wednesday of that week. I drove home knowing that the next two days would be agonising.

Wednesday came and went – no phone call.

By mid-day on Thursday I was perplexed – should I ring him and perhaps make him more irritated – or should I leave it? By 3pm I could stand it no longer. I telephoned his office only to be told that he was out at a meeting and would not be returning that day.

Friday morning – still nothing. By mid-day I had had enough. I rang again and was told that Mr Hunter was at lunch and would be back during the afternoon. I made quite sure the secretary had my name and number. At about 3.30 when I was just on the point of bursting Mr Hunter telephoned. He apologised for keeping me in suspense: he had discussed the matter at length with his fellow directors and they had all decided Rank would sell its lease to the District Council. It had worked. My last resort. I was so relieved for we had come so close to losing everything.

The phone was red-hot that evening. There was now so much to do and so much excitement. John and the boys were very very pleased. Shopping that Saturday morning I kept finding an excuse to have yet another look at the cinema in the London

SEVENOAKS

CHRONICLE

SATURDAY, JULY 16, 1983

ACE DEAL GIVES STAG A THEATRE

Cinema parking secure after secret meetings

by Keith Blackmore

THE main auditorium of the Ace Film Centre is to become a theatre for Sevenoaks.

This was ensured on Thursday when Sevenoaks District Council, Sevenoaks Theatre Action Group and the Rank Organisation agreed a deal after months of secret negotiations.

The anbitious plan will not only provide a long-sought town theatre but will also preserve the two smaller cinema screens and secure the long-term future of the 150 space car park behind the building.

A further 40 parking spaces will be provided on the Old Post Office Yard site previously earmarked for a STAG theatre.

The whole deal is likely to be seen as a remarkable coup for the district council which has, at a stroke, provided more parking and a ready-built theatre while preserving the threatened cinema and its vital car park.

LATE SCORE

The deal became public on Wednesday night after months of talks involving the district council, STAG, Fraser Wood Properties, Rank and the management of Ace.

There was a late scare when a rival group bid higher for the site but it is believed that Rank will honour the original agreement.

In a joint statement STAG and the district council announced that contracts had been exchanged to acquire the lease of the cinema building and car park from the Rank Organisation.

AT the time of going to press, Mrs Margaret Durdant-Hollamby rang the Chronicle to say that final negotiatons were being held up by a technical hitch involving the Rank Organisation. She was fairly confident, however, that it would not affect the deal between STAG and Sevenoaks District Council.

"The initiative for this scheme has come from STAG but has been made possible only by the financial help and willingness of the district council. Full co-operation has been given to STAG by all concerned including the Fraser Wood Properties and the directors of Ace."

It is hoped that the building will house a fully equipped theatre, two cinemas, a rehearsal hall dressing rooms and ample catering space.

A meeting of the council planning studies committee was held in private on Wednesday evening to approve the change of use of part of the Old Post Office Yard where an extra 39 parking spaces will occupy the site previously set aside for a STAG theatre.

Negotiations had to be kept secret to avoid rival bids from property developers who might have seen the Ace site as a valuable acquisition.

The car park behind the cinema has only been on short term lease to the council and was under a similar threat.

What is now the Ace Film Centre nearly closed last year before being taken over and although the new management has proved successful the cinema's long term future always seemed in doubt.

The deal brings much closer the prospect of a town theatre.

STALWART IS STAGGERED!

THE news that screen one of the Ace Film Centre is to become a town theatre provides a climax to the 17 year personal campaign of STAG chairman Margaret Durdant-Hollamby.

Little more than a year ago Mrs Durdant-Hollamby and other members of STAG were rejoicing that they had acquired a site on the Old Post Office Yard.

Now they actually have a building to make plans for. "It's unbelievable," said Mrs Durant-Hollamby this week. "It has been such a long time but this will mean an enormous amount for Sevenoaks because until now we have had nothing to offer people from the young upwards.

"We're going to bring entertainment of a much higher standard to the town and we intend to present evenings that will give people something worth getting up from the television to come and see."

Although STAG was founded only in 1981 Mrs Durdant-Hollamby has been campaigning for a theatre capable of staging professional entertainment for 17 years.

Once the deal is completed STAG hopes to erect a temporary stage to provide a six-month introductory period to show what can be achieved. There will be celebrity concerts and the best amateur theatrical groups performing.

The theatre will then be closed for full scale and permanent alterations.

It is not expected that it will be re-opened before the autumn of 1984 at the earliest.

The two cinema screens will be sound proofed and enlarged and will continue to be run by Ace. The theatre will be run by an arts director responsible to a management committee comprising members of STAG and representatives of other organisations.

It is hoped that if blockbusting films like ET are released in what are dead periods for the theatre they will be shown in the larger auditorium.

"We think it is very important to keep the cinema alive in Sevenoaks and we hope this ensures it has a much longer life," said Mrs Durdant-Hollamby.

Road – not the prettiest architecture but to me it looked wonderful.

Documents were drawn up, the lease was purchased from The Rank Organisation, the magnificent seven were gradually returning from their holidays and it was all go. The District Council after deliberation agreed to give S.T.A.G. a six month licence from the day we took over the building and everything was planned around that framework.

We had no money, we were very soon to have a building in which to operate and there was a mountain of organising to do. By now it was September 1983.

The lawyers were doing their bit, meetings took place constantly with either the S.T.A.G. Board or the District Council and I don't believe my feet touched the ground for several weeks.

My husband was wonderful, the greatest support, always encouraging me and spurring me on. He was really excited by the whole idea and was so very pleased that it was really going to happen. I was able to share all my ups and downs with him and that made it so enjoyable and exciting. He never begrudged my time or my enthusiasm for the project. He had never had time for people who started things and then gave up, so I had the right person to support me in all my wild ideas. I made sure family life did not become unbearable as a result of all the comings and goings – the boys were now all into their 20's and leading independent lives although we had the bonus of them living at home. My values were well and truly established – the family always came first. It made me extremely well-organised, an excellent planner of time and a juggler beyond belief!

Early that September Ian Wood rang me with a staggering offer. Deacons, the building contractors for Waitrose, would now reap the benefit of financial saving as the planned car park for the supermarket and theatre could now be simplified with S.T.A.G. no longer to occupy part of the site. They (Deacons) were prepared to build a stage for S.T.A.G. in the cinema building with the money which they would save. I was astonished and accepted the offer at once!

It was at this point that S.T.A.G. lost its dots! When Barry had first come up with the acronym, 'action groups' had been the flavour of the month. In the ensuing period public attitudes had changed – action groups now carried with them all the wrong associations. We had our four letters – STAG – and we all agreed that it would be an ideal name for the time being – The Stag Theatre.

It is important at this point to describe the Cinema. It had been built in 1937 in the days when Odeon built a traditional picture house in nine months flat. It seated around 900 people in total with a large stalls area and a dress circle holding approximately 450 people. It had ornate plaster work typical of the thirties and in its heyday had been a very comfortable and sumptuous cinema with a restaurant on the first floor. My father had often taken us as a family so I knew the building quite well. A Saturday treat was either to see a film in the afternoon followed by high-tea in the restaurant, or early supper in the restaurant followed by a film in the evening. In those days a full pro-gramme – the feature film, the news, often cartoons and a 'B' film – meant you really had your money's worth.

In the early 1970's it had been converted into a triple cinema by The Rank Organisation. It was only the second building they had converted and they had spent as little as possible on doing so. As a result it was very different. It had two small screens downstairs (the back of the old stalls area) and one large screen which served the old dress circle. Between the front row of the dress circle and the large screen was a gaping hole (the front rows of the old stalls no longer in situ).

Rank had expected to run a disco from the building – discos were all the fashion and Sevenoaks did not have one. As a result of anticipating planning consent they had ripped out all the front stalls leaving concrete and holes. Their plan had been to have a large disco behind the two screens on the ground floor and hopefully to keep rather late hours. However on the south-west side of the South Park car park behind the cinema was the boundary for Rockdale Old People's Home, where flats were being built for Sennockians to spend their glorious golden years in reasonable peace and quiet. There was no way that planning permission was going to be given for a discotheque ending sometimes at 2.00am in a building so close to elderly residents. A car park was one thing – a disco something else.

John Marsh, Ian Wood and I decided we would have to form a small group responsible solely for the building. There was talk of consultants of all sorts which made me fearful. I had heard from other theatres of vast sums of money being spent on consultants often with disastrous results, but I was no expert. Professionals had to be called in for certain things and both John and Ian were marvellous at getting us good advice from colleagues and friends. Their knowledge and experience too were invaluable. However we still had no money and anyone who needed prompt payment for their services was warned of our position. They either joined us or not!

We kept the press informed of our progress. One day they asked to take a photograph on the roof of the cinema with me, Ian Wood, John Marsh and members of the Lawrence Hewitt Partnership, Consulting Engineers. The picture appeared in the *Sevenoaks Chronicle* on the Thursday of that week and the following evening there was to be a meeting of our 'building group' in my house. We had by this time co-opted Frank Marshall (well known in Sevenoaks for his association with the Sevenoaks Preservation Society) and John Stillwell, one of our many young supporters who was passionate about lighting theatres.

On the Thursday that the picture of me on the roof appeared in the paper I had a telephone call from a complete stranger. He said he had been watching my progress over the years, was utterly astonished that I had succeeded in finding a building for a theatre and wished to warn me that once consultants got hold of the project money would disappear like water and did I know what I was up against? I said it was extremely nice of him to take the trouble to pick up the phone and asked if he knew anything about theatres? He explained that he had been involved with them in some shape or form almost all of his working life and that he was also passionate about cinema. I couldn't resist the opportunity. Here was someone telling me of all the pitfalls – so why didn't he come and help? I told him about the Building Committee Meeting the next evening and cheekily suggested he came and spoke about his anxieties and offered his experience. To my amazement he agreed to do so.

His name was Francis Price and he quickly became an integral part of our team.

Over the next few weeks we spent hours and hours discussing and debating the design and workings of the theatre in the dress circle of the cinema.

John Marsh came up with his idea of building an enormous stage (two storeys high) over the derelict stalls which would reach the front row balcony wall of the dress circle, thus creating two floors below it, the ground floor to be used as dressing rooms and the middle floor as the orchestra pit. An orchestra pit – wow – who had ever thought we would have an orchestra pit?

We sat evening after evening in our overcoats, muffled to the ear-lobes in a perishing cold dress circle (there had been no heating for weeks and the building had got really cold and damp) planning our theatre. Only our excitement kept us warm. Debate raged about all sorts of things – we were certainly not unanimous about many of the details (particularly about employing endless consultants!) but basically we were all working to the same end – a theatre for Sevenoaks.

The design of the stage was wonderfully simple. A 60 by 30 foot platform from wall to wall with no impediments – bliss. Amazingly, Deacons generously agreed to build the whole thing – foundations, steel girders and with a weight limit of, I believe, two elephants! There was only one snag. Deacons were to be finished on the Waitrose site by the week before Christmas and the offer to build our stage was on condition that I was prepared to accept it being built whilst their men were on site over the road – in other words in twelve weeks' time!

I was thrilled and terrified at one and the same time. Twelve weeks?!? That meant we would have a performance space before Christmas and nothing to put in it! I planned my campaign. I had to try to encourage the amateur societies to use the theatre for performances if the Council intended to give us a licence for six months. And now that licence would start from December 1983.

The majority of groups had already planned their performances for the next six months period and it was no easy task to persuade them to give Stag a try. I attended committee meetings telling them how wonderful it would be and nudging them to come off the fence and have faith! I arranged meetings with conductors on site who were mostly terrified by this woman who insisted on showing them the gaping holes and tried to get them to walk across steel girders to show them what the stage would be like when finished.

Anyone I could persuade to come in and have a look got a tour of the site. Almost enough to put anyone off. Dust was everywhere, large workmen were swearing and cursing as they bashed huge pieces of iron into the girders, the route was tortuous to say the least and there was that awful smell of damp dilapidation everywhere. But to me it was magic. Somehow I must have transmitted my enthusiasm to the visitors and very, very cautiously I began to put together a fragile programme of events which might (if it was finished) happen on that stage.

The District Council had by now agreed formally on a six months' licence. They did not really believe that Sevenoaks needed a theatre and this period would prove it once and for all. If we failed everyone came out of it with pride, having tried. Only Stag would have egg on its face. I had no intention of washing egg off my face in public.

We would have a stage two storeys high which meant that there would have to be temporary scaffolding staircases to get to

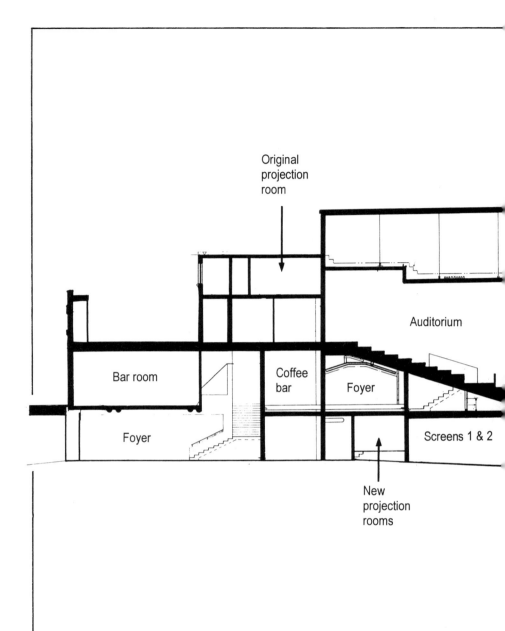

Original projection room

Auditorium

Bar room

Coffee bar

Foyer

Foyer

Screens 1 & 2

New projection rooms

Drawing based on those supplied to Sevenoaks District Council by Maunsell Consulting Engineers, reproduced by permission.

The Stag Theatre, Sevenoaks

A section through the building
from front to back as it was
for our opening in December 1983.
See endpapers for architect's
floor plans, which include the
Plaza Suite, drawn in March 1993.

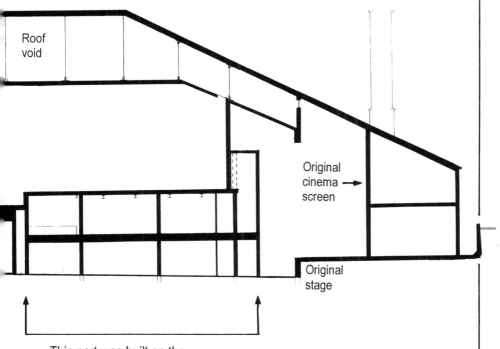

Roof
void

Original
cinema →
screen

Original
stage

This part was built on the
original floor of the cinema
stalls (note the slope) to
provide a new stage on top,
an orchestra pit and storage
immediately below and
dressing rooms on the lowest
level.

the lower floors. The agreement was that these staircases could remain only for the six month period – if there was to be a con tinuation after that those two staircases would have to be replaced by proper fire-resistant stairways. We accepted all these conditions. We all knew we had no choice and we had overcome far worse hurdles than a couple of staircases.

My next meeting with the Chief Executive of the District Council left me somewhat breathless.

"When are you going to have your opening night?" he asked.

"My what?" I replied somewhat aghast.

"Well, the Council has made all this possible. I think it would be nice to have a public thank you."

I sat there looking confident whilst my brain was whirling. He was quite right. There must be the correct recognition – it was just that it was about three months too early in my book. I had not even moved through the dust and rubble in my mind to consider an actual performance and an opening. I told him to leave it with me. I went home and had another think!

Meetings like that do concentrate the mind. That evening I ran through every possibility. The idea of a public thank you to the District Council was exactly right. They had made the impossible possible and deserved a high-profile sign of our gratitude. I decided that there would be an Invitation Only opening but that we would launch Stag with a performance (heaven knows what!) to which only our closest supporters and all the District Council Staff and Members would be invited. Black tie – well, it was easy thus far – but what next?

We were still penniless, although supporters at least were multiplying. The evening itself had to be exciting, glamorous and show-bizzie. It had also to have a middle-of-the-road appeal that would please an audience consisting largely of people who would probably never choose to go to live theatre.

Quite simple really! My thoughts turned to two very talented cousins who had moved to Sevenoaks in 1967. Robert Elliott and Robert Jones. Robert Elliott with his sister Joyce Hayhurst had established a very popular hair salon in Seal and was an excellent pianist and singer. His cousin Robert Jones was the Head of Music at Wildernesse School for Boys and had the most glorious tenor voice. He had been a fellow actor in *The Queen and the Welshman* when we performed it at Wildernesse School and I admired and respected both men greatly. They also understood show business.

John and I had been friends with them for years – from the first day Robert Elliott moved into Sevenoaks. We had had musical evenings with them, business discussions and social occasions, and we had a genuine rapport. They had been aware of my campaign for a theatre but had not seriously believed it would happen. They both had friends who were professional singers and I knew they would understand my dilemma. I rang Robert Jones and said "h-e-l-p!" We met to talk about this Opening and gradually the shape of the evening began to evolve.

Remember, no funds to spare, but it had to show the place off and be entertaining. A tall order. We came up with the idea of *They Sang for their Supper*. The plot was that Robert Jones would appear to have entertained some of his friends to a sumptuous banquet (notice the past tense so only the remnants of a banquet were left on the table!). In their turn his guests had to entertain him. A feast of glorious but popular music to please all ears(!) sung by artists with gorgeous voices. Nothing too solemn, too long or too boring, spiced with a little humour and looking as eye-catching as possible.

Ah, there was the rub. How do you make an enormous stage look eye-catching without a fairy godmother? I left Robert to contact his friends and one or two local favourites and to organise the precise programme. There were other more pressing problems to be solved in relation to the construction work and my time would have to be spent on more practical and pressing matters. The stage was taking shape. It was like Phoenix rising from the ashes. There was no money for acoustic experts or the like but we did employ professionals to hang our lighting rig. Scaffolding bars were suspended from the roof, it was crucial that the technical aspect of these was absolutely correct and there was huge excitement when proper 'riggers' appeared and swung like monkeys about the auditorium.

The generosity of Ian Wood during this period cannot be applauded enough. Without him Stag would not be there today.

Dust was everywhere. The old plush seats were filthy, the carpets were appalling (some from 1937), it was icily cold but it was magical. We were going to have a theatre at last and in not too many weeks' time!

Nevertheless there were some horrendous construction problems during those twelve weeks. A main drain was found to be completely blocked with concrete and there was no time to repair it. This meant that the dressing room area would have to work on two loos only – very little when you realise a show might have a cast of sixty. The facilities were exceptionally basic, very cold, no showers and water which occasionally ran warm if you were very lucky. We were really doing pioneering work. Those who were courageous enough to book the theatre in those early days, with no real proof of what it would be like, were pioneers in the true sense of the word. The phrase 'suffering for one's art' could almost have been invented here.

I was deeply involved in every aspect of the building work, though naturally when serious building problems arose I relied heavily on the advice of Ian, John and Francis. We had some nightmares.

The Opening date was now decided – Sunday 18th December 1983 (my mother's birthday: I hoped she would be looking on) and there was so much to be achieved before then. It really did not seem possible that the building would be habitable for the public by that date but as news spread about our progress more and more volunteers offered their help.

The front of the building was unattractive architecturally, the inside of the lower foyer looked gloomy and unwelcoming – not at all like a theatre – and the original restaurant upstairs had been turned into a Video Games Room by one of the cinema owners. These walls had been painted black to create the necessary atmosphere and the ceilings were orange and purple! So tasteful! So Sennockian! The surfaces of most of the walls in the building were 'pebbled' and in places great patches of this pebbling were torn off. There were cracks in the ceiling, flaking plaster and a general air of desolation. When the games machines were taken out the effect was extraordinary – a vast black cavern but with a parquet floor which we discovered under all the grime. The room had to be painted somehow – it was to be our new bar – a major source of income. However we had no actual bar and nothing with which to buy one, so my next job was to call up Charrington's Brewery with whom John and I had had contact during our years at The Moorings.

Many people had told me the brewers would be falling over themselves to help create new business in a theatre – perhaps I should have let those people try for me . . .

Charringtons were interested but their requirements nearly sent me crazy. They wanted me to tell them on paper how much barrelage (how much what?) I would sell over the next year and what I expected the turnover to be! How on earth was I to know that? No-one had ever run a theatre with a bar in Sevenoaks before, I had never run one in my whole life, time was desperately short and I had no crystal ball. I made guesses and told them they were guesses.

After about two weeks they telephoned me to say they were prepared to help fund the purchase of a second-hand bar which was redundant in a golf club somewhere in deepest Sussex provided we collected and installed it. They would supply us with the technical back-up for serving beer from the keg and a certain amount of stock. In those days they also gave us ashtrays, trays, beer mats – all advertising their company – and we were restricted to selling their beer.

It was much better than nothing although I had foolishly imagined they would be delighted to build us an attractive bar especially as John and I had been customers of theirs for about fifteen years at the hotel. Heigh-ho, never look a gift horse in the mouth unless the vet's right behind you. We accepted the offer and one filthy Saturday morning Peter Strother Smith, Ian Wood and four or five other strong men set off with Peter's trailer to dismantle the bar and bring it back to Stag. What a marathon task that was. They were all very wet and cold by the time they arrived back in Sevenoaks with the spoils but they set to and constructed that bar with only a few hitches and things not quite fitting where they ought. The wood at least was very good and over that weekend the old restaurant acquired a bar counter and some shelves behind it and the room started to take on a different aspect.

We set about painting the walls and very high ceiling. Long ladders were begged and borrowed and every day somebody with a few spare hours would be up those treads painting their bit of the bar. We had to put planks between the ladders because of the scope of the room and I became quite good at balancing. The painting was extremely hard work. The pebbling absorbed paint like a sponge and supplies of paint were limited – we still had no cash and had begged paint from a local businessman. There was the greatest feeling of excitement and anticipation about the place and the volunteers who gave up their time to be handy men and women must never be forgotten – without their enthusiasm and commitment we would not have opened.

So, we had a bar room with a second-hand bar, no longer with black walls (mushroom!) but not a stick of furniture and a filthy floor. We put out an appeal for furniture and what a wonderful assortment appeared. There was a handsome 1930's dining table about six foot long, one or two folding tables, trestle tables and white garden furniture, all donated by kind supporters. I cannot pretend the bar looked enticing but patrons could at least sit down!

It was during this frantic, hectic run-up that I was approached by the mother of a young man asking whether I could use his enthusiasm and practical help in the building. Barbara Nipper explained that her son was strong, passionate about the technical side of theatres and available. I jumped at the offer and

Rod Nipper came to see me. He was immediately enthusiastic and excited about the project. We also came into his life at a time when his direction was not clear so we felt it was meant to be. He was extremely practical, loved DIY, was prepared to work long and hard for nothing, like the rest of us, and he poured his heart and soul into the project – just the sort of person we needed. Anyone who offered help was welcomed with open arms, and the enthusiasm and joy of volunteers was breath-taking and quite amazing. People gave up their Saturdays and Sundays to help us and the camaraderie was heart-warming.

The lighting rig was now in position but apart from a very few lanterns we had begged or borrowed the rig looked pretty bare. We knew we would just have to hire every time we had a show – we had no cash to buy up front. We would simply have to make sure we sold enough tickets to pay for the hire of lights afterwards.

During the next few weeks every corner of that building needed work on it. I visited areas hitherto unexplored in my sheltered upbringing. I had not, for example, previously spent any time in a Gents Lavatory, but I soon learned a great deal about them. The urinals (another new word for my vocabulary) were original – and looked it. Beautifully tiled but neglected, with walls that contained some pretty explicit graffiti (an even bigger vocabulary!) but I am ashamed to say not nearly so explicit as that in the Ladies. Shock, horror. Some of that made my eyes open very wide. We were desperately short of time but there was no way we could have an opening night with frocks and chains and let the lady patrons see that stuff. Sevenoaks would have fainted.

We scrubbed with a vengeance. Much ribald comment from the men that girls were pretty, delicate flowers and not sup-posed to know such language. The scrubbing took ages and was not entirely successful. The Ladies had to have one coat of paint to obliterate the obscene words on the doors. My time spent in the Gents was to prove valuable. Whilst ensconced in there wearing overalls and rubber gloves I learned that this particular urinal flushed every twelve minutes – information which was to stand me in good stead in following winters when everything froze up. If I did not hear flushing regularly during the long hours on front-of-house duty in the upper foyer it meant big trouble.

Whilst all this was going on Robert Jones was busy preparing the Gala Opening. We had many conversations which assured me that the programme was well under control. I could relax about the show. All I had to do was work out how I could make a blank stage look stunning with just eight new black masking flats, no furniture and no funds.

There was also the question of a good grand piano. The need for that instrument created quite a problem. 'Burglars – Pianos our speciality' was not yet a heading in the Yellow Pages! Not only was the piano essential – it had to be tuned. There was no major access to the stage in those days except by the scaffolding staircases. If a piano was delivered to the back of the theatre it meant carrying it up two flights of awkward stairs. It would have to come in through the front. The Sevenoaks Music Club very generously loaned us their beautiful grand for the evening on condition that we had it tuned and paid for the cost of the transport to and from the theatre. It was coming only about a quarter of a mile but six men would be needed to deliver it to the front doors, carry it up the main foyer staircase, down the steps through the auditorium and then lift it on to the stage. Again, we had no choice but we had to find the money to do it.

We had made a particular effort to raise one sum of money and that was for the black flats (mentioned above) which would act as masking at either side of the stage. It would have been ridiculous to have had the side internal walls of the building visible and artists entering and exiting in full view of the audience. We knew the flats would be a long-term investment. As we were to have an 'open' stage, ie no front of house curtains (tabs), these flats would have to be made to specific fire regulations and be covered in inherently fireproofed material – we chose black velour. The excitement when they were delivered was almost overwhelming, although this sentiment may be lost on those of a non-theatrical disposition.

The stage was nearing completion, the lighting rig was at least hanging from the ceiling and the place was beginning to take on the atmosphere of a theatre. There was still an enormous amount of work to be done. The Building Inspector paid us regular visits and was always helpful but not optimistic that we would be ready on time. Everyone gave as much time as they could but the size of the project and the details that had to be dealt with were vast and numerous.

The weather was particularly seasonal, the draughts throughout the building felt like gales and, if there was a really torrential rainstorm, water came through the roof onto the stage. It looked as if we were going to have to pray for dry weather before every performance.

As well as everything else, I was trying to put together a pro-gramme which would carry us through our first six months. The amateur input was fairly easy – I either persuaded local groups to put their shows on at Stag, or I failed.

The professional side, however, was a completely different ball-game. I had never booked a professional artist in my life. How did you do it? How did you know what or who Sevenoaks would come to see? Above all how did you pay for them? All these questions and no-one to tell me the answers, so I just got on with it.

Soon I had the date of the Opening, a Carol Concert by the Kemsing Singers and in January a young people's group called Silver Lining (directed by John Marsh) had booked the theatre for a whole week to present *Grease*. My calendar (a home-made wall chart) had one or two spaces filled up already – marvel-lous. I bought a copy of *The Stage*, the newspaper of the enter-tainment industry, and on the penultimate page was an array of artists, their photographs and the telephone numbers of their agents. Would they commit themselves to coming to a new the-atre which was not even finished? Would they demand money in advance? I had not the faintest idea. I only knew that most people needed work and that many artists had a real compassion for anyone who tried to do something for the business – and we really were trying. So I picked up the phone and made the first of hundreds of calls I was to make in the future. The response was extremely encouraging. I explained about the Stag, was completely honest about its lack of experience and money, but my enthusiasm for our project obviously won through because everyone was so helpful. Every artist needed to be paid, but I did get some very special deals and for those I was very grateful.

I managed to book Acker Bilk (I hoped to goodness he had enough supporters in Sevenoaks) and Pam Ayres, then took my courage in both hands and contacted the touring arm of The D'Oyly Carte – Sevenoaks loved Gilbert and Sullivan. The man heading this tour was Kenneth Sandford, a very well known and popular performer with the company. I invited him to see the theatre before he would commit them to a performance and he accepted. He arrived with two colleagues on a very windy day. The inside of the building still looked pretty rough and there were workmen everywhere. The dust was terrible. Hardly conducive to the well-being of singers. We toured the site, me brimming over with enthusiasm and excitement because it really was all happening and the visitors wrapped in their overcoats and clearing their throats constantly.

I took them down to the dressing room area – now a vast open space with some donated mirrors, a few light bulbs and some donated chairs. The only thing going for it was size – one thing I did know was that most theatres had tiny dressing rooms – ours was at least spacious. Mr Sandford was charming but explained that if the company was to come to Sevenoaks the dressing room would have to be divided up physically for the ladies and gentlemen.

I was secretly astonished. In the 1980's the sexes needed to be segregated when changing? Amazing! I said that that should be perfectly possible – I had no idea how – and when I told the three visitors the story of Stag, they were most impressed. They could see the building had huge potential and loved the size of the stage, the acoustic and the auditorium, even looking as it did. They indicated their agreement to perform but said they hoped the dust would be cleared by the time they visited us! The D'Oyly Carte Opera Company coming to Sevenoaks – what a coup.

Time rushed by and during the second week of December I decided that we really had to do something about the seats. They were appalling. We couldn't have an opening with such dirty seats and so much loose dust flying around. Their singers would be choking and our audience would sue for cleaning bills. The contractors were able to use vast sucking machines to remove the dust from their part of the work but there was no time for cosmetics.

Rod Nipper and I put out an appeal to the Girl Guides. We asked if they would come on a Saturday with as many hoovers as they could muster (we did not possess even one at the theatre) to help us clean up the auditorium.

Bless them, they did. What a day that was. We had dozens of girls, not quite so many hoovers and one or two Guide leaders. What we had overlooked, of course, was the fact that the auditorium had no power points for hoovers, we had hardly any junction boxes and most of these hoovers were domestic with normal length leads. It was hilarious. There were Guides, hoover leads, hoovers and Rod Nipper and me all entangled in the auditorium and some Guide leaders in hysterics at our antics. It took us hours. I provided light refreshments, Rod spent all day dashing up and down the different rows of seats untangling leads, Guides and hoovers and by mid-afternoon, exhausted but exhilarated, we had broken the back of the work. The auditorium began to look a little better and those girls did a wonderful job in very frustrating circumstances.

By now invitations had been sent out (in itself quite a task, to draw up a list which would not offend!), replies collated, and it looked as if we would have a full house.

The amount of work still seemed never-ending. I had to order enough, but not too much, for the bar – glasses, optics, water jugs, coffee, disposable coffee cups that did not burn your fingers, milk, sugar, soap, loo rolls, kitchen towels, tea towels, washing-up liquid – the list seemed endless and I blessed my experience at The Moorings. We also needed staff for the Opening and we certainly could not afford to pay anyone. This was the start of our fantastic group of front-of-house volunteers, a group which exists today although some of the faces have changed.

Workmen were still on site but not nearly so many of them. Ian Wood, John Marsh and Francis Price kept a careful watching brief on the construction problems, although they all had full-time jobs themselves, and the local Building Inspector was extremely co-operative and kept us abreast on a daily basis of what still needed to be done.

In the week's run-up to the Opening everyone was at full steam. The adrenalin was flowing and a nucleus of volunteers turned up at all hours to continue with the painting, cleaning, putting in loo rolls and generally trying to make the interior of the building presentable. We had to have a programme for the evening, but could not afford to have it printed, so it was typed and photocopied by some kind soul. The local press agreed to send a photographer. The two Roberts had their friends organised and it was all systems go.

The grand piano had to be delivered on the Saturday for the Sunday performance. Sunday delivery would have cost twice as much. Watching it being carried through the front doors and up and down flights of stairs I began to realise that we were actually near to opening. The removal men did not enjoy this particular job but were impressed by the excitement in the place. We did not even have time to give them a cup of tea.

That Saturday a number of us worked the whole day with hardly a break. There was still so much to do . . . Because we had scaffolding staircases up to the stage at the back of the theatre every joint had to be covered in case anyone cut themselves in the event of an evacuation or even just hurrying. We had found some old carpet underlay down in the old cinema dressing rooms and everyone was tearing it into strips so that each bolt and screw on the staircases would be covered.

There was little sleep that night. Opening day dawned. Today was crunch time.

Dust was back on all surfaces. The Fire Inspector and Building Inspector both arrived about 10.30am with their list of outstanding jobs. They were not encouraging.

"You'll never finish today – there's masses to do."

"We will" we said, "we have to – we open tonight."

We worked so hard all morning, dusting every orifice, ripping up underlay, tidying, painting white lines for safety on stairs, preparing the dressing rooms – a million and one things. At about noon the two inspectors re-appeared. They were able to cross some things off their list. They were sure we would not be ready – we knew we had to be. No-one stopped to eat but sandwiches were passed round as we worked. The Theatre Licence would not be issued (and therefore we could not open) until the list of outstanding jobs had been completed.

We had about four hours left. The tension was electrifying. We became quieter and quieter as we got more tired. My hands looked like nothing on earth – ingrained with dirt and very rough. We meticulously ticked off each job as we completed it.

About 2 o'clock two men appeared in overalls. It was the Fire Inspector and the Building Inspector. We could not believe our eyes. "We're so full of admiration for your guts, we went home, had our lunch and have come back to help."

We were amazed. Amid the smiles, handshakes and hugs, we all set to once again. Those two men were marvellous. They were fresh and of course knew exactly what was required. At 4.45pm precisely I was called into the auditorium.

"The Building Inspector wishes to see you." I creaked up off my knees in the orchestra pit and went into the auditorium. Almost everyone seemed to be standing around. The Building

Inspector came over to me. By this time I was so tired I hardly felt anything.

"Mrs Durdant-Hollamby, I am delighted to hand you your Licence. Our requirements are complete. Congratulations."

Suddenly I was no longer tired. I danced round the aisles shouting "WE CAN OPEN" and everyone was wearily but happily celebrating. We put the finishing touches to the things that needed that final polish and at nearly six o'clock I drove home to have a bath and change, ready to receive the dignitaries and guests who were due at seven. I did not have the luxury of an hour to get ready as I had to be back in the building as quickly as possible to receive the volunteers, make sure the front of house was open and the bar ready. I was back at the theatre by 6.30 – the fastest bath and change in my life. For the first of what would be many, many times, I prepared to open the Stag Theatre to the public.

This Is Your Five Minute Call . . .

My first port of call on arrival was the auditorium. It's hard to describe my feelings. I just stood there and took a deep breath – it suddenly looked like a theatre. All the volunteers had gone, it was very quiet, the stage was enormous and arranged on it was the grand piano and the long trestle table dressed overall in silver satin with our new black velvet flats as the masking down each of the wings. It looked wonderful to me – economic but wonderful!

I wasted no more time dreaming. I could still taste dust but that was too bad. Too late now for anything but opening. *Chains off from all doors, lights switched on, programmes neatly stacked, milk, coffee, sugar, cups all at the ready. Floats for the coffee and the bar. Upstairs to the office, open the ancient and very heavy safe, collect the money, don't leave the keys anywhere for goodness sake, back down again. Put the urn on for coffee (no coffee machines in those early days, we borrowed an urn), check the loos, the fire exits and the auditorium*

– no ladders or bulbs anywhere by mistake! Someone's forgotten their jacket – remove it to the cloakroom and try to remember it later – and there are some sweet papers on the floor – get rid of those.

Even in all the rush I notice how draughty it seems. Check with Rod. Yes, the heating is on, such as it is, and nothing more can be done about it. Can hear voices rising from the dressing rooms practising – what a wonderful sound and how exciting – performers warming up in this theatre! Volunteers begin to arrive and I brief them on their duties. The excitement and nervousness are almost overwhelming. John, Kim, Noel and Barry arrive, all looking very smart, and we await the arrival of one of our Patrons, Sir Desmond Heap, the Chairman of the District Council and the Mayor of Sevenoaks.

Everyone remarked on how calm I looked (!) and many people asked if I had had a nice day. Nice day! If only they knew! I hid my hands behind my back whenever possible, smiled and said the day had been wonderful.

That was the first of many occasions when the public and even some of my friends had not the faintest idea of the panic and problems which had been overcome before they arrived. If you need to exude confidence in what you are doing you do not spill the beans about the worries to all and sundry. That is my belief and has remained so throughout some very turbulent years. Smile and the world smiles with you – how very true.

The dignitaries began to arrive and there was great excitement and anticipation. No-one quite knew what to expect and most seemed amazed at the size of the place. We made everyone feel very welcome. The cheerful volunteers were wonderful and the auditorium filled very rapidly. Everyone was talking about the size of the stage and I took my seat in the middle of the front row (A16) next to Sir Desmond. In order not to upset any precedents John had to sit on the gangway some rows behind – we simply couldn't manage it any other way – but he didn't mind and neither did the three boys.

It was freezing. The draught coming from the stage had to be felt to be believed. It seemed to whistle through everywhere.

The house lights dimmed (goodness, just like a real theatre!)

and onto the stage came Robert Elliott, followed by Robert Jones, Alan Bourlet, Ken Brown, Anna Cooper, Alexandra and Ivan Leigh, Jean Millett, Anne Weller and Nicholas Willmer. The ladies looked gorgeous in very glamorous evening gowns – there was a great contrast between their jewel colours and our black velvet flats.

Robert Jones introduced the performance with pride – the first on the stage at Sevenoaks' new theatre – and so it all began. The voices were superb and the acoustic in the auditorium seemed excellent. Popular arias from opera interwoven with piano solos and duets and humorous songs – a perfect mix. The first part of the concert over, we moved into the bar and foyer. It was very crowded, very noisy (always a good sign) and no ladies had complained about the graffiti! I had eyes everywhere whilst all the time keeping up conversation and answering so many questions from our guests. The other Board members were all doing their stuff and everyone played their part to perfection.

There were no bells to signal the end of the interval – Rod had only a walkie-talkie – so we started to usher everyone back to their seats at the appropriate moment. The second part of the evening was equally delightful and the applause at the end was rapturous. The first real applause at Stag. It sounded glorious. The artists took many bows and when I sensed the applause dying down it was my cue to walk up the central steps onto the stage. We had made it and here we were but even now there was room for one last unforeseen hiccup. As I walked up onto the stage in my new black velvet dress there was a slight murmur from the audience. Not exactly a titter – not as defined as a giggle – but a reaction which, wrapped up as I was in the excitement, I ignored. However, I sensed something, somewhere, was amiss when as I turned to face the audience a similar murmur came from the cast.

I delivered Stag's public thank you to the District Council for 'at last' putting some money into arts in Sevenoaks. I upset one councillor so much by saying 'at last' that I had to write and apologise later to the Chief Executive. I was being honest. I did think it very brave of them and I said so. Oh well.

The applause and cheers at the end of my speech were lovely. To my very great surprise my eldest son Kim appeared from the audience and presented me with a gorgeous bouquet. My family have always been good at keeping secrets and John loved surprises. I didn't know it at the time, but I was about to receive another. Standing there, centre stage, I was the focus of all the attention. Kim leaned over and gave me a kiss. His next seven words knocked me right off my perch:

"Mum, the price tag's on your bum!"

Everyone knew from my instinctive reaction that he had told me and it brought the house down. It was not the price tag for my new dress but a sticky white label which must have been on A16 and which had clung to the velvet of my dress. All dignity gone by this time, tears of laughter pouring down my cheeks, relief, excitement overwhelming me, I succumbed to the happiness and praise which showered down from everywhere.

My fellow directors, all the volunteers back and front of house were so elated – we had pulled it off against all the odds. Stag was really born. The longest gestation period I had ever encountered, and the most difficult birth – but what a result!

Tragedy and Triumph

From that moment Stag became serious business. We were without funds, had a six months licence from the Local Authority in which time we had to prove ourselves to the town, an outstanding debt of £100,000 to that Authority, no full-time staff, and my husband and I were running our small business in Riverhead.

The next two days after the opening, Monday and Tuesday, were kept free from bookings so that the lighting could be altered for the carol concert by the Kemsing Singers on the Wednesday evening. This was our first 'hiring' of the theatre by a local group and it was to be the last event before Christmas so that everyone's efforts could then be concentrated on preparing the theatre for the musical *Grease*.

Volunteers under the encouragement of Rod Nipper had agreed to help with the lighting for the concert and we had a second-hand tower (a tallascope) so that the lighting rig could be reached. Ladders were not satisfactory for two reasons – the height and the fact that every time a crew member wanted to move a light he had to climb down the ladder, move it and then climb back up again. Time-consuming and not altogether safe. Time was of the essence and the two or three young men who were more than delighted to offer their help on this occasion were very experienced at changing the rig at Sevenoaks School's Sackville Theatre.

About the middle of the afternoon on the Tuesday an ambulance went roaring northwards past our business in Riverhead, blue light flashing and siren wailing. I cannot pretend to know why, but I said "please God, don't let that be anyone from Stag."

The thought went almost as fast as it had come, but it surprised and worried me. John was at home doing our books and I arrived back just after five.

I entered the house to find John Marsh and three or four of the company of Silver Lining with John. My heart sank. There had been an accident at the theatre. One of the young men so keen to help us with the lights had fallen from a height of about 15 feet and through the cruellest act of fate had hit his head on the wall as he fell. He was in a critical condition. We were all devastated. The tears were flowing, we all felt empty and shaken up and it was with the greatest difficulty in the world that I had to assume the mantle of leadership at that moment. The young people had to have hope, we all had to pray as hard as we could and we agreed to confer again in the morning when we had more news from the hospital.

When everyone had left I did not know how to live with myself. I had spent all those years badgering away at people so that Sevenoaks could have somewhere for entertainment, somewhere for them to have fun, to enjoy entertaining other people, and what had happened? I might be the reason for a young life to be ruined, perhaps even ended. I was utterly distraught.

John was a tower of strength. We talked about nothing else until the early hours. There was no way I could sleep. My whole being was in that hospital.

What should I do about the carol concert? The accident was nothing to do with the Kemsing Singers. They were very excited (and very brave) to be performing at Stag in its early days and I had arranged to meet them at the stage door (a posh name for a back door at that time) at 8.30am on the following morning (Wednesday), so that they could bring in their rostra and prepare the stage for their concert. That night I went over and over it in my mind.

The temptation never to set foot in that building again was almost overwhelming – but how many people would I be letting down, and should I really admit defeat? I thought of all those who had helped me over the years who would be relying on me to do the right thing. I also knew that there would be some for whom I could never do the right thing again.

I decided to let the concert go ahead. I arrived at the back door at 8.25am to greet the representatives of the Kemsing Singers with my heart very heavy. The Singers' mood that morning could not have been more different from mine. Excitement and anticipation for their first ever concert in the town's new theatre. It was with the greatest sadness and reluctance that I informed their Chairman, Robin Edmunds, and their conductor, Chris Knox-Johnston, of the accident. I did not want to spoil their evening but those two people had to know why I wasn't revelling in their excitement.

I know for a fact that had I not kept that appointment I would not have gone back into that building.

The news from the hospital was not encouraging. Everyone was on tenterhooks and having three sons ourselves our hearts went out to the parents. The young man, Martin, had received a terrible blow to the head and was on a life support machine.

We could not think properly about anything else, but we went through the motions that day. That evening an excited audience of over 200 people arrived for the concert and had a wonderful time. It was very hard greeting people who were congratulating us on our wonderful achievements whilst we felt sick to the stomach. How ghastly life can be – two days before we had all been so full of hope and now . . .

In my heart of hearts I knew Martin would not recover. It was truly a freak accident with the most appalling consequences imaginable and we learned later that week that the life support machine had been switched off. I realised then that there would be inquiries by the police and the Health and Safety Executive. Apart from being absolutely honest about the circumstances it was a situation with which I had never had to deal in my life. I had no idea how harrowing it would be over the next few months, particularly for those people who had been present.

We were questioned individually and as an organisation and after one such session with the police when I was feeling about as low as one can be, the officer present did his best to reassure me. "You must not feel personally responsible. This was an accident which had totally unexpected results. People have fallen fifteen feet before and not even broken their wrist. No-one could have foreseen such an outcome."

It helped a little but it was ages before I could come to terms with it. To this day I cannot see anyone up a tallascope without thinking of Martin. I am always very relieved when the crew member is safely down.

Christmas passed and the arrangement with Silver Lining was that they could rehearse in the theatre during the holidays. They had long, long discussions about whether they should continue with their production of *Grease*. They finally decided that Martin would have wanted them to, that he loved the theatre, so they agreed that the performances would be dedicated to his memory.

It was about the only compromise that could have been reached and I admired their stoicism. It also helped me.

The show was almost a sell-out. Its success was inevitably coloured by what had occurred but the enthusiasm, energy and talent of the young cast helped to lift our spirits during those very dark days. The tears that were shed every night through the triumph of the show and tragedy of the accident further reinforced the adage 'the show must go on', and it did, because the company wanted it to. For Martin.

We had many hard times to face, not least of which would be the Inquest, but each individual felt he or she had done his best for Martin.

The Introductory Season

Somehow I managed to cobble together a programme for that first six months, the first month of which we were now well into. D'Oyly Carte appeared on our stage and their singing and presentation were superb. Sixteen voices in all but in the auditorium it sounded like sixty, and I was mesmerised by how wonderful they were.

Stag now had a part-time secretary, Maria Strother Smith whose husband Peter had been one of the early 'magnificent seven' and was currently on our Board of Directors. At first Maria came in two half-days per week – that was all we could afford – and before she was able to work in the building a very good friend Vernon Law had given us space and a typewriter in his office in Pembroke Road. It was amazing how kind people were.

I had managed to persuade some amateur groups to perform at Stag and the Sevenoaks Players asked if I would direct their first musical in the theatre.

I accepted willingly and we decided on *The Merry Widow* by Franz Lehar, a box office success if ever I saw one.

One evening in this six month period we held a public

meeting to drum up more support. Very few people attended but a very special thing happened that night. At the end of a question and answer session a lady from The Sevenoaks Concert Band approached me.

"You're going to need all the help you can get. Here's a fiver – I would like to be your first friend."

In an instant she had sown a seed. The Friends of Stag was born and individuals seemed more than pleased to give us a five pound note for a home-made membership card. We explained that it would pay for our postage and maybe help a little with publicity and that source of income, however small in those early days, frequently saved us from bankruptcy. From that day the support and encouragement of The Friends grew and grew. Stag owes them a great debt of gratitude.

The months of rehearsals were really hard work. Quite apart from trying to run this theatre with virtually no staff, keeping a tight hold on the purse strings and keeping up morale on every possible occasion, I was also responsible for the musical.

I loved directing. However tired I was by the evening, somehow rehearsals were a release. My musical director was Tony Gould, an excellent musician and well known in the town. We had a splendid cast headed by Jeanne Millett and Ken Brown. We did our best with advertising but again all the publicity for the theatre was done by one or two volunteers and there was still no money to do all the things we would have liked.

However, ticket sales were tremendous and I knew that although it was by now March (three months into our precious six months), with the success of *Grease*, the D'Oyly Carte, *The Merry Widow* and other events which were drawing excellent audiences, at least a few thousand people would have been made aware of the Stag and hopefully would realise that Sevenoaks at last had a proper theatre, sparse though it was.

I also had my failures. Two particular disasters stick in my mind. The first involved the Gas Company, whom I had per-suaded to give a cookery demonstration on the stage. At that time demonstrations were being put on all over the country and I had been to one or two of varying kinds and thought the female population of Sevenoaks would love it. Segas had only agreed to this suggestion after thoroughly inspecting the stage.

They did not charge us, they were simply promoting gas, and although they told me that their demonstrations were normally free to the public, I decided that I ought to try and make at least a little profit out of the event. I priced the tickets at £2. We had already checked from the auditorium that almost every seat had an excellent view and we guessed that a lot of people would come on the night, rather than buy tickets in advance.

The equipment that arrived that day was beautiful. Cookers with overhead mirrors and tables for the food preparation. The stage looked stunning, the Gas Company staff were charming and efficient and although we had not sold many tickets in advance I was fairly hopeful that we would have a good house. We did not. We had sold about 20 seats in advance and not more than four or five people turned up on the door.

My other real disaster in the Introductory Season was The Mermaid Molecule Theatre. One day I received in the post some excellent publicity about an educational and entertaining show called *The Snatch* which was being toured by this company. I had been a great admirer of Bernard Miles and The Mermaid Theatre in the City of London, to which I had been many times and taken the children, and I rightly surmised that a touring arm of such a theatre would be of high quality and of the sort never before seen in Sevenoaks.

I thought back to when our three sons were small and how I would have loved to have taken them to something in our own town instead of travelling by train to London, so I thought Sevenoaks mums would fall over themselves to find such enter-tainment on their doorstep.

The Company had only one week left on their tour and that was in the Easter holidays. Being fairly green behind the ears I asked whether shows in the holidays were successful or were they really only for school parties? I was told that Molecule sold almost any time they performed because of their good name. I had to take the show for a week – eight performances which at least would give me time for word of mouth advertising. It was expensive, almost £2,000, but it would be a coup for Stag to have such a prestigious production and it would certainly help parents out during the holidays.

I booked it, explaining all about the theatre, and the deal was signed. We wrote dozens of letters to the heads of all the local schools, delivered photocopied leaflets and distributed the Molecule's own publicity which was excellent.

The bookings were very very slow. I had asked the various schools to distribute the publicity to the mothers as I knew there would not be school parties in the holidays, but I also knew there were lots of families in the district with nowhere to take the children. I remained optimistic. The show opened on a Tuesday morning at 10.45 with performances twice a day.

I arrived at the theatre just after 9.30 to get out the table which served as our box office and the tin which housed the cash and sat myself down in the lower foyer. On the seating plan we had three people booked in – one mother and two children – in a 455 seat auditorium! I remained calm but quiet, it was a nice morning outside and I was ever hopeful.

Rod Nipper came down the main stairs and said the company manager would like to see me. He muttered something about Equity rules but I could not quite hear what he said. Presently a slightly fierce young lady came down to the 'box office' and asked how many people had booked.

"A few" I replied, my fingers crossed.

"You do know the Equity Rules, don't you?" she asked.

"Oh yes," I replied. "Which one in particular?"

She looked me straight in the eye.

"The one which says there must be more people in the audience than on the stage."

"Oh, that one," I answered. "How many of you are there?"

"Eleven, including the stage manager, and we mustn't break the rules."

I thought very fast. I had never read an Equity rule in my life but I was paying the company and weren't actors supposed to be grateful to be in work?

"Don't worry" I said calmly, "there will be twelve people in that auditorium and even if there are not, just remember that I am paying your bill and you can treat this as a dress rehearsal."

I felt quite cross but not sure whether I had overstepped the mark. Now to find some more people! I did something which Sevenoaks would find hard to accept had it known – I went out into the street to try and bring people in – anyone, anyone. London Road had little passing pedestrian traffic at the best of times and that morning was no exception.

I spoke to anybody who was going by – but I think they thought I was quite mad. There were very few people about but quite suddenly they all seemed to have appointments at the dentist! What they thought of this strange woman who was offering them free seats for a children's show I can't imagine. I went back inside.

Suddenly, two small boys appeared outside looking at a poster. I shot out and invited them in. They both looked extremely guilty.

"Are you supposed to be at school?" I asked.

"Well, yes and no. We've got a dentist appointment (more bad teeth!) but we don't have to be back at school until a bit later."

I told them about the show, offered them free seats and said I really needed them.

"Alright" they said, looking somewhat nervous.

"I won't tell on you if you don't tell on me" I winked. To my relief they both came in – two more. At that point the Fire Officer arrived in full uniform just to see if everything was alright. He often paid an unexpected visit and this particular morning I was very pleased to see him.

"Are you very busy?" I asked.

"As it happens, no."

"Oh good, I need you to stay and see the show!" – so there was another one.

It was by now only about two minutes to curtain up and there was still no sign of the mother and two children who had pre-booked. With about half a minute to go the doors swung open and a very harassed lady and two small girls came into the lower foyer. She came straight to the table.

"I am sorry to be so late, we were unable to park. Will we be allowed in or have we missed it?" Two anxious little faces stared up at me. I had to come clean.

"Do you mean you are putting this show on just for us?" she asked with her eyes wide.

"Well, I had to take a decision. You were either going to leave this building with two tearful children who would probably never forgive Stag if I called it off, or you were going to go away and remember us for ever. I decided I would prefer you to remember us for ever." I often wonder whether she did. I press-ganged Maria and Rod Nipper into being audience and we ended up with nine of us. Would you believe that the show (which was really excellent) was one of those that required audience participation.

I booed, hissed and shouted very loudly to make up for the lack of people. At the end of the performance I could have been wrung out. I was exhausted but we had got through it without the company going on strike. A mother and two little girls were so happy and grateful and she promised to tell her friends how wonderful it was.

The other seven performances were better attended and word of mouth did improve things towards the end of the week, but it was a financial disaster and taught me a very important lesson about booking shows. I was also told what a mistake it had been to write to the heads of schools as many teachers told me they had heard nothing about it. In future we would direct our publicity to specific teachers who were not quite so swamped with paper pouring onto their desks.

Time was moving on apace and the few of us involved were running to stand still. There was simply so much to do, so much to organise and all on tiny sums of money. It was crucial that any professional event which I booked more than broke even because there were certain overheads that even we could not avoid. The dilemma was knowing what to put on that the local population would come to, especially when they knew they were going to be in a draught!

It was an exciting challenge, but a very very tough one. I decided to aim for the biggest names I could afford (huh – I couldn't really afford anyone) in the hope that the man in the street would be drawn to the name and pay to see them. As a result on most performances we made money – not a lot but enough to help keep us afloat during that first hair-raising six months.

One of our early jazz evenings was Mr Acker Bilk, a name I had picked from the inside back page of The Stage. I explained all about the theatre to Mr Bilk's manager and struck an extra special deal – after all if the group was too expensive we would not make money and if that was the case I would not ask them back – so it was in everyone's interest to make it work. That's how I saw it anyway, and I must say that when people in the business heard the story of Stag they were very generous and helpful and that vein ran through all the years I was in charge. Theatrical people can be very generous, helpful and kind and I found that so long as I was completely honest about the building, what it lacked but what we were trying to achieve, everyone almost without exception was prepared to give a little in whatever way they could. If it happened that they could reduce their fee a bit, then so much the better.

It was by now April and Rod Nipper and I had learned a great deal about the time of artists' arrival and their several requirements. On the day that Mr Bilk was due I had been in the building until about 2pm (it was a Saturday) and the band's technical crew were due to arrive about 4 o'clock for a sound check. Rod would meet them and see to their needs. I would return in time to see the end of their rehearsal and prepare the building for opening. We had sold about 300 seats – a lot – and Stag was going to make some money. The telephone at my home rang about 5 o'clock and a slightly anxious Rod told me there was no sign of anyone from Mr Bilk's outfit. There was a sound check to be carried out, lights to be focused and all the usual things that are done long before an audience arrives.

I gave Rod the number of Mr Bilk's manager, put down the phone and waited: Rod called me back about ten minutes later. It appeared that Mr Bilk and company had flown back that day from Abu Dhabi and had been very badly delayed. Not only delayed but much of their luggage had been lost, they had not been able to eat the food on the plane, they were tired, cross and hungry – and they were coming to Stag! I remained extremely calm, told Rod that I would prepare some food for them as a welcome and would come up to meet them as soon as I was able.

I prepared a whole brown loaf of sandwiches (we had little other bread in the house and shops mostly closed at 5o'clock in 1984), bought a welcome card on my way to the theatre and set it all out in the dressing room for them. I was determined that the evening would be a happy one – we had sold so many tickets!

They eventually arrived but had had an appalling flight. They were of course totally professional jazz musicians to boot – about the most laid back type of performer it has been my pleasure to meet. They were thrilled with their welcome, woofed the food, drank the beer we provided and seemed to be most impressed with the stage and auditorium.

That evening when Mr Bilk appeared on stage to thunderous applause he explained to the audience all about their trip. Fortunately their instruments were safe but half their clothes were missing and they were wearing each other's trousers and waistcoats. He had the audience eating out of his hand at once. He also said they had never tasted such good sandwiches or had such a warm welcome from the staff of a theatre – cheers all round.

The audience loved him and he has since paid many visits to Sevenoaks.

The programme in that Introductory Season was diverse if nothing else. Through the kindness of Rod's parents we were able to have a visit for nothing by Marilyn Hill-Smith and her husband – a most glorious feast of music but not well attended, and of course we had to get that piano back in again!

Rod's brother was a member of the Band of the Royal Corps of Signals and again, by dint of favours to this new theatre, we were able to have a most stirring and wonderful evening of music for very little money. The men looked superb in their scarlet uniforms on that vast stage with a black background, and the excitement when they arrived in their coaches for rehearsal with all their equipment was quite something.

Our three sons put on a pop concert for us – they were young professional musicians hoping to make it in the pop world and we wanted to show the young of Sevenoaks that the theatre was for all ages. They produced a startlingly professional evening – it was certainly different from the Royal Corps of Signals! The very important lesson the pop concert taught me was that on that type of occasion the bar takings were always excellent – young people wandered in and out of the auditorium constantly, had a drink then went back inside. The poor front-of-house volunteers didn't know whether it was Christmas or Easter! It was almost a trouble-free evening – the exception being a minor tiff between two young Romeos over their Juliet – and the event went off without a hitch.

For every event I tried to prepare myself mentally for what would need to be different from the last event. Amateur dramatics I of course knew very well. I had directed, acted, been front-of-house, sold programmes, made coffee – in fact done just about anything – but this was now quite different.

Now it was not just friends and relations paying money for a performance but complete strangers, and I had to be prepared. Having run an hotel was an enormous help, and whenever I wondered whether I could cope I would tell myself it was just like running The Moorings only slightly bigger (!) and that people simply wanted to be made welcome, see a show of a high standard and be comfortable.

Apart from the technical side of the operation I was able to do all and any of the jobs that I persuaded other people to do. We could not afford regular cleaners and I learned precisely how long it took to clean that building (including under all the seats) from the front doors to the front of the stage. Rod was responsible for the stage and dressing rooms. We often ended up doing it all – but together.

There were many occasions when I thought that audiences would have had a fit if they had known that an hour before they arrived I was often to be found cleaning the loos, putting in loo paper then washing and changing in time to receive them as if I had a staff of dozens. But it didn't matter. I had started this project, it looked as if it was really going to take off and it would only succeed if I was prepared to do anything and everything. It had been my foolish idea so why should anyone else have to take the responsibility? It never once bothered me and, although I was often extremely tired, I loved it and that's why I was able to do it.

The Introductory Season was coming to its crescendo. The Licence with the Sevenoaks District Council allowed us six months from 18th December 1983 at the end of which the theatre must close, the temporary scaffolding staircases must be removed from the back of the stage and certain fire regulations had to be met before we would be allowed to operate again.

I had had meetings with Mark Pyper, Artistic Director of the Sevenoaks Summer Festival, and we had agreed that Stag would host certain performances in the Festival. This was another coup for the theatre. The Festival's reputation in the town was high, their publicity and marketing covered a far greater area than we could afford and the link between the town's new theatre and the Summer Festival was exactly right.

I suggested to Mark that perhaps we might have a 'company' this particular year that would produce a show which could involve actors from any of the societies in the area. This was agreed. It was decided that an actor named David Cole, whom I knew reasonably well through the Players and who had in fact been a professional actor for many years, would direct *The Heiress.* Life really is strange – my first leading role all those years ago and now it was to be performed at the Festival. I would have loved to do the part again but twenty odd years on was too late!

The cast chosen was excellent and Ray Russell, one of the directors on Stag's Board, was chosen to play the part of Maurice. The set was one of the most handsome I have ever seen on our stage. It was designed by a young man called Peter Hall who has since gone on to become a successful professional designer.

It sold well, especially with the use of the Festival's publicity machine, and it helped greatly with the profile of the theatre. It was most unfortunate that due to circumstances beyond his control Ray Russell had to relinquish the part of Maurice at the last moment. David Cole stepped in to save the situation.

In that Festival we also hosted Donald Swann. The atmosphere that evening with a completely full house was very exciting. It was very rewarding to see someone so famous on our stage in our town.

We were also privileged to have Surrey Opera's production of *Peter Grimes* by Benjamin Britten. It was superb in every respect and it was particularly nice for us because the part of Peter Grimes was played by Ken Brown, one of Stag's most avid supporters and who was to become our Chairman some years later. Ken and his wife Heather were two of the greatest 'achievers' for Stag in those early, vulnerable days. They not only talked about the theatre to their friends but they also raised money for us. Instead of conversations beginning: "Why don't you try . . .?" Ken and Heather got on and did things. They also motivated other people to do things and that kind of support was precious.

All during the Introductory Season we had in our minds that we had to raise the £100,000 to repay the District Council. It soon became clear that that target would be impossible to achieve in the time. Negotiations continued between Stag and the Local Authority. We could only impress on them that the building was being used, that people seemed to be really enjoying it and that a large part of the population of the District was benefiting by this wonderful facility.

It was tough negotiating. Some Councillors were very scathing about Stag, and the local press carried stories about whether we would ever have a future, but we could not be daunted. We now had the bit well and truly between our teeth and I think it would have taken an earthquake to wrest the theatre from us after all we had been through. Besides, the excitement and goodwill was building day by day.

Although we never found that person with the magic wand who would heap riches on us and persuade others to do the same, we struggled on. And struggle it was. Not only were we supposed to be raising the large sum for the Council but we also had to raise money to replace the back-stage staircases and pay for the new fire precautions.

Heather Brown went into action. The fund-raising committee, made up of people who believed in Stag but who did not have spare financial resources, had a target under Heather's leadership to raise £3,000. Heather decided that she would cajole 100 people into raising £30 each in whatever way they wished. The idea behind it was that it would involve large numbers of people, thereby spreading the Stag gospel, it would stretch individuals' imaginations to raise the money differently from their friends and it would mean that the committee itself would not have to do all the work.

It was a brilliant idea which succeeded. We were constantly astonished and delighted at the schemes people invented to raise the cash – quite often more than £30. There were the usual coffee mornings and bring and buy sales but we heard of ideas in people's homes where they had table tennis competitions, sold trout from a local farm, paid to swim in someone's pool, played cards, served dinner – all types of events – and it engendered an enormous amount of fun and goodwill towards the theatre.

Boot Fairs were at the beginning of their popularity and I decided that it would be a good thing to have one in the South Park Car Park (behind the theatre) to raise funds. We could promote the theatre at the same time. I chose a Sunday in September and it took quite some little while to get the necessary permission from the Council to close the car park to the public for a whole day (I hadn't thought of that!).

Rod Nipper worked out how many cars we could cope with, we agreed we must provide food (and make more money!) and in case of bad weather we had to borrow a small caravan for someone to sit in with the Stag publicity. We none of us had any experience of Boot Fairs, hardly anyone had then, and fortunately Rod arrived at the car park at about 7.30am to get the notices up and generally prepare for the day. It was a good thing he did! Cars were lined up in South Park waiting to get in and the places which had not been booked in advance were soon taken up. The volunteers did not know what had hit them – the place was buzzing from about 8 o'clock.

My eldest son Kim had agreed to be in charge of the barbecue, a huge monster we had begged from a local school. When we had discussed the arrangements we had assumed that people would be getting hungry by about 10 o'clock and that it would peak around lunchtime and then die down. I had purchased dozens of baps, burgers, sausages, tomato sauce and mustard and Kim agreed to turn up about 9am to start the barbecue. No sooner had he set a match to the firelighters than he had a queue of cold, hungry people waiting for hot food. He was amazed. He started cooking as soon as he was able, had to send for help because there were so many customers and did not stop cooking and serving until about three in the afternoon. His eyes were streaming, he stank of barbecue smoke and he took loads of money – he did a wonderful job.

Everyone worked like trojans and the day was very successful. A little more cash towards our staircase!

Ken Brown initiated a covenant scheme on which we relied for many years and, whenever time permitted, we ran events of any kind that would raise money – but they were usually fairly small sums. I was so busy keeping the whole thing together there was never time to concentrate solely on fund-raising but at least the word was spreading. Slowly, slowly catchee monkey.

Finally, and much to our relief, the District Council agreed to grant us a five year lease at £4,000 per annum and it was only then that we felt reasonably secure. The debt was still owing but five whole years gave me the chance to plan, it gave the theatre some credibility and hopefully it would encourage more and more people to support us.

The scaffolding staircases were taken away – just so many poles and planks of wood now despite the fact that we had hand-wrapped every bolt on that opening Sunday. After September 1984 the auditorium was unusable. There was no access to back-stage. Somehow we had to continue to keep the building alive despite it being 'dark' as a theatre.

Whenever we could hold anything in the bar, we did. We exploited any excuse to get people into the building. The place was cold, pretty unwelcoming and not very presentable, but we made up for that with our enthusiasm.

Through a professional actor, David Barry, we managed to get Christopher Timothy and Valentine Dyall (to name but two) to come to the bar one Sunday for a 'Poems and Pints' evening. It was great fun and reasonably well attended, but of course raised only a few pounds although the artists had been generous enough not to charge us a fee. In return I had agreed to drive Mr Dyall home after the event to somewhere in deepest Sussex.

We set off at about 11pm. There were very major works being

112

Personalities

John Marsh – architect extraordinaire.

Willing hands and money raisers – John Tanner and Linda Fishenden.

'Very Important People' – our Patron, Sir Desmond Heap, with Lady Heap and Albert Granville.

John Lurcook – we go back a *long* way.

Patrick Pascall – who took over the Chair from me.

In-house Productions

Right
'If this doesn't pull them in, nothing will!'
The programme cover for *My Fair Lady* designed by John Marsh.
November 1986.

Below
'I put it to yer, Guvnor.'
Paul Barnes and Ted Denman in *My Fair Lady*.

Opposite page
'Who's this geezer, Hitler?'
Cast photograph for *Blitz!* in November 1988.

Top: Programme cover, designed by Christopher Holgate, sponsored by the company who built our stage.

STAG THEATRE
PRESENTS

my fair lady

STAG THEATRE

Books and Lyrics by ALAN JAY LERNER
Music by FREDERICK LOEWE
Adapted from George Bernard Shaw's Play
and Gabriel Pascal's motion picture PYGMALION

6–15th NOVEMBER 1986

'I hate seeing stage sets broken up.'

VIP Visitors

Bill Finney, Mayor in 1985 – he was on our side.

Our MP was in the house – Edna Wolfson.

A real trouper – Glen Dunlop.

Joyce Thomsett, Chairman of Sevenoaks District Council 1985 – a charming lady.

Louise and Harry Williams – ardent Stag-goers.

Bruce Cova, Chief Executive, Sevenoaks District Council – a firm friend.

Opposite page
Not a seat in the house!
Who cares – it's going to be wonderful!
December 1992.

Back on Stage

Above
The hills are alive . . . the set for
The Sound of Music and the children
who became the Von Trapp family
on alternate nights.
November 1989.

Right
Five minutes please –
Lonnie Christophers and
Ray Howell in *The King and I*.
November 1994.

Opening and Closing

Left: 'We passed the Fire Inspection!'
– Francis Price and I celebrate.
Below: The invitation to our
'Switch On' ceremony performed by
The Beverley Sisters in October 1991.

I can't bear to part with *any* of them –
the staff just before we closed in
November 1992

STAG THEATRE and SEVENOAKS DISTRICT COUNCIL

request the pleasure of your company at the

'SWITCH-ON' CEREMONY
and celebration of our facelift

MONDAY 21ST OCTOBER 1991

on the London Road at 7.30pm for 8pm

followed by a reception in the Stag Theatre Bar

R S V P

The Stag Theatre, London Road, Sevenoaks, Kent TN13 2QA

Set Design and Building

Julian Adams with the model of the set he designed for *The Matchgirls*, presented by StagTech in June 1994.

and, as a representative of many set builders over the years, Peter Galbraith.

done to the very new motorway. At the best of times my navigation is appalling. Mr Dyall relaxed totally. I didn't. Having that "Appointment with Fear" voice from the radio next to me in the car was quite spooky although he was an absolute dear.

I got into the wrong lane just through Riverhead and we were stuck going miles out of our way. I cannot recall how we got back onto the right road but I do know it was a cold, foggy night and it seemed like an eternity before we arrived at his home. He was extremely grateful for the lift (almost a world tour!), I thanked him for his kindness and set off home.

I could not find my way back. In the dark and fog it was ghastly. I eventually arrived home about 2.30 in the morning. John was fast asleep when I crept in. The family had a good laugh in the morning when I told them what had happened.

Our immediate aim was to raise enough money to open after Christmas in 1985 but the target seemed to get further and further away. The Council realised we did not have a hope of raising the £100,000 towards our part of the lease and they very generously decided to put it on hold for the time being. They knew we were doing our best.

I pored over lists of companies in the Yellow Pages, earmarked some, made people give me introductions to one or two and went round pleading for help in kind.

Sometimes it worked. A company on the Vestry Estate gave me one flight of an iron staircase. Another company the second flight. So, we had our staircase for the back of the stage – all we had to do now was raise the money to install it properly.

Once again, Ian Wood generously helped us out and we now had enough for the staircase and fireproof wall which had to enclose it.

Plasmarc, a company in Riverhead, agreed to give us worktops and mirrors for the dressing rooms and Mobil Oil kindly donated a large number of free-standing plastic screens with which it could be partitioned. It was coming together but time was slipping away.

The Sevenoaks Town Council had listened, with some scepticism, to my pleas for years, but they finally agreed to make us a loan of £7,000 towards the necessary works – a vast sum of money to us but quite crucial in order to carry out the necessary fire precautions. We had donations of paint and then persuaded loads of volunteers to come in in their spare time and paint the inside of the building for us. There were endless discussions about colour (everyone had different ideas!) but in the end I took whatever decisions were necessary. It was impossible to take advice from every direction. At least they would have one person to blame!

John and Jane Mitchell from Impulse Lighting Shop had come to a performance during the Introductory Season. They had admired the show enormously but Jane had been appalled by the conditions in the Ladies (she should have seen it in 1983!) and felt that the upper foyer could be much improved.

To our delight the Mitchells offered to provide new carpet for the upper foyer and new lighting, and John Mitchell came and repainted the whole area with the help of my husband. We discovered an original coat of paint of a dark bluey green on the doors in the foyer and the whole scheme was decided around that colour. The carpet was very 30's, as were the light fittings, and the effect was so different it was wonderful.

The Amherst Rotary Club provided us with the money to have a coffee bar built in the upper foyer and my hairdresser, Linda Fishenden of Chamille in Riverhead, decided that she would take on the Ladies Powder Room.

One Sunday members of her staff went round the pubs dressed as lavatory attendants and raised money. Linda's mother Joan painted, wallpapered and made curtains. The money raised by the girls bought us new wash handbasins and lavatories. Extraordinary dedication.

The men were very jealous and often complained to me how awful the Gents was. I agreed and suggested one of them might like to do something about it. The idea obviously didn't appeal because apart from more scrubbing and painting the Gents was not refurbished properly until 1993.

Individuals never ceased to amaze me. There are so many unsung heroes and heroines who did pioneering work for us. In the months that we were closed different people kept popping up to do specific voluntary jobs for us. One of my old friends, the son of the Verger at my beloved St Mary's Church Kippington and someone I had known from my teens, was one of these heroes. His name was John Lurcook. He loved woodwork of any kind, was a professional photographer and was closely involved with The Holmesdale Players on the technical side.

John polished old poster frames which he rescued, old handrails covered in years of grime and when he had finished they looked beautiful. Touches which were all important in the building and added to its 'glow'.

He spent many, many hours on Stag's behalf. He had a real feel for the genuine article and restored so many things for us. He also explored the history of the building and became a fount of knowledge when we needed information on dates or people connected with its past.

By now a totally dedicated supporter, John introduced to us Christopher and Margaret Holgate. The family name had been prominent in Sevenoaks for many years and my path had crossed that of Chris's father in my teens. John Holgate was an authority on drama, coached many aspiring actors and encouraged anyone interested in theatre. Chris's speciality was book design. Over the ensuing years he and Margaret not only acted as front of house volunteers, but Chris designed more and more of our publicity. Generous to a fault, he understood our precarious finances and on so many occasions made the impossible possible.

Our financial records were not in the most desirable form. George Knott had very generously done a mammoth task for us keeping track of what was going on, but he was a full-time accountant. Most people involved with working tasks in the theatre were not that careful about keeping their records straight or keeping George informed. Life was very difficult for him. If he discovered that the electricity was about to be cut off because the bill had not reached him, he was wonderful about phoning me and letting me know, but it was hairy!

Lots of folk were making history but no-one had time to think about that during that period, they were far too busy.

Gradually the necessary work was completed, but only the necessary work. There was no money for frills and there were dozens of things which we needed but knew we had to do without.

My husband spent hours painting skirting boards, walls, the general office and anywhere where it needed attention to detail and careful finishing. He was a perfectionist and always reminded me that if the public saw sloppy paintwork they would treat the building carelessly and regard us as a real bunch of amateurs. He was so right. The pace was increasing daily. We finally decided that we would be able to re-open the theatre in June 1985 and that we should make it special. Everyone would have to be involved.

It was during this period that I was introduced to a man by the name of Peter Othick, who with his wife Betty and daughter Joanna lived in Chipstead. Peter had recently retired from Lloyds Bank and, although he had no real interest in theatre, he relieved George of the time consuming job of keeping track of our accounts. He started proper records for us on an almost daily basis and gradually became more and more involved in the life of the theatre. He was outspoken but never bitchy, had a great sense of humour and – most important of all – he had time to spare. Not only did he give us invaluable hours with book-keeping but he became one of our bar volunteers, full of useful advice about what people drank and almost always available when I had a crisis. As it was to turn out both his wife Betty and daughter Joanna became totally involved with Stag – a real family commitment.

The team was gradually assembled for the Grand Opening (can you have a second one?) and the excitement again was tremendous. We tried desperately hard to get TV coverage for the evening. As luck would have it London TV said we were just too far out for them to cover the story and TV South, as it then was, said we probably ought to be covered by London TV – neither of them really wanted to know. It was most disappointing.

However there was no time to fret, still so much to be done, but at least the building was looking more respectable than it had on its first opening in 1983. There were also many, many more people willing to help and put themselves out.

Once again, Mark Pyper and I had agreed that the Festival Players would be a most appropriate company with which to trumpet the slightly revitalised building, but we wanted to come up with something really special that would involve a cast of thousands!

New on our Board of Directors was a man called Michael Cormack. Michael had written a seven page letter to me soon after our Introductory Season, telling me that I had mountains to climb, asking me if I realised quite what I had taken on and what my policy was for the theatre. He explained that he had been the Deputy Head of the Rose Bruford School of Speech and Drama for the last twenty-odd years.

I telephoned him.

"I have just received your letter. It was very kind of you to take such trouble. I've never had time to think about the mountains but you're probably right. My only policy for the theatre at the moment is survival and please, if you have so much experience, will you come and help!"

Michael did and it was he who suggested a wonderful drama for our opening. *Inherit the Wind* with a cast of thousands! Well, not quite but it seemed like it on occasions.

Small groups of people were frantic with varying parts of the production and different teams of people were busy with the administration of the Opening, the reception and all the things that go with such an event. Everyone seemed to be having such a good time. It was wonderful to see how our numbers had grown and how many people really wanted Stag to succeed. All it needed really was holding together and that is how I seemed to spend most of my time.

I had had no intention whatsoever all those years ago of running something like this. I had simply set out to acquire a site, but having got one I could not then walk away and say "OK chaps, there it is, get on with it." It really would not have worked.

I couldn't be in the play for the Opening, there was too much else to do, so my role had to be 'out front' keeping up the morale, thanking everyone who did anything and generally looking after the 'business'. I loved it. I don't pretend for one moment that I did not, but it was not what I had actually meant to happen.

On 25th June 1985 Stag re-opened.

Dozens of special guests had been invited for 7.30 for 'BUBBLES & BALLOONS' followed by *Inherit the Wind* at 8 o'clock. Ken and Heather Brown had had a most horrendous day trying to organise the helium balloons and equipment on the roof. There was little space and a high wind, and trying to get the timing right was giving them nightmares. As always, they coped admirably.

There were the usual dramas throughout the day – programmes arrived only in the nick of time, milk ran out and we nearly forgot to collect the ice from Barry at The Anchor pub across the road. He had acted as our 'deep freeze' from the beginning. We were unable to buy our own freezer and Barry had accommodated us all those months – collecting a bag of ice was quite a joke! Peter Othick was in charge of drinks in the lower foyer on arrival and he had a bevy of beautiful girls on hand to serve them. The goodwill everywhere was almost overwhelming – there was absolutely no doubt whatever in my mind that Stag would go from strength to strength – this was just the beginning, well, the second coming so to speak.

The evening was a great success both artistically and from a public relations point of view. We were all exhausted by the end but very happy and quite ecstatic to be open again.

No-one liked the battleship grey paint which was everywhere but as we had been unable to afford an interior designer and had no money anyway, I had taken professional advice to choose this particular colour so that as soon as we could afford a designer the very least we would have would be a quality undercoat on the walls!

We sailed through the next few days on cloud nine, the euphoria was catching and people generally seemed to be delighted that we had negotiated with the Council, come to a sensible arrangement and got ourselves a lease, if only for five years.

After Re-opening

My opinion was that Sevenoaks would never be the sort of town that would come to live theatre during the summer holidays, and we negotiated with the cinema company downstairs that they could hire the main theatre auditorium during the summer to show the blockbusters which are usually released at the holiday period. It was a sensible arrangement – we could not provide live theatre and the cinema could use 455 seats each performance for popular films. We agreed a very cheap rent – they had little money too – and we had our first cinema letting in the theatre.

I had not quite appreciated how different theatre and cinema audiences were. Some of the young people who paid to come in had only one thing in mind – vandalism. By the end of that summer period some paint had been stripped off the auditorium walls, seats had chewing gum on and under them and one or two seats had been damaged. Also the mess in the auditorium had to be seen to be believed. Cans, sweet papers, Maltesers rolling between the rows, cigarette ends (although smoking was banned), rubbish of all kinds was strewn across the auditorium. I could not believe my eyes but I soon learned that it was a fact of life in cinemas.

Rod Nipper was often heard to say to me "it would be fine if it wasn't for the people" and I know that we have almost all said that at some time or another in our working lives. But we were in a 'people' business and although the cinema was not our personal concern, we had to check every day just to make sure what sort of state it was in.

Maria Strother Smith was now able to do her secretarial work in the smartened-up but very cold office near the top of the building. She came in for two and a half days per week and was marvellous. Courteous with clients and totally loyal to Stag. I could not have asked for anyone better.

We were given a typewriter, had a telephone and that was about it. Photocopying was done at Lorimers Stationery Shop in the High Street. We still had no money. When we needed equipment for shows we hired it – I was absolutely adamant about not getting ourselves deeper into debt with monthly repayments for anything not vital.

Almost all the bookings were done from my home. Evenings were spent talking to prospective hirers (often local people that I knew) and it became my routine to spend the whole of every Saturday in the building because that was the day when most of our clients wished to discuss bookings with me and talk about front of house and technical requirements.

Interest in the building was growing. In a typically British way many people had waited to see how others got on before they were brave enough to book the theatre, but some of those barriers were now being broken down and the important thing was that the audiences loved the place. Naturally there were the complainers, but on the whole, despite the chill and the odd mix of furniture in the bar, our audiences were more than enthusiastic in their response. It was much more like an evening out – they could have a drink in the interval usually served by me plus volunteers, have coffee and always see and hear what was going on on the stage – a luxury denied them in most local flat floored halls. The happy and excited atmosphere in that building was down to the growing group of people who were pulling together and working exceptionally hard to make the place succeed.

Very slowly I built up a bigger programme. Wide-ranging events that would attract almost any member of any family in the district. As long as the standard was high I was prepared to try it – we had to discover what people in Sevenoaks wanted. Ideal in theory, difficult to carry out in practice on no money. I still had to balance what I thought would sell with things that we ought to be seen doing and this was extremely difficult. I had been talking to South East Arts for many months hoping that they would be able to give us a grant towards running costs and although I achieved a little, it went nowhere. I hammered away at them and eventually Chris Cooper, Director for South East Arts, said he would try and arrange for the Minister for the Arts, Mr Luke Ritner, to pay us a visit so that he could see for himself what we had achieved, what our potential was and how great was our involvement in the community.

One Monday Chris Cooper telephoned me to say that Mr Ritner was doing a whistle stop tour of the South East in two days' time and that one of his calls would be to the Stag. I was delighted. I knew that I only had to get Mr Ritner in that building, fire him with enthusiasm, show him round and he would at least have to give the place some thought. The day and time were very inconvenient for me but there was no way I was not going to be present, and both my staff(!) were briefed.

It was a bitterly cold day and eventually Mr Ritner and Mr Cooper arrived. Talk about whistle stop! We shot round the building like rockets being launched and without pausing to take breath I told the Minister about the project. It was impossible to dwell on anything – there was no time – but I did delay minutely on the stage because I knew it was so impressive. I skated over the merits of the bar because I was well aware of the impression that would leave! Mr Ritner had to leave. I went out of the front doors with my two guests. Mr Ritner turned to me with his hand outstretched. In a fairly condescending way he said "Good luck – keep up the good work" – and was gone. I was to learn many months later that he had told Mr Cooper in so many words that "they don't stand a chance – it will probably be gone in six months." I know for a fact that those few words spread quite a fear in the South East Arts and created an extra mountain for us to climb, but I was unaware of it at the time.

At the end of November 1985 I did what I really had been wanting to do all the time. I took part in a play on my stage in the theatre. The Sevenoaks Players under the direction of Joan Lloyd had decided to perform *Whose Life Is It Anyway?* I took t he part of the Ward sister. The play is very moving, arouses a great deal of debate and centres on a patient who is quadraplegic and does not wish to go on living. An actor called Paul Barnes played the lead, and his partner, Terry Shaw, was also in the cast. The two of them were a delight to work with. Both of them had been professionals on the stage in different ways in the past and it showed. I had a ball. Acting in the new theatre on such a wonderful stage was something I was begin-ning to think would never happen to me – I simply could not find the time without something suffering – but I loved every second. The play was a great success and audiences were most impressed. Another great choice from Joan Lloyd.

A Stag Christmas show was out of the question that year. There were not the resources or anyone with the time to do it, and there was no way I could afford to risk a professional show. I knew Stag would never be able to compete with the big guns who booked major pantomimes with TV stars, and if truth were known I was not interested in competing. I simply had not worked out quite how Stag was going to cope with Christmases. It had not been a problem up to then and I could jump only one hurdle at a time. Numerous questions were about to rear their heads and they would need decisions but I was determined the place should walk before it tried to run. We had to consolidate our position, get more people prepared to hire the theatre and take risks only if we knew we could get back on course – there was absolutely no point in losing everything we had worked so hard to gain. No-one disagreed with my 'policy' – good heavens, perhaps I had one after all – and I continued to take all the major decisions with regard to programming.

One of the artists I booked in that December was George Chisholm. He was getting on in years but was still much loved and extremely popular with his fans. Again, on the night he came, it was freezing cold. As was normal, during the evening I popped up to the back of the auditorium to make sure everyone was where they should be and that all was well. It was the beginning of the second part, just after the interval. Mr Chisholm came on stage blowing breaths out of his mouth, rubbing his hands together and generally making signs that he was cold.

The audience began to laugh. Mr Chisholm: "How do you feel out there? Are you cold?" "Yes" was the reply with much laughter but I would like to have disappeared. I was quite hurt hearing someone criticise the theatre from the stage. Mr Chisholm: "Take my advice – do what I did, go outside to the car park for a warm!" The place erupted with laughter and after much foot stamping and general fooling around the concert continued. I was not really pleased because I was afraid the only thing our audience would say to their friends afterwards was that the theatre was cold and that would not do our ticket sales any good. However, there was nothing to be done. As much money as was available had been spent on heating and there were no funds for such a major expense. There were numerous occasions after that when I would listen to such remarks from the stage. I became rather more immune as time passed.

I booked the famous film star Miss Constance Cummins to do her one-woman show that winter. I genuinely thought that the more senior members of the population would flock to see her. She had been so popular and so glamorous in the thirties and forties I thought we were on to a winner. Again it was freezing. I caught flu and for the first time was quite unable to be on duty.

Only thirty-two people bought tickets for the vast auditorium and Paul Barnes and Terry Shaw were two of them. The Theatre Club (our Friends), had suggested that Miss Cummins might come round to the bar afterwards and meet the audience(!) and she agreed quite happily. Rod Nipper told me that as he was bringing her up the two flights of stairs from the dressing room to the stage she said "Excuse me, young man, could you remind me, is this place being rebuilt or demolished?" Rod told me he nearly pushed her back down the stairs. Another anecdote from that evening came from Paul Barnes. When he and a few other people gathered round Miss Cummins in the bar after the show Paul was delighted to be able to meet her. Paul, 'oozing charm from every pore', took Miss Cummins' hand and said: "Miss Cummins, that was quite wonderful. You made me feel as though I was the only man in the audience." Miss Cummins was quick – "Young man, you nearly were." That event did not add to our coffers!

In January 1986 Silver Lining once again booked the theatre for a week to perform *Anything Goes*. Their reputation was secure and once more the seats had sold well although the show did not suit the company as well as *Grease*. However they were young, full of enthusiasm and energy, and that transmitted to the audience. Humphrey Lyttleton came to the theatre for the first time and we almost sold out, such was his popularity. We asked every artist who came what they thought of the place. It was fascinating and very rewarding to hear them say how much they loved performing in the building because the atmosphere was so good, the acoustic excellent and everyone so friendly and helpful. At least we were winning on some counts.

In late 1985 it became obvious that someone would have to run the building full-time. The business had grown enormously and it was perfectly obvious that daily involvement was needed if Stag was to continue to be successful. I was still Chairman of the Board of Directors (as I had been from the start) and although I had never intended to do full time work in the theatre, it was beginning to look as though it would be essential. John and I talked it over for a considerable time. As a family we needed an income and I could not afford to work for nothing. Stag could not afford to pay a full-time member of staff.

Michael Cormack understood the dilemma and suggested that he could take on the administrative work on a part-time basis. I jumped at the offer. For a few months it seemed to work, but it then became obvious that with Michael's other commitments on Drama Committees the workload was far too great. At the time I was temporary private secretary to the Finance Director of Associated Newspapers.

One evening John and I finally decided that the only way forward for Stag was for me to become fully involved, however little the pay. I was excited and nervous at one and the same time, but the options were plain. Two days later at my desk in London I was introduced to a friend of my boss. He was very charming and asked many questions about my role. I thought nothing of it until I was called into the office next morning and asked to sit down by a very happy looking Finance Director. He explained that yesterday's visitor was the Mayor Elect of the City of London and he wished to know whether I would become his personal assistant for his year in office. Life can produce conundrums sometimes. The offer was very tempting, the promised salary high and the prospects of an exciting year were dangled before me.

I turned it down. I had taken the decision to run Stag, John was fully behind me and I had no intention of changing my mind. It was a decision I never regretted.

The programme remained varied and exciting and as I was there every time there was a performance I began to realise that the audience was mostly upper-middle class. I thought about this a great deal. Why didn't I ever see our milkman, or coalman, or postman – what was stopping them coming to the building? It was quite plain to me that we had to increase our audience and I had hoped that what I was putting on would attract people from all walks of life, but apparently this was not happening. The next time we had some coal delivered at home I collared the coalman, a man we had known for years.

"Have you been to the Stag yet?" I asked.

"Me? No. Wouldn't go there."

"Why not, don't you like anything that's on?" I asked.

"Oh yes, but it's too toffee-nosed for me."

"Toffee-nosed!" I exclaimed. "What makes you think that?"

"I went past the other evening and saw this bloke in a stuffed shirt – that's not for me."

I explained that he had seen the cinema manager wearing dinner jacket because it was the uniform but that we weren't in the least bit toffee-nosed even if someone was dressed up. It was sometimes necessary for identification and it was occasionally just fun to dress up. However, this conversation set me thinking. How many other people thought Stag was stuck up – and how on earth could I get to them?

Our finances were not getting any easier. I was now being paid as little as I was able to afford to live on and the only way we made any money was from the bar.

Running the bar was part of my daily job. I ordered the stock, cleaned the pumps, the optics, any work which was needed became a routine part of my day. Had I not done that Stag would not have survived. The bar profits, small though they were, actually paid my fee for one whole year. We persuaded volunteers to serve customers whenever the theatre was open and again they did sterling work.

It was usually staffed by men (it did not appeal to the ladies overmuch) who often came straight from their jobs in London, had no supper and were on duty until well after ll o'clock. They were real troupers and again an enormous debt is owed to them all. Most of them had great fun but it was very hard work. We had no glass washers and the kitchen in which all the washing up had to be done was tiny. Two people in there at a time and the place was bursting.

A typical bar duty went like this. Arrive at least 45 minutes before curtain up. The bar would be all ready for use with lemons sliced, ice and orange juice out and float in the till. On a full house members of the audience would be pouring in from about thirty minutes before curtain up. They would not only have drinks then but also order for the interval and pay in advance. At curtain up the bar volunteers would move into action to clear the room: dirty ashtrays, odd bits of rubbish and glasses by the dozen. These had to be washed and dried ready for use for the interval orders – I had not had spare money to order too many glasses.

About five minutes before the interval was due the stage manager would ring from the 'corner' to warn the bar staff. Sometimes this was not possible. It was quite out of the question when we had only a walkie-talkie! All orders were by then out on the table (hopefully) and the volunteers and I would stand ready for the rush.

Twenty minutes of mayhem would follow. No time to look up and greet people properly, just head down and pull pints and serve as fast as possible. A sea of faces, occasionally the odd hostile one, but mostly very friendly. Get the brain moving fast, everything had to be totted up in one's head, use the till and give the right change.

Curtain up for the second act. The room looking as if a bomb had hit it. Dozens and dozens of glasses, a repeat performance with ashtrays and rubbish and then washing up and more washing up. We possessed only a few tea towels too (more economies) so it was not easy putting a polish on those glasses. Often, too, the little gas water heater would collapse with exhaustion and the washer-up would despair. A kettle would be boiled and unnecessary delays created.

In no time at all it seemed it was the end of the show. If the cast was large and there was a full house, the whole process would be repeated but without the benefit of advance orders. Those helpers worked so hard. It was often nearly midnight before I was able to cash up. I would frequently end the evening feeling terribly thirsty and wondering why. I realised that on occasions I had not had a drink all evening!

Still fretting about our lack of income I put my mind to solving the problem of appealing to the man in the street and raising some money. There was no doubt that local audiences flocked to amateur musicals and that with proper financial control in every department a popular musical could make money – just. I decided that if I directed a musical that had major box office appeal not only could I make some much needed money for Stag but I could possibly draw in those members of the public who had not yet set foot inside the building. I reasoned that if someone wants to see a particular show they will come – who is doing it and where being hopefully of secondary importance.

I settled on *My Fair Lady*. It is such a famous English story with a most glorious score and a well-constructed script. It had not been performed locally for some considerable time. It was an undoubted box office draw – I felt that if we could not make money on that show, we were in the wrong business.

I suggested it at the next Board Meeting. I had no private money to finance the project. Naturally I did not expect to get paid for directing it but the theatre would have to take the risk. I further suggested that we should have ten performances over two weeks, with one on a Sunday afternoon. This was a radical idea for an amateur production. The norm was six performances in one week. I had done the figures, knew that a long run increased the expenses as well as the takings, but was certain that if I could introduce three afternoon performances I stood a very good chance of large family audiences. The Board was sceptical. Could we really afford it and would it sell? Even Michael Cormack, the only member of the Board with any real theatrical experience, had grave doubts. I left the room to give the Directors the freedom to discuss it and stood outside in the corridor for some little time while they debated the issue. They called me back in and were unanimous in their decision. They agreed to take the risk!

If I were to be right with this show, not only would the

coalman, milkman and postman need to come and see it – so would another 3,500 people – and that was just to break even. I fully understood the Board's initial doubt. Notices of Open Auditions were posted on the building, we advertised locally, in Tunbridge Wells and also in The Stage, making it very clear that this would be an amateur production and that no-one cast would get any money. Nicholas Willmer agreed to be the musical director. I had known Nicholas for many years. He was a well known local organist who led church choirs over a very wide area and knew many of the performers in the locality. He was also very pro Stag but led a busy life and had not conducted a musical before. He generously agreed to conduct for nothing.

Open Auditions were the only way I could possibly approach such a gigantic task – a cast of fifty and a crew of amateur volunteers. I needed the creme de la creme of local amateur talent as so much was riding on this production. If it succeeded Stag could continue in business. If it failed . . .

The applications came flooding in. People applied from miles around and I was astonished. The talent that appeared was of an exceptionally high standard and we could not have been more delighted. There was no auditioning committee, just Nicholas, myself and a pianist, and we had a very exciting time. Auditioning people from early morning to late afternoon on two Sundays was as exhausting as it was rewarding.

Another surprise was the number of parents who wanted their small children to be in the show. *My Fair Lady* had no parts for children. My business instinct showed me a hitherto unknown opportunity. Children in the cast would create ticket sales so, without misleading anyone as to their roles, I agreed to have a small 'crowd' of children who had to be prepared to dress the stage but not speak at all and sing very little! The number that applied necessitated two teams of children, and we had to work out which team would perform which night so that parents could book for the right performance – one good deed results in endless complications.

Applicants for the principal roles were excellent. Paul Barnes

129

and Alexandra Leigh were chosen for Professor Higgins and Eliza and we had two such equally wonderful Doolittles (Ted Denman and Geoff Charrot) that we cast them both for alternate performances. A very talented and popular actor with the Holmesdale Players, Patrick Harper, was cast as Colonel Pickering and John Marsh agreed to be the designer. The performances were to be in November with rehearsals from September onwards.

This was to be the first in-house production and I planned no further ahead than coping with the tasks for that year – I had not the least thought in my head that the autumn musical might become an annual money-raising event. Life was becoming ever more busy and the last thing on my mind was forming a company at Stag, although one or two people did suggest it.

We continued with our programme throughout that spring and early summer and one of the highlights was Kentish Opera's production of *Carmen*. This company under the direction of Sally Langford had a fine reputation and normally performed at the Churchill Theatre in Bromley. I was thrilled that they decided to book Stag. It was of course much cheaper for them but our seating capacity was smaller.

The production was stunning and we felt privileged to have had them in the theatre. Francis Price knew Sally and her husband Richard and he helped Rod Nipper with the mammoth task of bringing in the set. The crowd scenes still linger in my mind. The company were lovely, very excited about Stag, very critical about our poor dressing room facilities but full of admiration for what we were trying so hard to achieve.

In the May of that year, 1986, the two local authorities agreed after much complex and protracted negotiation to help fund us for a further three years. What a relief, and how grateful we were. It did not mean that there was any spare money, but at least we could pay for further essential fire precautions and improvements to the building for the safety of the public.

The other public bodies were very good. All the inspectors

(fire, building, health) were sensible and insisted on specific items but they never pushed us to a position where we would have to close. They knew we were doing everything in our power to comply with their requests and whilst they made quite sure that no-one would be in danger they never quite asked the impossible, and for that we were extremely grateful. If we had a problem we sought their advice and personally I found them co-operative and understanding. Of course we were all on the *qui vive* if a uniform appeared in the lower foyer during a perform-ance but it was equally reassuring to know that someone was actually taking the trouble to keep an eye on us. Looking after the public is the most enormous responsibility and one that has to be taken very seriously, so I for one was more than grateful for any help.

September came and we swung into rehearsals for the show. I had worked hard during the summer months in preparation. I knew exactly what I wanted and the cast was very excited at the start of this new venture. The rehearsals whizzed past and, just as we had thought, our choice of principals could not have been bettered. Paul Barnes *was* Professor Higgins and all the others rose to meet his high standard of performance. I just knew it was going to be a knockout.

A costume-hire company in Wimbledon needed a new set of costumes for *My Fair Lady* and I struck a wonderful deal with them. If they would let us submit our designs and colours, would they make them and thereafter keep them for hire? They agreed and a very talented and long standing friend of mine, Gwen Bewsher, who had designed my very first production – *Patience* – agreed to design the costumes for the musical and to oversee the fittings.

Things had changed in the world of costume hire for ama-teurs since the days when I had been fitted and corseted for my part in *The Heiress*. Although amateur companies were still important, economics meant that hire companies had neither the time nor the resources to be so particular as to the final result. More often than not amateurs paid one visit to the costume company, saw sets of costumes, placed their order and then waited for them to arrive on the day of the dress rehearsal. Many's the time when clothes have been missing, did not fit or were not what had been chosen in the first place.

We had none of that. The company in Wimbledon were proud of their standards and our leading ladies had proper fittings overseen by Gwen Bewsher – just like old times. We did not have the same luxury for the men. There was some difficulty in finding suits of the right period for Paul Barnes as he was very tall, but, with a lot of goodwill and chasing around by various people, we managed to dress the show beautifully.

John Marsh and I had endless meetings about the set. His idea was to have a vast study with all its paraphernalia which opened like a book. It was very exciting. The opening and closing of the set would have to be done manually, there were no luxuries in those days, but it would intrigue the audience and, provided it would not hold up the action, would work very well.

Rehearsals continued but were simply part of an ever increasing and rapidly expanding workload. That summer we were afforded a wonderful surprise. An official looking letter arrived one day from Knocker and Foskett, Solicitors in the town. On opening it we found that Stag had been left £7000!

Now £7000 was a fortune especially as we were to do with it whatever we liked. It had been bequeathed to us by Miss Ella Sutton, a well known Sevenoaks resident who had run Miss Sutton's School of Dancing in Argyle Road for years and a place where I had had lessons. We thought long and hard about how best to use it. I had never been able to book classical ballet into Stag because the floor of our stage was quite unsuitable and we had no sound system. To hire both these things put the cost beyond our resources. We decided to buy a dance floor and a basic sound system. The thrill and the responsibility of choosing those two items seemed enormous to us and we were very picky. The companies who were asked to give us quotes were nearly driven to drink by our parsimonious attitude. It was a wonderful feeling knowing that we had chosen something for the theatre of which Miss Sutton would have fully approved. Classical ballet in her home town – what a pity she could not be in the audience.

The workload was increasing daily and Rod was under enormous pressure. He was so conscientious, had become fairly obsessed with the place and put in the most enormous number of hours simply to help me keep it afloat. When jobs needed doing he would do them – we were so lucky that he enjoyed DIY. Of course we had no tools of our own and no money with which to buy any and Rod often brought in his own as did other people. It was a dangerous path to go down but we had no alternative.

I continued to fill the slots in the programme wherever I could, with things I hoped would appeal to the public, and pressed on with the rehearsals for the show. My family were ever supportive and did not begrudge the time I was giving to the theatre – I have a feeling they probably felt more proud of it than I did.

Our three sons were now adults with lives of their own but all still at home with us. They were all creative. Kim, our eldest, went into advertising and Noel and Barry were completely set on succeeding in the pop music world. We were anxious about the two younger boys. We knew the competition was fierce and they would need as much luck as talent, but I had never forgotten not being allowed to 'go on the stage' and John and I both agreed completely that if they wanted to do something we should give them all the support we could, whether we agreed with their choice of career or not. If they were not successful they would at least have had a go. What's the point of looking back in later life and saying "if only . . . "

Tickets for *My Fair Lady* were selling like hot cakes. I had no doubts whatever about the quality of the show. The excitement of rehearsing and polishing a large cast was exhilarating and I believe people really enjoyed those rehearsals. The opportunity of directing a large group of people on such a big stage was a real pleasure.

Opening night came closer and closer. My visits to where the set was being built and painted (a small building in the town) left me with the collywobbles. Could it ever be ready in time? It was *huge*, very elaborate, quite magnificent and would amaze our audiences. But would it work? Either way, no-one would ever have seen anything like it in Sevenoaks.

Tempers became more and more frazzled. It happens every time in the run-up to a show because there is so much to be done by willing helpers who can spare only a few hours when they are not doing their full time jobs.

The set arrived on the stage in the same way as it would eventually leave – in pieces – at the weekend before the opening night, the following Thursday. By the Sunday evening one thing became glaringly obvious. It did not fit. It was six inches too high. Disaster followed by panic.

The idea of 'opening' the study simply did not work – it hit the lights as soon as it moved. John Marsh was away on a professional assignment and whoever we could muster had to sort something out. The pressure was very great.

I was fully occupied with cast, props, costume fittings and all the loose ends that needed to be held in one hand in that vital three days before opening, as well as keeping an eye on all front of house preparations. Rod was working all hours and looking more and more fraught as each hour went by. The dress rehearsal was a nightmare. People were still banging and sawing and it was obvious that some would have to work very late into the night if we were to open.

Thursday dawned and there were still several problems to be sorted out. Rod spent hours on the stage working and supervising others. Electricians were still focusing lanterns, everyone was getting in everyone else's way, there was lots of shouting and, with such a lot at stake, a real feeling of panic.

During the afternoon whilst people were still banging on the stage the electrician simply had to have the lights off. Rod was working with a piece of electrical equipment, did not hear the

134

shout 'lights going out' and was plunged into darkness. That, for him, was the last straw.

Rod exploded, stormed off the stage into the auditorium and was ripping out his equipment before anyone realised what was going on. Peter Othick, in the auditorium at the time, tried to reason with him but Rod had quite obviously had enough. Our first night was on the brink of disaster. I felt quite sick.

There was now only one priority. We had an almost full house turning up in a matter of hours, a sponsor and other important guests who needed to be shown just what the theatre could do and the show *had* to go on.

Before I left the building for my hair appointment I explained to Francis Price, who had just arrived, what had happened. He really understood show business and we had built up a small and excellent team of volunteer helpers who could react well in a crisis. When they heard what had happened they were wonderful. Led by Francis and others they rescued the show by begging and borrowing sound equipment and setting it up ready for that night. Stag owes them a great debt and three names that come immediately to mind are Steve Wiltshire, Paul Kutchera and John Harris.

Forgive me if you think I was absolving myself of all responsibility by sitting in a hair salon. There was nothing I could have done on that stage that would have made any difference whatsoever. Far more technical expertise was needed than I possessed – and I had a first night to contend with. I also knew that, even if the roof had caved in on that show, we had the most marvellous production to offer an audience. We could have done it in a field! My view has always been that if the cast is excellent, the production strong and close attention is paid to detail, a show will succeed. Occasionally so much centres around the technical brilliance of a show that an audience forgets what it has actually come to see. You cannot ever do that to George Bernard Shaw!

Don't ask how, but that set was made to work. I was completely knotted up inside, mainly about Rod, but with so much else on my mind I had no time to pause for thought. As the director I could do no more than stand out front and watch. How little the audience knew of what had gone into that first performance.

As it turned out, the first night was an outstanding success despite one technical hitch from the sound department. In the famous Ascot scene where the racegoers sing that wonderful number *Every Duke and Earl and Peer is Here* they have to pretend to watch the horserace happening in the auditorium (the fourth wall). We had rehearsed it over and over again as the direction of each head on stage was crucial and was synchronised with the thunder of galloping hooves over the sound system. Unfortunately, that night, our horses finished the race before the cast finished the number. Everyone heard galloping horses, a sort of glooping tape sound, dead silence but with rows of faces on the stage still following the race! It looked so funny, it was impossible not to laugh. It's my second strongest memory of that production.

I was very sad about Rod. He was young, younger than any of my sons, and on the morning after the first night he came to see me. He was distraught at what had happened. He knew very well what a frightening position he had placed us in. We both shed tears in my office. We had been through so much together, he had worked so hard and lovingly on that building, but he had been pushed just too far.

Perhaps I ought to have realised it and for that I apologised to him. I suggested that he step back and take a long hard look at Stag from a distance. I was concerned about his seeming possessiveness of the building. I explained all these things to him, told him it worried me deeply and was something everyone ought to try to avoid. He agreed and understood. He did not work for us again but I was pleased to learn that he made a very successful career in the entertainment business in Nottingham.

I had considered carefully the doubts raised over my desire for a Sunday afternoon performance. My reasoning was straightforward. Sundays in winter when the weather is bad can be rather dull – surely there would be many families keen to come out to the theatre after a leisurely lunch and yet be home in time to prepare for Monday morning. In addition our hard-working cast could have a Sunday lie-in as well as an early night. It worked like a charm. It was the first performance to sell out. Families poured in, most of whose children knew all the songs.

Throughout the run, before every performance, I went down to the dressing rooms to make sure everyone was happy. I was particularly careful on the Monday night. After four performances I guessed the energy would be at its lowest and there were still six performances to do. Amateurs were not used to this level of pressure so their morale had to be kept high. I reminded them that the audience had paid good money for their tickets, it would be the only time they would see the show, and the company must give of their all, however they felt. Their faces were an absolute picture when I announced to them that the house was completely sold out. On a Monday! No one was tired after that. John Lurcook, the butler in Professor Higgins' household, was the member of cast deputed to 'open and close' the study, that enormous set which had given us so much grief. I watched every night as he, with stiff upper lip and ever stiffening back, walked to and fro across the stage pushing this huge wall. I know he wore tracks in the floor because it became slightly more difficult every night! However it looked stunning and our audiences were enraptured.

My gamble had paid off – £1,700 net profit and as many as 4,000 people had come through Stag's doors, including the coalman and the milkman! The following extracts from Peter Othick's ensuing letter dated 9th January 1987 have remained embedded in my mind:–

"I enclose the final figures in respect of *My Fair Lady* . . . Looking at the overall position the profit appears to be due to ten consecutive performances, as a break in the continuity could have led to a reduction in audiences in the latter stages. This is apparent as receipts from all

137

sources were basically higher in the last few days and although some expenses could have been reduced by a shorter show, I am convinced that the final profit would have been substantially reduced. The Sunday matinee was an excellent idea and although the box office was lower than some other nights (due to party rates) it was a full house and gave the impetus needed to keep the show in front of the public. It also saved the cast the problem of two shows on one day (Saturday) with the inevitable deterioration of performance in the evening show.

. . . There is no doubt that the show made a very favourable impact on the Town as well as providing a further seven and a half weeks' life for the Stag Theatre . . ."

I felt that said it all.

From the way I have told it, it makes it sound as though the only thing happening was *My Fair Lady*. That could not have been further from the truth. I was experimenting with all kinds of things as part of the programme and, to emphasise my belief that we had to try to appeal to someone in every household locally at least once a year, I decided to go for a sporting event.

At that time our television screens were filled with snooker tournaments from the Crucible Theatre, Sheffield. I decided to see whether snooker would find its niche in Sevenoaks. Of course I tried to get Steve Davis (I always believed in starting at the top) and approached our friendly brewers, Charringtons, to see whether they could give me any introductions and also to try to persuade them to sponsor the event. That was hopeless. They would not sponsor Mr Davis in any venue smaller than a 1,000 seater, so that avenue closed. However, being quite a snooker fan, I knew there were other names that would attract the public. I approached the event from an entirely different angle. I found an advertisement in The Stage, a very large advertisement, for a company who specialised in providing 'stars' for spectator sport events, and I made contact. The bluff

Yorkshireman who dealt with my request was very kindly, told me he knew everything there was to know about such events and agreed to come to see me and the theatre before I signed a contract.

On the appointed day this large, fatherly man in a sports jacket came down to see the theatre. I gave him coffee in the office, told him the history of the place, that we had no money and how we desperately needed a big name for our first event. I took him into the auditorium from the top doors near my office. He gasped.

"Eee lass, this place is *wonderful!* Is it really true that it's taken all these years?"

He looked round the auditorium grinning – "It's smashing, I'll buy it, I'll buy it. I could make a fantastic place out of this."

I laughed. "It's not for sale," I said, but I was very comforted. I knew he would help with our snooker evening because he was so smitten with the place.

As a suggestion he offered *An Evening with Ray Reardon.* I accepted. I asked about the shape of the event. I had never run a snooker exhibition before, what did one do? He suggested that in our advertising of the evening we challenge amateur snooker players to pit themselves against Mr Reardon in a match. Apparently it was possible to manage about three challenges in one evening and the final part of the show would be Mr Reardon's trick shots.

It sounded good to me. He told me not to worry my head about a thing. He had organised more of these evenings than I had had hot dinners and he said everything necessary would be provided by him. The contract arrived, I signed it and we exchanged.

On the day of the event a large lorry arrived with all the snooker lighting and enormous slabs of slate to make up the table. The stage did look wonderful. I had arranged for extra seating to be borrowed from Sevenoaks School so that some members of the audience could sit close to the action, and by the time everything was in place we were delighted.

There was, however, no sign of my kindly Yorkshireman.

I returned very early that evening to the theatre. The seats were un-numbered and unreserved and I suspected that the real enthusiasts would be queuing before the doors opened. As I was preparing floats and the usual bits and pieces I was told that Mr Reardon would like to speak to me in the dressing room.

I went down to give him my usual warm welcome and he was enthusiastic about the venue and the interesting challengers we had managed to find for him. (One young challenger was I believe from Hastings and was fourteen).

He then said "Now, tell me how you would like the evening to run. How many frames do you want me to play and for how long, when is the interval and who is the referee?"

I think I must have turned a shade of green. *I had no idea about any of these things. I thought they were all being done for me!* Thank goodness some of my mis-spent youth had been at the family snooker table. I might have thought he was talking about a picture-frame otherwise.

I came clean and explained my predicament. Mr Reardon was very helpful and did not seem that surprised.

"Oh, don't worry, we'll muddle through somehow and if there's a real problem I'll do some extra trick shots."

I was very grateful to him, all the while silently cursing the man from Yorkshire who had obviously let me down with a crash. I needed to get out front to see what was happening. There was a queue in the upper foyer and I was relieved that we had an audience but very nervous that the evening might be a disaster and that snooker would never be seen again at Stag.

I was dealing with the queue, chatting to people and asking how far they had come because there were very few faces I recognised (always interesting) when a man came up to me and asked me to step to one side.

I did. He said very quietly and out of earshot of the others – "Have you got a referee for tonight?" I couldn't believe my ears – how did he know?

"What makes you ask?" I replied.

140

"I'm a snooker fanatic and I follow Mr Reardon all over the country. Nine times out of ten they've not got a referee. I've my white gloves and bow tie in my pocket if you could use some help – I won't charge."

I nearly hugged him, but didn't, and quickly took him back stage and down to the dressing room.

"Mr Reardon, this angel has appeared out of the blue. I'm so busy out front, could I leave you two to decide the shape of the evening – I really don't mind so long as it works."

It did. Ray Reardon was the perfect personality in such a situation. I think he and my rescuer had met before. The audience was spellbound by his skill and his constant commentary. To this day I have not seen the same sports company advertising and, although I complained about the contract not being fully carried out, I didn't have a leg to stand on. We made a few hundred pounds that night – mostly in the bar. The audience was not huge but I was learning from each new experience.

Also that autumn, before *My Fair Lady*, we had our first visit by a ballet company. London City Ballet were an up-and-coming ballet company, building a fine reputation. They contacted me because they were doing something rather unusual. Half the company was going on a tour abroad and the other half on a tour of England.

They had heard about the size of our stage, they knew we had no flying facilities and could never therefore book the whole company, but they were anxious to 'bring ballet out to the people' and provide an evening of high quality dance. The evening would consist of three separate items. This suited us perfectly. We could use Miss Sutton's dance floor for the first time plus our new sound system. The performances sold very well.

They arrived a day before the first performance as there was much lighting to rig and rehearsals to be held. The company manager complained in no uncertain terms about the draughty conditions on stage and in the dressing rooms. Equity rules were such for ballet dancers that a specific temperature must be maintained and we were nowhere near those requirements (those Equity rules again!). After much heated discussion (obviously not heated enough) we had to provide extra warmth or no performance.

The building was vast and the only way to help was to hire gas blow heaters which cost the earth. Sevenoaks Hire It did us a special price. We did not quite know how it was to be paid for but it was that or no show.

By early evening of the first performance the auditorium was like a turkish bath and a number of the audience complained about how hot they were! One of the many occasions when I knew it was not possible to win.

I continued to keep a variety of events on show at the theatre and sometimes they worked and sometimes they did not. I chased sponsorship whenever I had the time. I was usually successful, but there were not enough hours in the day.

'People'

Within the twelve months spanning 1986-87 Stag was joined by four people who were to play a very significant part in its future success.

A young, enthusiastic man came to us through the then Manpower Services Commission. He was passionate about the technical aspect of theatre, had some experience, lived locally and had been a major player in the rescue operation on that first night of *My Fair Lady*. His name was Steve Wiltshire and he very soon became totally involved in our pioneering work, and was indeed a major part of it. He was one of the only people on the staff who really knew where the crucial services went in and out of the building and what we had to do when a pipe burst or a drain blocked. Over the years he gained enormous experience in the real hard slog of achieving miracles on no money. He gradu-

142

ally took on more and more responsibility for designing lighting for shows, not only our own but also some of our clients'. He became a real part of Stag and stayed with us until 1995.

We had to say goodbye to our secretary, Maria. Her husband Peter was to be relocated to Bristol and a replacement had to be found. We also had to rethink our workload somewhat. I spent hours of time counting endless bags of money (not vast sums but lots of coins) with the help of Peter Othick and I really ought to have been doing more important things.

We decided we must have an administrative assistant rather than a general office secretary. By sheer good fortune we interviewed a man named Dennis Gilkes. He had taken early retirement from the GLC, lived locally, had sufficient income to allow him to take a very badly paid job, was passionate about music, had had experience in the administrative side of the Royal Festival Hall and was prepared to work in the pretty awful conditions we could offer.

It was the best choice we could have made for the work. Dennis could be obstinate but he was meticulous to the nth degree over money. I knew that whatever we earned by sheer slog it would be safe in his hands until it arrived at the bank. He had a wicked sense of humour which I shared, his knowledge of classical music was extremely helpful on occasions, and both his wife Jean (a knitting wizard and costume expert) and his daughter Emma (a talented young musician) became involved and very supportive about what we were trying to do.

Dennis was not a fit man but he would never admit to his poor health. He grappled manfully with our flights of stairs daily and we all admired his spirit. He took a tremendous amount of the daily chores off my shoulders.

When we had exceptionally busy weekends, Monday mornings would find Dennis and Peter Othick at two desks upstairs, money everywhere, money bags spilling onto the floor and we tried very hard not to interrupt. There is nothing more infuriating when you are counting money than to be disturbed. How many times have we had to start again from the beginning, cursing the whole time.

Dennis also helped me with the contracts (he had been involved with them in London), kept manual box office records meticulously and became a tower of strength. He stayed in the team until his death in 1994. The project owes him a great deal.

Throughout these months Francis Price had become more and more involved even though he had a full time occupation of his own. Whenever there was a major crisis (like the whole building freezing up in the middle of the night with a concert the next evening) I could always call on him for help. He never queried the hour I phoned him or why the problem had arisen, he just got on and helped me over it. He always spoke his mind, often to the discomfort of other people, but he was obviously full of admiration that the building was now a theatre and in his home town and he seemed pleased and happy to help whenever possible.

We spent hours discussing progress and strategy, but the theatre was still without a production manager on the staff. The programme was increasing weekly, standards were expected to rise, more money had to be raised annually and the whole place needed to go up a notch. I could do only so much. I had never run a theatre anyway, had no experience of doing so and had only amateur experience backstage.

One day Francis telephoned me from London and asked if we could meet. To my absolute delight he said he would like to work for Stag. His business commitments were no longer a problem and he could not think of anything he would like to do more.

I questioned him very earnestly. I reminded him of the conditions, the lack of money, lack of security and the number of amateurs he would have to deal with. None of it daunted him. He became our production manager and, by dint of sheer slog, like everyone else he gradually raised our image and standards backstage.

He was fully aware that we were desperate for technical

equipment but could afford nothing. We also needed staff to man the shows. He decided that if we could find volunteers for front of house, then he could do the same for the technical side of the theatre: he formed StagTech.

The principle behind this group was to train up volunteers in all aspects of technical theatre work and then go on to raise funds for technical equipment. He knew that 'technically minded' people would pull their weight if they thought they would get better equipment and young people were more than pleased to learn all aspects of backstage work.

StagTech went on to put on shows of a very high standard under the chairmanship of Francis. They raised large amounts of money for the theatre and without their input and enthusiasm we would not have acquired the equipment we did. We had *Round the Clock* fund-raising events (in which I roller skated for the first time in my life), annual musicals and masses of free help with set building and numerous other tasks.

The fourth of my 'people' came to us through an organisation called REACH with whom I had registered. We were now anxious to have professional accounting help to meet the growing demands of the business. Some months earlier we had been publicly criticized at a Council meeting. The words of a Councillor made the front page of the Sevenoaks Chronicle: "I believe we are dealing with a bunch of amateurs incapable of organising their finances." Those words stung, but we had no resources to employ an accountant. All our financial helpers were volunteers.

Albert Granville made an appointment with me through REACH and expressed his interest in the financial aspects of our operation. We met in our very cold bar and I knew this man was going to be right for us. We had a long talk. He was an extremely experienced businessman with time on his hands. I learned that he had been awarded the CBE for his involvement in helping to raise the *Mary Rose* some years previously. He was astonished at the size and potential of the project even in its raw state, was full of energy and wanted to help! I held nothing back from him and he agreed to take over the responsibility for our accounts.

Albert came into that building for two days every week for nothing and, working with Peter Othick, Dennis Gilkes and Richard Shirtcliff who at the time was a director on the Board, he improved our financial image beyond belief.

He had never been involved with the entertainment business before, had never worked with regular volunteers or people who were being paid a pittance and there were occasions when he longed to shout at someone because something had not been done on time, but he very soon learned with some graciousness that we would not be in existence without our volunteers and few staff. It was hard for him but he was the first to admit that it was a way of life which *had* to be stomached at Stag.

He had a very enquiring mind and asked questions about everything, not only concerning figures but how things worked on the stage and how people handled technical equipment. He was always willing to be shown. Little had he realised that he would even end up shifting scenery for a week during a tour of *Postman Pat* because we were short of stage hands! He took it all in good stead. He became our Chairman in 1993 but still continued his two days a week, sharing my office, my problems, my joys.

He even got the acting bug. When I directed *A Man For All Seasons* in 1992 Albert was cast as Signor Chapuys, the Spanish Ambassador. It was his first ever performance on a stage and he thoroughly enjoyed himself. So much so that he also appeared in *Amadeus* at Stag in 1995. His wife, Jocelyn, has been very long suffering over Albert's commitment to the theatre. Often we would be working at the office and Albert would suddenly remember that he was supposed to have bought the salmon for supper and would dash out and be very relieved when he found the shop still open!

Those four people became vital to the whole scheme of things and Sevenoaks should be indebted to them. Other individuals, far too numerous to name, helped with everything. Wherever their strength lay we used it to the full.

146

If I Hadn't Laughed . . .

We kept pushing forward, all the time struggling for money but all the time enjoying ourselves. Our standards were improving in every area, more and more people were becoming involved both as audience and performers, there were increasing enquiries from groups wanting to hire the theatre, but still that lack of money dogged us and occupied a very large part of my thinking time and energy.

We did not seem able to get the business community in the district to acknowledge us. Sevenoaks has never had a large industrial base, which is probably one of the reasons why it is so attractive, but we had some good-sized companies in the area. The problem was that most of their Head Offices or parent companies were in another part of the country altogether. It was exceptionally difficult trying to persuade local managers to get behind the Stag.

I decided to hold a series of 'Business Men's Suppers'.

One of our great supporters was Ray Gulliver of Gulliver Timber Treatments. When I spoke to him about my idea he encouraged it. He said that I should invite any local businessman I knew to one of these suppers and ask that person to bring at least one or two of his peers. Wives were of course included and we would aim to have about sixteen people per supper and run about four. Another 64 converts hopefully!

It took a great deal of time and effort. To begin with we had to get the guests to agree to come which wasn't easy. I think people were afraid we were going to jump on them for money, and they were not far off the mark, but it would be done diplomatically and they could always refuse!

We had no catering facilities. I prepared very sumptuous suppers at home then had the fun of transporting them in a car which was not made for carrying food! The bar was, as ever, chilly and it had to be paper tablecloths and napkins. All this cost money. However, once more our enthusiasm overcame all the obstacles and with the help of at least one or two directors on each occasion the suppers were an enormous success.

Guests were given a large drink on arrival. We would then make the introductions. I would start the 'business' of the evening with a brief chat about our aims for the theatre. I had what passed for a flip chart showing our shopping list of needs in order of priority, and when I hoped they had had time to absorb the facts we sat down to supper. It was very friendly, there were lots of laughs and at least we had persuaded busi-nessmen to come through those front doors. That was the first step.

After coffee we set off on a tour of the building. That made the greatest impression of all. Everyone who came to those evenings gasped with astonishment when they saw the size and potential of the project, regardless of its basic state. They simply could not believe that we had taken on such a mammoth task. It suddenly became a 'real' project, not some little hut that we were trying to convert.

We did not get cash from those suppers but lots of gifts in kind and a great deal more understanding from the business community that we were serious about what we were doing.

I was forever thinking up ways and means of raising money. One of the areas where we had so far not succeeded at all was getting a large commercial organisation to book the theatre. We needed people in that building who would spread the word once they had seen the place, and a few commercial bookings would really help. How to get them? We had so little to offer. No catering facilities, a large bar room filled with an odd mixture of furniture, an auditorium which worked well but was by no means glamorous, a large stage with little technical equipment and a reliable box office with very pleasant staff.

As one young secretary friend of mine said when I asked her to look round the building, "My boss wouldn't entertain anyone in here – he's used to plush furniture and warm surroundings."

148

I knew she was right – we all thought the place was wonderful but if you were objective about it it was in fact tatty – very well-loved, but tatty!

One day, quite out of the blue, a telephone enquiry came from a national corporation asking about the facilities in the theatre for a conference. A conference! I kept remarkably cool, promoted like mad and it was arranged that the prospective client would come to see the theatre.

When they arrived, I first took them to the auditorium. The size of the stage delighted them.

They explained to me that these management conferences had been held in very large hotels up to then but that the technical facilities were poor and the audience sat on chairs in a flat floored hall. For projection and stage presentation using professional equipment which they would provide Stag knocked everything else into a cocked hat. They were careful about their budget but our 'commercial' rent which I had carefully calculated, though higher than our normal rents to struggling groups, was very favourable compared with costs at hotels.

They wanted to accommodate about 400 people. We finished our discussion in the auditorium. As we made our way out the senior man said "Now what can you offer us in the way of catering?" My mouth went dry. Catering for 400? Oh dear, oh dear. I thought very fast on my feet.

"I'm afraid we cannot offer a proper sit down lunch as we simply do not have the room. May I suggest that we provide a boxed lunch, have the bar and coffee bar open and endeavour to serve your managers as quickly as possible in that way."

They asked if I would object if their own caterers were brought in. I had to show them what passed for a kitchen and we agreed to talk about it a little later when they had had time to report back. Several telephone calls later, they asked if I would provide cheese and pickle rolls to be served from the upper foyer and the bar. I simply could not afford to let this opportunity slip through our fingers – we needed that money so badly.

Just the logistics of getting 400 people queuing into and out of that bar room filled me with terror but my clients were prepared to take it in 'shifts' because the appeal of the large stage to them was too great to be lost.

No time to be negative. I said that we would be delighted to provide what they had asked for now that they knew our limitations. I put the phone down and then began to think how *on earth* we would be able to cope. I must have been mad.

Nothing in the world was going to jeopardise this opportunity for the theatre. I worked out that if everything was made without employing outside caterers Stag would make quite a lot of profit – the choice was made for me. I priced blocks of cheese, catering size jars of pickle, catering butter, and did a special deal with Plaxtol Bakery for 500 rolls (in case we broke some!).

There was only one way that 450 rolls could be prepared for the day. They would have to be done in batches weeks ahead of the conference, sealed and frozen in almost every freezer round Sevenoaks. The grapevine spread the word that I needed freezer space and willing hands at certain times. Lots of offers of freezer space, a very few offers of help because there were specified times when it had to be done – there was no time to portion everything, deliver it to other people – so I raised the question at home. Who on earth had the time to spare and would actually enjoy doing hundreds of these rolls, not to mention the manual grating of pounds and pounds of cheese?

Well, bless him – my husband – what a sport. Weekend after weekend when I was at the theatre he would come up with me and spend hours preparing cheese and pickle rolls. Grating the cheese itself took ages and he used to end up with stiff shoulders and an aching back, but he never gave up. I would never have managed without him. As each batch was completed it was sealed and popped into someone's freezer – a mammoth task!

There was great excitement in the theatre that we had at last cracked our first commercial booking, and at least two technical meetings were held with our clients to ensure that the day ran smoothly.

John finished the cheese and pickle rolls about two weeks before the event and I was so grateful to him. Freezers all round Sevenoaks were bursting, even the second-hand one which had been donated to the theatre had more than its fair share – that freezer had also to play host to the ice for the bar and occasionally ice creams for the theatre, so there was not that much room. But the rolls were done – we were ready.

During one extremely busy day about ten days before the great event, my clients telephoned. They wished to cancel. You could have knocked me down with the proverbial feather. Once more I had to think very fast on my feet. I could not allow this conversation to end without making sure the theatre was properly compensated. This had never happened to me before. Just as important to our reputation, I had to be very careful not to let on about the food having been prepared so far in advance – that really would have given the impression that we were a Mickey Mouse organisation – heaven forbid!

I struck a deal – the best I could manage on the spot. The theatre rent would have to be paid in full, there was no doubt about that as the contract had been broken. I explained also that I had had to order certain quantities of food in advance and that at least the cost of that would have to be covered. My clients agreed – at least the theatre would not lose out.

But how would I tell John? . . .

Once I had arrived home that evening I seemed to keep finding lots of things to do to avoid our usual matey conversation about my day. Suddenly even domestic chores held a previously unfelt charm – what on earth would I say to him after all those hours of boring slog?

In the event, I just blurted it out over a cup of tea in the kitchen. I could contain myself no longer. There was absolute silence. I could feel John seeing himself grating all that cheese and smelling that pickle for hours – I felt awful.

"What reason did they give, darling?" he managed eventually.

"It was more than their budget would run to," I replied. "Apparently Head Office suddenly decided that a conference of any kind was simply not possible."

"Oh well – get a packet out of the freezer and we'll start on them for supper!"

We were always able to see the funny side and on this occasion John really needed his sense of humour. I was also desperately disappointed because I had hoped it would be the beginning of some serious commercial bookings for Stag, but it was not to be.

So, how then to use up all those cheese and pickle rolls? I decided that from then on, whenever we had a show in the theatre, we would offer our audiences refreshments. Cheese and pickle rolls appeared over the months from various freezers and sat in baskets on the bar before, during and after shows. They were very scrummy – John had not stinted on the filling and they were much appreciated. In the end we threw away about three dozen which was not bad after such a fiasco. We had also made a few extra pounds for our coffers.

The Saga Continues . . .

The months flew by as did the years and our foothold in Sevenoaks grew stronger and stronger. All the time money remained exceptionally tight.

StagTech under the leadership of Francis was constantly raising money for technical equipment and one or two wonderful individuals gave us donations. These always seemed to appear when we were hanging on for dear life. One man, whom I had known since my teens, always told me I was wasting my time trying to make a theatre work in Sevenoaks. He ran a large company locally and was very sceptical about our future. It was doubly rewarding, therefore, when many years later he made a sizeable donation to Stag and was gracious enough to admit that he had been wrong – Sevenoaks obviously used its new theatre.

If there was ever an opportunity to raise funds, we took it, but this mostly brought in very small amounts. We were certainly not profligate – if anyone wanted to spend £1 Dennis quite rightly queried it, and this attitude helped to build up a most wonderful spirit of achievement and camaraderie.

As a volunteer for StagTech a young man called Peter Fleming began to be trained in all aspects of technical work. His parents, Ian and Penny, became stalwart members of our group of front of house volunteers, and from then on Peter was never far away from anything that was going on. In later years he became someone we relied on, passionate about the place with lots of common sense and a friendly personality which endeared him to all who worked with him. He helped us in a big way with a number of the large shows and if he was available he was always prepared to help us out. He eventually became a member of our paid staff and stayed with the theatre until 1996.

StagTech also drew to its widening group of enthusiasts the Galbraith family. Peter, his wife Valerie and daughters, Alexandra and Sally, became devoted followers. It was Peter who instigated our magnificent scenery builders and created some of the most exciting sets Sevenoaks has ever seen.

One of our greatest and most memorable in-house successes was *Blitz* by Lionel Bart, suggested by Francis. I had never seen it during its run in the West End (I think I was too busy having babies at the time) and it was very difficult to obtain the rights.

Francis made one or two trips to London, and by dint of much charm and persuasion he was able to go into some attic room above the agent and practically scrape the score off the floor.

The music was in a terrible state, there was no proper orches-tration, yet for me the idea of the show had enormous appeal. It was so British, it had not been seen for years, was hardly ever performed by an amateur society, had a large cast and had enormous box office appeal.

To my delight Terry Shaw agreed to be the musical director. He spent months of his free time orchestrating a score and writing out parts, and although it was a huge job I believe he quite enjoyed it.

We all had a marvellous time doing that show. Everyone became so involved. Pictures of the second world war appeared at rehearsals, people gave us gas masks, tin helmets and army belts, and there was a great family feeling among the company. As we rehearsed it brought it all back to those who had lived through it, and the young were swept up in this great feeling of pulling together.

The preparation was very exciting and somewhat nerve-racking. In the show itself there had to be bomb sounds, sirens and a final serious explosion which would tip up trestle tables. I spent some happy but concentrated hours with a stage maroon expert and Francis and Steve, sitting in the auditorium and deciding the precise volume of sound that we would require from various bangs. It had to sound real but it must not upset the audience. It was a fine line to tread – but fascinating.

We called in the local fire brigade to show us how to mount a ladder correctly for a rescue operation, how to roll out the hose (how heavy that was) and John Lurcook researched pictures and books both for publicity purposes and to get the real atmosphere on the stage.

It was wonderfully successful. We ran for 10 performances (I was still repeating what I had started with *My Fair Lady*) and audiences flocked from far and wide. Because the show had not previously been released for amateurs we had groups from other societies coming in coaches from places as far away as Plymouth and Bristol.

The atmosphere during that show was quite special. Everyone seemed to sense the tension whilst experiencing that wonderful spirit which is essentially British. Standing at the back each night and feeling that excitement always brought a lump to my throat. We were very honoured to have Mr Lionel Bart and Mr Richard Harris, the author, in the audience one night. Mr Bart was hoping to re-write the show for the West End and he was most complimentary about what he saw. Another artistic and financial success – almost 94% capacity audiences.

We were moving in the right direction. The instincts were still working well.

I now found the task of being Chairman of the Board, as well as all these other commitments, very taxing to do properly. I had never pretended I was a great chairman – I had led the Board more by default than anything else – and I was very anxious that Stag should broaden its public image. I was highly relieved and delighted, therefore, when Patrick Pascall agreed to take on the role.

It's An Ill Wind . . .

In 1987 Sevenoaks became internationally famous overnight.

In the terrible gale that October our town became One Oak. Six of our seven magnificent oak trees on the Vine Cricket Ground were uprooted – it looked as though there had been another blitz.

The evening leading up to that night was rather eerie. We had a performance in the theatre and, as was usual, Francis, Steve Wiltshire and I were the last to leave the building. It was nearing midnight. As we were walking down the side path we all noticed how strange the atmosphere was. It was almost as though the world was holding its breath. Exceedingly warm, almost oppressive, very, very still. Even on the windiest corner of Sevenoaks, at the edge of the car park, there was not a movement.

We all remarked upon it, said goodnight and went to our respective homes.

John and I had been living at 16 The Close for some time. It was a house built in part of the old Montreal Park Estate which had been so beautiful many years before. In the garden was a very large, very old oak tree. We went to sleep but I was woken by the strangest flashing light sometime during the night and the weirdest, creepiest sounds I have ever heard. Everything *felt*

155

wrong. The wind was incredible and within seconds I was wide awake. I could think of nothing except the old oak tree outside, and memories of diving under the stairs for cover during the blitz were flashing through my mind. I shook John.

"Do you think we ought to go downstairs under the dining room table? I'm scared."

"Scared? In bed with *me?* My darling, you're in the safest place. Cuddle up. If your number's on it you won't know anything about it anyway. What's the point of going downstairs and getting cold?"

There was a certain logic in what he said and I burrowed under the clothes but I shall never forget that noise as long as I live. It seemed to go on for about half an hour.

Suddenly there was the most tremendous crash. With bated breath I waited for the ceiling to come down – it did not. I instinctively put out my hand to switch on the bedside light – nothing. I tried the radio – dead silence.

Even John was now a little concerned. He reluctantly got out of bed, picked up the torch and said he would just look out of the bedroom door. He went across the hall towards the back of the house where the spare bedroom and bathroom faced the garden. I heard him go into the spare room and come out very quickly. He then opened the bathroom door. As he did so I could hear smashed glass being pushed back by the door.

He came back. He put out the torch and climbed back into bed.

"I shouldn't go into the spare room, the window's out. I think the bathroom's a bit of a mess too but there's nothing either of us can do now with no electricity. We're both still in one piece – thank God none of the boys was staying here. Let's go back to sleep."

Talk about calm in a crisis. I was very relieved about the boys. I knew they were all safe in different parts of London that night and I said a prayer of thanks. We eventually got back to sleep – by now it was once again quiet. I was first up in the morning. The spare bedroom window had smashed and a branch stuck drunkenly through the gaping hole. The bathroom was terrible. Its windows had been shattered by a large part of the oak tree and there was glass everywhere.

In a somewhat dazed state I went downstairs not knowing what to expect. The lower hall was intact, the front door still closed. I opened the door to the living room. It was very dark. The whole of the french doors and windows were a scene of leaves, branches, twigs and general mess. I could not see out at all.

I went into the kitchen. From there I could see an enormous branch of the oak tree which had split and smashed into the back of the house, burying itself in the lawn and creating havoc. I put on the kettle and stared out of the window. What a ghastly mess, but how fortunate we had been. I made the tea and saw some branches moving on the lawn. I could not believe my eyes. There, among the leaves and looking anxiously up at the house, was Francis with our next door neighbour. Everyone was very relieved that we were OK and it was tea all round.

We hardly dared express our thoughts about the theatre. Would it still be standing? Could it be possible that in maybe half an hour nature had undone all that we had strived so hard to achieve? Francis went ahead of me just in case. He came back with wonderful news. Stag was alright, still standing and apart from some small damage that building had withstood the night's onslaught.

John and I counted our blessings too. Had that oak tree been uprooted and fallen on the house we would not have been around to tell the tale. God moves in a mysterious way.

Our district was devastated. Acres of land had been laid waste. The magnificent trees in Knole Park and surrounding areas looked as though a great hand had swept across them uprooting them in a fit of real rage. No-one could quite take it in. If that wind had come six or seven hours later when people were up and about their business the loss of human life would have been unspeakable.

So, we all thanked our lucky stars and got on with the business of repairing the damage and coping as best we could with what had been handed to us. Compared to many we were very fortunate – hundreds of people in rural areas were without electricity and water for many days, but the British spirit once again rose to the surface. Everyone helped everyone else wherever they could.

The town became the subject of media attention. Our Chief Executive of the District Council, Bruce Cova, did an excellent PR job and made sure that Sevenoaks was well and truly on the map. Sevenoaks featured on television and radio and became the comedian's topical joke – "you know, the town they've renamed One Oak!" People came from everywhere to stare at the sights and arrangements were made to plant seven new young oaks on the Cricket Ground. This was carried out with a deal of media hype and once again we had seven oaks.

We all felt a bit better. After all, it was a very strange feeling losing more than three-quarters of the foundation for our town's name and it was more comfortable to have seven oaks back in their rightful place.

Our relief was short-lived. Within a few months most of our new young trees had been vandalised. They had to be replaced and this time carefully protected. How senseless and mindless some people can be.

Very slowly and often quite painfully, Stag continued to make progress. We strove to be as professional as possible and under Francis and Steve our technical facilities and services improved in leaps and bounds.

I continued with my 'policy' of something for everyone and decided to try Wrestling. I knew it would look good on that stage, it was gradually being taken off our TV screens on a Saturday afternoon and maybe local people would appreciate it on their doorstep.

I booked a complete evening package (not from my Yorkshireman!), arranged for stage seating to be available and contracted to have the best names we could afford. It sold reasonably well, we had a very different audience that night and I was quite intrigued. I had never been to a wrestling match, I had heard the grunts and groans on TV and was very interested to learn how they could do all that and seemingly not get hurt.

After about ten minutes into the show, I walked into the auditorium from the foyer and stood on the few stairs leading up to the seats. I was quite amazed at the theatricality of it all. The wrestlers' skills could not be denied but it was a real performance. From the noise one would have thought each man was being murdered, yet he got up and came back for more. Well-dressed ladies were shouting their heads off, waving their handbags and generally joining in.

I got the giggles. I had to leave the auditorium fast. What a spectacle – fantastic, but not very well attended. I would have to think carefully about a repeat performance. The problem was that I needed to run these types of shows for about six times before I could take a decision as to whether Sevenoaks wanted them or not. Sadly, I lacked the funds to do so.

A few days after this event I was doing an unexpected stint in the box office. Dennis or I would often relieve staff and this particular day it was my turn. A couple came to the window. I was marking off a previous sale and had my head bent but said "Good morning, I won't keep you a minute" and finished the last ticket sale. The gentleman spoke immediately. I did not recognise him or the lady with him.

"We were appalled to see that you had wrestling in this theatre recently."

"I'm sorry to hear that" I replied, hoping not to reveal my role in the matter.

"When we started to support this theatre we were very impressed with what was programmed – but to have wrestling – how could you?"

Still not wanting to identify myself, I said I imagined it was to give the public a wide variety of events. The man leant down to look me straight in the eye.

"Mrs Durdant-Hollamby, when did you last see a theatre in the West End putting on wrestling? If this is the sort of thing that is going to happen Stag will not have a future."

Bother, they knew who I was. No escape there then. I then tried to explain my policy, thanked them most profusely for comparing Stag to a West End theatre and told them I would bear in mind their complaint. Another instant where one cannot win.

Still, you can't change your tack because someone criticises you and I was completely confident that I was taking the theatre along the right lines.

Our amateur clients, at first horrified by what seemed to be exorbitant rental charges (compared with their usual venues), soon began to realise that when they considered the 'whole' package offered to them for the money, and how much of the aggravation was removed from mounting an entertainment, Stag was not at all over expensive.

My instinct over the years had been to persuade groups to use the theatre because I knew they would find that their audiences demanded a decent night out; but, because I had such an understanding of their financial limitations and because the theatre needed them desperately to use the building, our hire charges did not in fact make us any profit at all. They helped only to keep the building open and serviced. Our overheads were still as low as low.

I now had to earn a slightly more reasonable salary and the Board members agreed that I should become a consultant administrator full time for the theatre. Stag could not afford to pay my national insurance or tax so I remained self-employed.

I still ran the bar myself, apart from the super volunteers who worked when the theatre was open, and although I badly needed paid help in that quarter, it was out of the question.

Volunteers were not that easy to find for serving behind the bar. A lovely one, Gill Maier, agreed to take on the role of enlisting people for bar duty. She worked very, very hard herself behind the bar and for a long time was extremely successful. But as with everything, people were becoming more and more busy, their spare time was in great demand and we were finding it harder and harder to get volunteers to do what was in fact quite a tough task.

I am amazed at how many folk did put up with what was often a very stressful ordeal.

We had our moments, of course. One evening I was very busy serving customers when a couple approached the bar and ordered drinks. The woman said "I must say this place looks so much better now. We came in the early days and it was really grotty. There was a woman here then who did Business Men's Suppers – I think she had quite a lot to do with the project. Have you any idea what happened to her?"!!!!

It suddenly struck me how white my hair had turned in the intervening years and how much I must have aged. I could not help smiling to myself but took the coward's way out.

"No," I said, "I'm afraid I have no idea at all!"

The Cinema

Whilst we were improving our standards up in the theatre, the two cinema screens downstairs were run by a separate company and we were beginning to have problems.

The company operated a video games room as well as the cinema. This room, situated at the side of the building where the Costume Hire is now housed, was often crowded with youngsters, particularly at weekends, and complaints were being made about behaviour and under-age drinking. Supervision was not always as tight as it might have been and on too many occasions loutish youths would hang about the alleyway ('vomit alley' as it was nicknamed by us) and very often shout abuse at audiences who were attending the theatre. It became so bad that many of our female volunteers refused to park in the car park behind the theatre.

There were discussions and requests to the cinema company to control the use of this room and, although efforts were made, in general the situation worsened. My fear was that we would begin to lose our hard-won audiences who were not prepared to put up with such intimidation on what was supposed to be a 'night out'.

The thorny problem as to where the young could go in Sevenoaks was by no means new to me. We had brought up three very lively sons in the town and had had to work very hard to help them find things that would occupy them in their leisure time. I had a deal of sympathy for the dilemma but I could not afford to let the theatre suffer. I had no objection to a video games room if it could be properly and adequately supervised. I felt in fact that we would be doing a service to the town if we could provide an outlet for the young. However I had no resources or desire to staff it. I paid a visit to the police station and suggested that perhaps a retired policeman might be persuaded to take over the running of the room. I explained the quite serious problems to the officer I met, particularly my anxiety about very young people drinking from bottles of spirits in the alleyway below the side path. I asked who would be responsible if anyone met with an accident in that alleyway and to my consternation was told that it would be Stag.

My suggestion was dismissed. The venue was apparently a thorn in the side of the community, was not really wanted, and it was suggested that Stag would be doing everyone a favour by closing it. I had at least tried.

I was quite relieved when I had time to consider it. The theatre was in great need of its own 'wardrobe' and we also needed more income. I suggested to the Board, and it was agreed, that we should terminate the permission to the cinema to run the games room, convert the space and have our own wardrobe and costume hire.

I knew that we would not be very popular with the young and, although there was a little friction from one or two people, some parents actually thanked me for putting an end to a slightly unsavoury activity. The company running the cinema was not too pleased – it was a large part of their income – but business is business and we had to survive.

Our wardrobe was born and was set up by someone who had helped us for some years as a volunteer mostly backstage, Margaret Walton. She worked exceptionally hard, often in very cold surroundings, and by dint of charming persuasion began to gather a collection of items that we could hire out. She made many of our costumes and eventually ran the wardrobe for us for a pittance. We owe her a lot. She now has her own costume hire company in Colchester.

1988 – 1992

This four year period was to see many, many changes, a great personal sadness for me and a suggestion to the theatre which was to change its face entirely.

Money was still very tight – boring but true. However successful we were, we ran on a shoe-string. The programme was of necessity limited by what we could afford.

One day an agent in London rang me to ask if I would like The Turkish State Dance Company. He explained that they were touring England for a very limited period. I said of course I would but I could not possibly afford them, we seated only 455 people and I had seen advertisements which showed they were going to venues seating thousands.

He offered me a very special deal. The company had one Sunday free and if Stag would host the event the price would be minimal. How refreshing – an agent who would rather earn something for the company on a free day, however little. I jumped at it.

A few months later I opened the *Daily Telegraph* and there in a huge advertisement was The Turkish State Dance Company. Proudly I saw, in the list of vast and important theatres where it was touring – The Stag Theatre Sevenoaks. What a thrill. Stag was at last on the map. All sorts of people told me (many with surprise) that they had seen our theatre in various national papers and our morale was raised another notch. The bookings flooded in and we were very soon sold out. The performance was for 3.30 on a Sunday afternoon. We were all in very early to be ready for our full house.

The town was quite a sight. There were lots and lots of people about from around 2 o'clock, many wanting to come into the theatre early, and we were quite delighted to see so many foreigners in what looked like Turkish national dress arriving at the theatre. They came in families, the little girls looking enchanting in their very pretty and unusual clothes, and the atmosphere in the building was buzzing.

The performance was breathtaking. What a troupe of dancers, and how the audience reacted to their energy and style. Sevenoaks had never seen anything like it and we made money! That was a real success. Offers like that were few and far between but when they did come, if I could accommodate them, I grabbed them.

I managed to arrange another special treat. Richard Briers, one of my most favourite actors, agreed to appear on a Sunday afternoon for a 'question and answer' session on his life in the theatre. He persuaded Peter Egan to accompany him and together they provided an eager audience with an insight into their professional lives. It was a delightful occasion and one for which I was *particularly* grateful – they did it for nothing!

I began to think about running the cinemas downstairs. I had kept a careful watch on the dwindling audiences that patronised them, and ideas were popping around in my head. I was convinced that, run in the same style as the theatre with a warm welcoming staff and films that were chosen occasionally to suit Sennockians as well as first releases, it could become more successful. We were receiving a rent for that portion of the building. I knew that we could do better if we had the courage to take it over.

I broached the subject with Albert Granville. He was not over-keen but had an open mind and was prepared to help me do some investigating. We started making general enquiries about the running of cinemas. One or two larger companies approached us with a view to taking it over themselves. Their figures were impressive. We thought if they could do it, why not us?

The Board of Directors raised eyebrows. Run cinemas? We had no knowledge of what it involved. I gently reminded them that we had never run a theatre before either. My view was that the theatre and cinemas should be part of a whole – not running in competition with each other, particularly as one aspect of the operation was pulling the other downwards. I must have believed in it passionately. The Board finally agreed.

The first two or three years of running those cinemas were not without their own nightmares.

We were fortunate in being able to employ qualified technical staff (even if some of them had come out of retirement) but in the early days it was touch and go. I set to work to learn the pro-gramming of films and I did it with as much care and attention as I gave to the theatre.

I knew it would be quite unfair to expect our band of volun-teers to help us on a regular basis with the cinemas. It was after all a seven day a week operation with sometimes three shows per day. Even I would not have expected anyone to give up their spare time so regularly. We had to find new staff, in particular a chief projectionist, and for a while the man who had run the cinema when it was independent, Sandy Sanderson, came onto our payroll. He taught me a lot and I never ceased to ask ques-tions about the business.

We had no cinema manager so the bulk of front of house fell on my shoulders. I did not mind at all – I had suggested the idea and I was really enjoying improving the atmosphere down-stairs. We began to see customers coming into the cinema who had not paid it a visit for twenty years or more.

I learned as I went.

The previous owners of the cinemas, Peter Dobson andTim Partner, acted as our 'bookers'. Bookers deal directly with the distributors and Peter and Tim had been involved with them all for years. They carried more clout than some female in Sevenoaks who had never run a cinema in her life.

I read about films till the information came out of my ears. I talked to avid filmgoers, watched Barry Norman on the television and generally absorbed as much information as I could. I found it very difficult to understand the principles of business in the cinema industry. I had one or two quite fierce arguments about what I knew would sell in our cinema and I often fought quite hard against having to have a film which I knew would do no business. Frequently I had to take what I considered no good in order to be considered favourably for a product which I desperately wanted. That really stuck in my throat.

I discovered that as far as the distributors were concerned, all cinemas were in a 'pecking order'. We seated so few patrons in the existing two screens that we were well down this list. I decided then that whenever I could, and if I thought the film would do the business, I would put it upstairs on the big screen in the theatre. The distributors were almost always very accommodating when they knew we could seat 455 at each showing!

My workload was now beginning to be impossible (though still enjoyable) and we decided to employ a professional person to manage the cinema but one who would also take on the theatre front of house duties to give me some added relief.

We advertised, spent hours interviewing and finally chose a man who had managed cinemas most of his working life. We explained precisely what we were looking for, particularly someone who would enjoy being 'out front' and a person who would become a major part of our team. Our chosen applicant appeared delighted. He said he had a great passion for theatre as well as cinema and the one thing he had always wanted to do was be involved in both. He began his job with us in the spring.

I decided that that summer it would be safe for me to have a full week's holiday. My new cinema manager would have learned the ropes from me, there would be little theatre activity after the Summer Festival and all would be well. What a relief.

I spent many many evenings with our new man, careful not to let him feel pressured but leaving him to cope whenever possible, and he seemed to be enjoying it. Our operation was nowhere near as sophisticated as he was used to and the 'hands on' approach was fairly different for him but I was hopeful. There was a great responsibility in 'running the house' when two screens and the theatre were open. Someone would invariably run out of change (and that meant a dash up two flights of stairs to the safe), someone would have lost their tickets or be going into the wrong auditorium or the beer would suddenly run out. You had to have your wits about you every second, and our volunteer front of house manager for the theatre was an enormous asset during those evenings. I made quite sure that our new member of staff was au fait with all contingencies and took my week's holiday.

I returned in the afternoon of the following Sunday because I was going to relieve him after his week. We passed in the car park although I was not late. I asked how everything had gone. He looked uncomfortable.

"I'm afraid I'm resigning. I've handed in my notice. It's not going to work."

I was astounded. Here was someone with years of experience, longing to run both a theatre and a cinema, and after a few months he couldn't stand our pace. Colleagues' words of advice kept ringing in my ears – "You must delegate, you'll wear yourself out." What was the point of delegating when people simply didn't do the job?

The summer holidays were fast approaching and I had budgeted to show films at least twice if not three times a day in the theatre. Great help for our cash flow, desperately needed, but now I had no manager.

We had by now recruited two or three part-time projectionists, all very mature men, two of whom had been projectionists in their young days when Sevenoaks had three cinemas. For the eight weeks of the holidays we needed projectionists seven days a week, a front of house manager, kiosk attendants and ushers, not to mention the cleaning that needed to be done daily between shows – and I do mean cleaning.

That summer holiday period was an experience I would not wish to repeat.

We were completely over-stretched on the cinema staffing side and out of sheer necessity I learned to turn the projection equipment on and off, not as simple as it sounds. We were never able to get two projectionists on duty at once which was really necessary with three screens running, the projection box of one being up three flights of stairs. The scheduling of films, ie the start time, had to be really tight. Each programme in each screen had to start 15 minutes after the other in order for the projectionist to start up each one. The sheer logistics left me breathless.

One Sunday evening when I was front of house the projectionist knew he had a problem with the film on the big screen upstairs and he had taken me through it two or three times. The film had what is known as a 'rack' which means that at a particular point the picture goes skew-whiff and out of focus. There was a special lever which cured this problem so long as someone was sitting there waiting and dealing with it on the spot.

I had rehearsed this operation and was fairly confident. We had a really good audience that evening upstairs, lots of tourists, foreign students and school pupils. My projectionist set the other two screens going downstairs and then started the programme upstairs. An usher downstairs was deputed to watch carefully and to come and get the projectionist should anything happen downstairs. All was well, the programme was started and my projectionist went down the three flights of stairs to deal with the Intermissions which would follow one another on the two screens downstairs.

I remained 'equipment sitting' upstairs waiting for the 'rack'. I knew precisely where it was. We had no communication what-

168

soever between the upper projection box and the lower ones. If you needed to send a message you had to run. The rack appeared and I raised the arm gently to restore the picture. Nothing happened. I gently pushed the arm again and the rack got worse. The picture on the huge screen was looking like a jumpy early black and white. The audience started to whistle, boo, hiss and stamp.

I felt terrible. I could not just go and leave it and I knew there would be at least five minutes before my projectionist could come back upstairs because he was busy. I wanted the floor to open up and swallow me as the noise became louder from the auditorium. Thank goodness they couldn't see me – I had visions of being lynched.

It felt like a lifetime before help arrived and the whole thing was rectified by a completely puffed out projectionist. To me it was like being in the middle of a stage performance and forget-ting all my words. Simply ghastly. I arrived home that night like a washed-out dishrag. I felt the same as I had all those years ago when our cook had not turned up at The Moorings. However, my convinction remained that we were absolutely right to be running the cinemas despite the problems.

In 1988 John, who had always been a heavy smoker, had a really serious cough which simply would not go. To our utter dismay he was diagnosed as having emphysema. All other nightmares faded into nothing by comparison.

John had never been ill apart from a mastoid operation when he was nine. He had a very positive attitude to good health and believed passionately in mind over matter. "Look in the mirror every day and tell yourself you're fine," he would say. "If more people could do that there would be a lot less moaning about aches and pains."

He had always been physically strong and extremely athletic and had not the slightest conception that he might have a serious condition. Emphysema meant nothing to him. So far as he was concerned, he had a cough which now had to be taken seriously, it was becoming difficult for him to breathe properly on occasions and if the medical profession told him to give up smoking then he would do so – not because he wanted to but because he did not believe you should ask an expert's opinion then disregard it.

He had a very serious bout of pneumonia which put him into hospital. Whilst there he reacted strongly against an antibiotic and for twenty four hours it was touch and go. I geared my work round my time with him in hospital. He was adamant that Stag should not suffer because of this 'slight inconvenience'. It made it quite difficult for me. Had I insisted on giving up the theatre he would have become highly suspicious. He was nobody's fool but he was quite sure this little problem would go away if he did as he was told. As far as he was concerned there was no reason in the world why I should change my routine.

He recovered very well from the pneumonia and with the aid of a puffer, which he could not bear anyone to see him using, he began to learn to lead the life of a man who could no longer do everything he set his mind to. He was so disciplined it always amazed me. This was a man who had been trained in the Special Air Service, who never thought about being unwell and who was completely fearless. He was a real example to us all.

However, as the months rolled into a year and the breathing did not become any easier, I knew that he was beginning to question the point of doing what he was told. He had no idea that emphysema could kill. He was sure it would clear up and I certainly wasn't going to prick his bubble. Hope is the greatest factor in the world – if that is taken away there is little left.

He remained disciplined although he questioned his consultant each time they met – I think he was always hopeful he might be allowed just one or two cigarettes! He tried asking to have a pipe perhaps just once a day, or even a small cigar (always with that wicked twinkle), and each time it was refused. He accepted with good grace whilst in the presence of the consultant and then we would have long talks about the whole problem. He never lost his sense of humour and only on rare occasions would his optimism desert him. Luckily I was always around when that happened and I would jolly him out of it.

In the meantime, Stag became more and more busy. My staff were excellent and very understanding and as John's health began to deteriorate, albeit very slowly, I could always rely on them to accept that I occasionally had to change an appointment. They all provided the greatest support I could have asked.

My greatest difficulty was keeping up a front with John. He insisted that I stuck to my routine of work at the theatre as much as possible – I knew that the minute I gave him any indication of my fear for his health it would undermine his confidence completely. It was like walking a tightrope.

Each day I would unobtrusively observe his condition and then decide on a course of action. I could trust only my instinct and my complete affinity with him. I would watch the slow 'getting up' process, no rushing, the attitude towards the day and then decide whether I 'wasn't expected in until later' or whether it was obviously better to go, get things done and be back as early as possible. I was always back for lunchtime. We had moved from The Close and were within ten minutes' walking distance of the theatre. If I was in doubt I took the car.

John was hospitalised again in the autumn of 1989. He had a massive fit at home very early one morning. It was so frightening. For many weeks he remained in hospital. There was a short period when, although he recognised the immediate family, his mind was completely confused. Conversations at his bedside had to be heard to be believed. We had none of us experienced anything like this in our lives and the boys were so good with him. When we visited him we agreed with everything he talked about, much of it making no sense whatsoever. Sometimes we simply *had* to laugh.

One particular afternoon I was sitting with him and he said, very quietly – "Why do you think they have put me in with so many gay men?"

"Gay? Why do you say that?" I replied, thinking only to

humour him.

"Well, most of the people in here are wearing high heels and they keep walking up and down the ward waving to everyone."

Somewhat startled I looked around. On all my visits to John my one thought was him. I made a beeline for his bed every time never knowing quite what to expect and I had taken no notice of what was going on around me. The truth dawned. He was in a mixed ward with a preponderance of women! It was pointless to explain at that stage, his mind simply would not have accepted that he was in bed in the same room as women, but we had a really good laugh about it when he had recovered and was once again at home.

My routine during that period was to work all morning and through lunch, spend the afternoon with John then return to the theatre. Work was my salvation.

That autumn I was in the throes of directing *The Sound of Music* for Stag's in-house autumn musical so my evenings were tied up with rehearsals as well as front of house and other jobs. Although I was exceptionally tired I am convinced that having other people to think about kept me sane. I had to concentrate at rehearsals, so much depended upon it. As long as I knew John was well looked after and the hospital knew exactly where I could be found I could relax as much as was possible.

I so enjoyed working with the cast on that show. I had two sets of children for the Von Trapp family which made rehearsing extremely complicated but fascinating – two quite different families.

John did not even know *The Sound of Music* had been performed until it was well and truly over. It was the first time he had ever missed one of my shows.

That Christmas, when he was allowed home, seemed extra special.

During the latter part of 1989 it became apparent that the District Council was taking Stag very seriously. More and more people were using the building and this had filtered through to the Local Authority.

The Blighs Development project, a major town-centre rede-velopment, seemed fairly imminent which would mean that the Kings Hall next to Blighs Hotel would be demolished. This would leave the town without the flat floored hall in the middle of Sevenoaks with its access for the disabled and its nearness to the bus station. There was a great deal of criticism in the press about losing such a central large hall and the District Council decided to replace the building elsewhere.

The problem was where? We at Stag were asked if we would consider the addition of a hall on the back of our theatre in the South Park Car Park. But that was not all. To my absolute aston-ishment Stag was also offered the prospect of having the existing building completely refurbished to the tune of about one million pounds.

I could not believe it. They were talking in telephone numbers as far as I was concerned. One million pounds?! We had never had any spare money unless we raised it ourselves or someone kindly donated something to us. Here was an offer to refurbish the building and ensure its future for generations to come. What more could I want?

From little acorns . . .

It was by no means cut and dried. Anything could happen in the coming months, but the District Council had started the ball rolling so we needed to consider the matter in real earnest even if the whole scheme of things changed.

Once I had recovered from the shock we had to get down to the serious business of considering all the implications. We had two options:

we could say thank you but refuse, and work ten times as hard to try to raise the necessary money for the never ending list of things that would have to be done;
or
we could accept, but ensure that by having the additional hall at the back of the building its presence did nothing to ruin all the years of work we had put into the project.

We adopted the latter course.

The excitement was unbelievable. Staff and volunteers and our supporters of all kinds were as amazed as I was. Stag was to have a secure future, and it vindicated all their hard work and the passion they had put into the project.

Endless meetings were held, agreements discussed and provisional dates fixed. The scheme had to take its natural course through all the Committees of the Council, but there was a certain amount of pre-planning which had to be done regardless of the outcome.

The Board of Directors decided that we should hold an Open Meeting in October of 1990. As well as members of the public we would invite the Leadership of the Council, the Officers and as many members as wished to attend. We decided it was time to make a proper business presentation and show people just how we made our money, how we spent it, who was on our staff and thank our many, many supporters for all their help. The date was fixed five or six months in advance and invitations sent out to the District Council. As a Board we had agreed to spend a little of our hard-earned money on a simple reception after the presentation so that Councillors and Officers could meet our staff and our Directors.

At the end of January 1990 our first grandchild was born to Barry and Winnie. A girl, after all those men! Anna Louise Grace. I wasn't convinced that I was ready to be a grandma but I sooned changed my mind!

In the summer of that year John had two serious setbacks. In June, one week before we were due to go to the West Country for a week's holiday, he had a partial collapse of the lung. Very, very frightening for him and so disappointing because he had been doing everything he had been told. He simply could not understand why he was not getting any better.

He made a good recovery however and returned home from hospital after about five days. The consultant explained that it was rotten luck. I privately asked lots of questions about

174

whether it could be repeated and what was I to do. I was told that it was possible that it would happen again but not in the same spot. John was 'fine' again and determined that life should go on as normal. He listened to the possible refurbishment plans and, whilst he was delighted that such recognition was being given to something I had worked so hard on, he did question whether it was what I really wanted. He was not completely convinced that Stag needed it and he knew that it would carry with it much greater responsibilities.

In late August he had another partial collapse of the lung in precisely the same place. He was very poorly. His consultant eventually decided that there was only one option left – the removal of a large part of his damaged lung.

Once more we experienced the agony of hospital waiting lists. The Brook Hospital at Sidcup was the only one where this type of operation could be carried out locally – it was three whole weeks before the operation was performed. He came through it very well, much better than I could have hoped, and that evening I was very surprised and pleased to see him sitting up eating ice-cream in bed. I went home relatively cheered.

The next four days showed me a great deterioration in his condition. I asked to see the consultant. He explained that at John's age and with the shock of the operation it was natural he would appear so ill but that he, the consultant, was very optimistic about his recovery. Somehow I simply could not believe him.

Four days after his operation, on Sunday 30th September at 2.30am, John died. A large part of me died with him. We had been two halves of a whole, the greatest of friends with the same values in life. We had had a great time together. Often unpredictable, sometimes hair-raising, frequently hilarious – but never, never boring.

The Open Evening at Stag when we were going to impress the world (well, at least, Sevenoaks) had been fixed for Wednesday 3rd October. Patrick Pascall, Stag's Chairman, was in a dilemma.

The Open Evening had been prepared down to the last detail.

Different aspects of running the theatre were to be explained by different speakers with allotted times. As the person in charge of the business it was natural that I would be speaking about the major part of the project. We had all spent a deal of time preparing our presentations, it was a really important occasion for the theatre and we had no idea how many people from the general public might turn up. I told my three sons that I would prefer it to go ahead. One of them rang a very relieved Patrick for me.

I didn't really want to do anything or see anybody at that point. I felt completely drained, quite numb, weepy and very tired. The alternative was to cancel the evening and that was virtually impossible. It also meant that my private loss would have to become public in a very public way and that I could not face. Sympathy in great waves at that time would have finished me off. Much better to try to be matter of fact.

I also knew what John would have said – "It's got to be done, darling – get on with it."

I took care with my appearance that evening. I was usually fairly well groomed and though I had no interest whatever in my clothes just then I was careful not to look any different. Kim, Noel and Barry took me to the theatre and sat in the auditorium during the meeting. As far as I was aware only the members of the Board and Francis knew about John. Everyone was very businesslike which helped tremendously.

Apparently the evening was extremely successful. There was a good turnout, lots of questions were asked by interested members of the public and I learned afterwards that the Officers, Leadership and Members of the Council were most impressed. As soon as the stage presentation finished the three boys collected me unobtrusively on stage and we disappeared backstage and went home. No felicitations, no obvious signs of sympathy on that night. I was very relieved. It was over and it had gone well. John would have been pleased.

It was not until some days later that Bruce Cova, Chief Executive of the Council, asked why I had not been in attend-

Some of the best

Peter Othick – one of our money men.

Jane Giffin – our Volunteers Organiser.

Ann Spencer and Janet McEwen – wonderful wardrobe mistresses – dressing our *Hans Andersen* (Noel Durdant-Hollamby), November 1991.

Designer of our publicity material since 1986 – Christopher Holgate with his wife Margaret.

The worker of wonders in the workshop – John Meredith.

Staff – past and present

Steve Wiltshire

Peter Fleming

Bob Slaughter

Sarah Thompson

A party of projectionists – the Cinema staff.

Sarah Hope

Donald Campbell

Douglas Julyan

Eleanor Hartland

Karl Davey
Ann Gaston
Rodney Dawson

Gongs and things!

Me and the boys – and the MBE! Buckingham Palace 8th March 1994.

Lest I forget! Francis Price set this up with Royston Edwards, local signwriter.

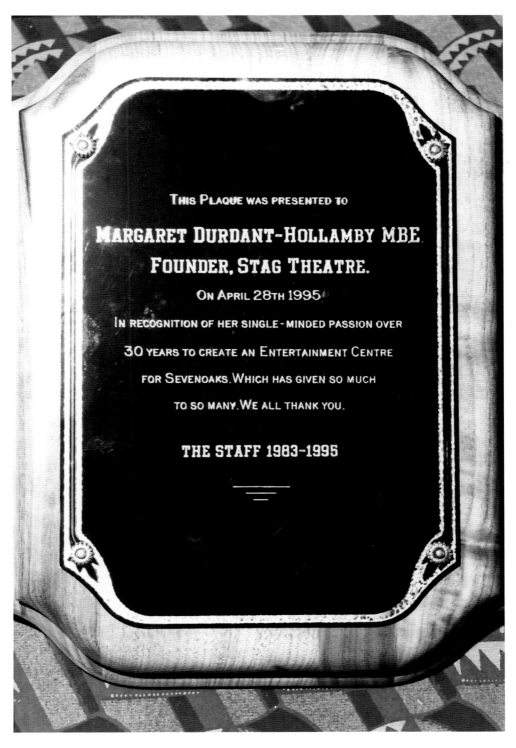

THIS PLAQUE WAS PRESENTED TO

MARGARET DURDANT-HOLLAMBY M.B.E.

FOUNDER, STAG THEATRE.

ON APRIL 28TH 1995

IN RECOGNITION OF HER SINGLE-MINDED PASSION OVER

30 YEARS TO CREATE AN ENTERTAINMENT CENTRE

FOR SEVENOAKS. WHICH HAS GIVEN SO MUCH

TO SO MANY. WE ALL THANK YOU.

THE STAFF 1983-1995

A plaque presented by the staff which still hangs in the upper foyer at The Stag.

Cheers and Good Luck!
The hand-over to Terry Shaw in 1996 with the staff:
left to right from the back: Rodney Dawson, Bob Slaughter, Donald Campbell,
Peter Fleming, Ann Gaston, Linda McPaul, Emma Cattermole, Joe Burrows,
Karl Davey, Don Knight, Guy Wrenn, Graham DeKoningh, Douglas Julyan,
Francis Price, Eleanor Hartland, Tracey John, Sarah Hope, Sarah Thompson,
Jane Simpson and Noel Durdant-Hollamby.

ance at the reception afterwards – he was quite astonished when I told him the reason.

The feeling of exhaustion over the next month really puzzled me. By about mid afternoon every day I felt shattered. Quite unbeknown to me the same was happening to the three boys. Kim finally saw his doctor in London and was told that this was a very natural reaction to grief, that it would pass and that he should not try to fight it. When Kim told the rest of us we all felt much better but quite surprised that we had all been having exactly the same reaction.

Some days later I started back at the theatre. I was so lucky that I had something so huge to occupy my mind. No more going home at lunchtime to give John his lunch, no more tension as to what I might find when I arrived home – but a gaping hole left just the same. I could only thank God that John had not been made to exist in unhappiness and what to him would have been misery. He had had no idea that his future would have been oxygen cylinders around the house, great fear of catching colds, very limited mobility. He would have loathed that and we all had to be grateful he had been spared. *But I had lost my best and only mate.*

I made one resolution. Although it was wonderful to have all the problems and excitements of the theatre and cinema to cope with, I decided there and then that Stag would not become my life. I had seen what obsession and possessiveness could do to people and I was not going down that path. I would now have time to give my whole energies to the project but I was going to be quite firm about it taking over my life to the exclusion of everything else.

That first Christmas was strange. The family came to me on Christmas Day and we all did our utmost to make it as traditional as it had always been. Our new granddaughter was the best diversion in the world. John had loved Christmas and his tree decorating was second to none, so Noel had collected a big tree and decorated it. All the old decorations brought memories flooding back but we were right to do it.

Christmas Day lunch was the same as always and I reached that last twenty minutes just before serving when everything is almost ready but not quite and you need eyes everywhere to get things just so. We were all making conversation, trying to sound natural and Christmassy, when suddenly there was a big BANG!

All the lights went out. Startled I turned around – the oven and hob were out and everything had come to a standstill. After much searching (we had never looked for a fusebox before) we discovered a fuse had tripped and it took only seconds to restore order.

I said out loud to the ceiling, "John, just because you can't be here to carve the turkey, there's no need to be like that!" The tension snapped, we all had a good laugh and the rest of Christmas Day was much more natural.

In early February 1991, five months after John's death, I broke my right wrist in two places. We had had a heavy fall of snow for some days, it had begun to thaw and had then frozen hard. I was walking home from the theatre in supposedly non-slip boots. There was black ice, which I could not see, on the corner pavement at Pembroke Road and in order not to slide under the traffic I tried to break my fall. The resounding crack echoed around the High Street. Seven hours later in Tunbridge Wells my injury was treated. On that particular day in February large numbers of people were breaking limbs and the hospitals were at breaking point. I arrived home about one o'clock in the morning and burst into tears. No John to give me comfort. The bedroom seemed particularly empty that night.

On 22nd February1991, Sevenoaks Rotary Club presented me with their Vocational Award in recognition of my 'service, over many years, to the Sevenoaks district'. I was very proud and flattered. My right hand still in plaster, I asked Francis to accompany me. The Rotary Club made me feel very special – someone even cut up my lunch! At the photocall later outside the theatre the plastered arm was well and truly hidden behind my back.

The Refurbishment

After many, many months and more meetings, it was eventually decided that refurbishment of Stag could go ahead. I still found it very hard to believe that our rather grotty building was going to be made beautiful.

We agreed to run the building at full stretch until November 1992. It was anticipated that it would take just over a year to complete. The District Council were to request tenders and to be responsible for overseeing the work. It was agreed that I should have a large input into how I wished the building to look when completed and that no decisions about its appearance would be taken without consultation with me. All aspects of running the building once refurbished had to be discussed with the technical staff and there were a hundred and one things to tie up.

One major aspect to be decided and discussed was the type of heating system which would be installed. The heating engineers commissioned by the Council came to see us on two or three occasions to make their suggestions and to learn how the building worked. At these meetings I listened attentively but left the technical aspects of the problem to Albert and Francis. I was determined that no money should be wasted and was always questioning the why's and wherefore's (sometimes quite naïvely) but I did want to understand everything we were doing and why we were doing it.

It was finally suggested that we should have a Swedish heating and ventilation system – not air-conditioning because experience gained in many West End theatres had proved that it did not work satisfactorily. All three of us questioned the need for a Swedish system. Why not British? Surely that would be much cheaper? The Consultants continued to press for the Swedish system and we asked where else in England it was installed, could we please see it in action and make our own decisions as to whether it was really what was required for what was going to be a small but rather complex building. It was agreed that a visit would be arranged to a working site – where at that point they could not tell us, but we were quite prepared to travel the length or breadth of the country in order to get it right. About two weeks later my phone rang. It was the Consultants.

"Mrs Durdant-Hollamby, we would like you to come and see the system in action to satisfy yourself and your colleagues. Are you available in the early part of February?" (this was February 1992, nine months before we closed). Having consulted my diary I said I could be free and asked where I would be going.

"Sweden" was the reply.

I nearly dropped the phone. They could not be serious! I had been quite prepared to go to Manchester or Edinburgh or Cardiff but Sweden had never crossed my mind. The Consultant could not understand my laughter.

"Yes, yes," I said, "Wonderful. Now pull the other one."

"I'm quite serious," he said. "We do not have this particular system operating in a similar sort of building in this country so we want to prove to you how efficient it is. We can only do that in Sweden."

My mind immediately flew to wasting money. Stag certainly could not afford a trip to Sweden. I asked who would pay. The Consultants said they would pay for me only. I told them I would let them know.

What a conundrum! I did want absolute proof that we were choosing the most suitable and economic system for Stag but with my lack of technical expertise there was no way I was going to go to Sweden by myself to take the decision. I could just hear the remarks when everything was decided. If I did not choose it, the men would say "fancy letting a woman decide on something she knows nothing about." If I did choose it, probably those same men would say "they must have given her such a good time in Sweden she couldn't say no!"

I described the problem to Alfred and Francis and then to the

Chief Executive of the District Council. They all understood that one person should not be made to take the responsibility of such a huge decision and yet it would be foolish to turn down the free flight and accommodation when so much was at stake.

In the end we reached a British compromise. The company making the system would pay for one of us and the District Council would pay for a second, the money for which would be deducted once more from the final cost of the refurbishment. It was agreed that Francis would accompany me. He was as sceptical as I about accepting a foreign system and would also have many questions to ask about the future maintenance and operation of such a system.

The trip was fixed. What fun! A free trip to Sweden to feel the heat! All my well-travelled friends told me that Sweden in February would be freezing so I took my thermals and my warmest clothes, wearing as much as possible to save too much packing.

We spent two nights and two and a half days in Sweden and *I have never been so hot in my life.* Our days were crammed with visits to the factory (where it was so pristine you could have eaten lunch off the floor), lectures on the principles of the system, laboratory tests and finally an 'on-site' test in a theatre building where I sat in a mini-skirt and Francis took off his socks so that we could really test the efficiency of this under-seat heating and ventilation. We gave our hosts no quarter. In return they were charm and kindness itself.

Francis and I had both had experience of 'salesmen' in our lives and we had to admit that if this was salesmanship they were exceptionally clever at it. They were not in the least pushy, were very intrigued and amazed at the story of Stag and seemed to be really genuine in their desire to get it right for us. After all, if we did have it in our theatre, it would be the first one of its kind in England in our sort of building.

As hosts they were quite delightful and showed us as much of their country as was possible in such a short time. One evening we were taken to a 'needle' ice hockey match for which our host was the chief sponsor. We had the special sponsor's seats rinkside and it promised to be an exciting evening. I was warned to wrap up well. I did and it so happened that my outfit was black and white. Little did I know that these were the colours of the opposing team – everyone was sure I would be lynched.

Francis and I were impressed with the system. We were very concerned about its future running costs but basically if it could be afforded we genuinely felt that it would work well. On our return to England we submitted a report on our findings with a special note about these concerns. After many more exploratory visits to Stag by the Consultants, it was decided by the Council that the Swedish system would be installed.

The District Council decided to employ a young designer by the name of Sara Alberici. She was to work closely with me about every detail of the building. Ken Davies, chief architect to the Council, was to be responsible for the planning and again was to work very closely with those of us who would be at the sharp end once we re-opened.

I had preliminary discussions with Sara. When I met her first I was not over-impressed. She seemed so young and had had no experience of designing the interiors of theatres. She had designed interiors of nightclubs and other smaller places of entertainment, but I did get the impression that the project really grabbed her interest so I kept an open mind. We had a very good discussion and I explained to her that wherever pos- sible I would like the 30's appearance of the building to be retained. It seemed to me common sense to use and enhance the best bits of the building and she was completely in tune with what I had in mind.

The new hall at the rear of the building worried me some- what. I had an awful feeling it would simply sit on the back like an overlarge shoe box without any real relationship to the the- atre and I was sure that would be quite wrong. Somehow it needed to become part of the whole project if it was to work. Sara understood my concerns.

As the weeks progressed during 1992 I was very surprised to learn that the hall at the back was to be designed in the same way as the rest of the building. This was not what we had expected. If this was to be the case we could integrate it into the whole scheme of things. It would not sit there like an empty box.

We had to think about finding temporary accommodation whilst the work was in progress.

In late October 1992, another girl was born into the family. My second granddaughter, Sophie Alice Rose, a baby sister for Anna. Two girls – how wonderful.

We had decided that throughout our closed period, a core staff should be kept on as there was still plenty to do. It was agreed that Dennis Gilkes, Francis Price, Steve Wiltshire, myself and Jane Simpson (publicity) would remain. All four were paid a pittance. If we lost them because of the closure we would never be able to replace them. Each individual would be invaluable because of their knowledge of the project and the building itself, and so much help was needed on all aspects of the work. Albert Granville as our finance director was also prepared to share whatever accommodation we managed to find. His two days per week were invaluable, particularly with engineering decisions and problems raising their heads, quite apart from the financial juggling we would need.

Our costume hire department was a critical part of our operation and I felt that if at all possible this must remain open. It would be the only section of Stag which could earn anything during the closure, so this needed to be housed reasonably conveniently too. I thought finding temporary premises would be easy. Over the years Sevenoaks seemed to have endless charity shops moving into premises for short periods of time, so I walked round the town one day looking at all the empty premises (and there were quite a few). I rang the agents, most of whom were outside Sevenoaks, and explained our predicament. I received fairly short shrift. I had hoped that as we were a charity and required premises for only about one year we would receive a sympathetic ear. Not really. It appeared that landlords would prefer to have their premises sitting there empty and wait for the asking rent than have them occupied for twelve months at a slightly lower rent. Some of the shops and offices which were empty had been standing idle for months but no-one wanted to do a deal.

As luck would have it we noticed that offices almost opposite the theatre were suddenly vacant. I looked immediately, explained our position, and after much negotiating it was agreed we could rent the premises for one year at a cost of £10,000. We didn't have that sort of money to spare so the District Council offered to pay it for us and take it from the sum to be spent on the refurbishment.

These offices were by no means ideal but we might be able to have our costumes in there too – that was important. Not only would we be just across the road from the building but we could all remain under one roof for the closed period. The rooms would just about accommodate five people at a pinch, the dresses could go in one room (with Steve, poor thing, squashed in the corner). The suite was up one flight of fairly steep stairs – not ideal to encourage customers but we had little choice. We had a shared kitchen and a ladies' and gents' loo.

During the coming months we made endless lists, and even though we were still running a busy theatre everyone was making mental notes of what would be left and what would be packed.

The last performance in our theatre was a concert by the Philharmonic Choir of Sevenoaks. Sunday 30th November 1992. It was a moving occasion for us all. The theatre would never again look the same, our performers would no longer have to put up with basic facilities backstage and our hopes were very high. All the painting and tender loving care which had gone into that building would disappear for ever, but our friends' and volunteers' efforts would never be forgotten. Their work had lasted for about seven years and that was quite a long time in a public building. The old golf-club bar would go for good, all

184

that furniture that we had borrowed and been given by kind people would have to go or be given back and our building would become a building site.

There was both sadness and anticipation on that evening. As soon as the concert was over we began the gigantic task of moving.

Getting It All Out

The organising of the move had to be seen to be believed. I had pages and pages of LISTS.

There were four separate sections to consider

1 the paraphernalia that goes with moving administrative offices
2 the cinema equipment
3 the bits of scenery, props, lanterns etc which we had amassed over the years – most of which we could not afford to discard
4 our precious costumes

Our priority was to remain up and running as a business. Although we knew we would be 'dark' for twelve months we had to keep a presence in all the right places. We could not afford to lose clients and we had to plan for when we reopened.

The District Council kindly lent us four men for one day to help with the office move. We needed them to carry the photocopier and word processor. There was no way we could have carried all our office equipment down all those stairs from the top of the building. Unfortunately, the weather decided not to be friendly. It was very damp, the building suddenly became icy cold (even worse than usual with doors open to the elements) and it rained like it had never rained before. Just crossing the London Road to our new home was a hazard. You could not afford to let your grip slip halfway across that road, particularly with traffic turning out of South Park.

I donned my dark blue working overalls and ended up wearing them for four days. We completed the office move. The staff were marvellous, anyone who had a spare hour and a good back was asked for help and Peter Fleming and Steve Wiltshire did sterling work. We made quite sure that Dennis did not hump anything too heavy. We put him in the new office and asked him to organise. He did it very well.

It was astonishing how fast the contractors moved onto that site. As we were carrying things out of the offices, they were passing us on the stairs bringing in all their clobber. I almost felt as if I was being chased out but that's the way it happens.

The next priority was our wardrobe. Some of our costumes were exceptionally heavy – Elizabethan dresses and tunics which Ann Spencer had carefully and meticulously made over the years, precious gowns which we had been given and hundreds of different clothes.

It still rained. Peter and Steve crossed the London Road hundreds of times bearing frocks, shoes, hats etc. Ann Spencer and Janet McEwen, our wardrobe ladies, exhausted themselves also. Remember, it had to be carried up the steps near the stage door at Stag, all along the side path and then across the road. We were able to bring some things through the cinema but before we could blink there was dust and rubble in the way.

Dress rails were set up, clothes were hung and the wardrobe was at least safe. There was no room to move, but apart from that . . .

Steve had to check that the floor of our temporary home would take the weight – fortunately it was a sturdy building – we just made sure the load was spread carefully.

Then to the backstage. Contractors were already appearing at the back of the theatre. Workmen's huts had appeared and a section of the car park was being fenced off. That would make us popular with the public!

By dint of favours from one of our biggest sponsors and help with transport from Robert Knight in London we had organised roughly where our technical equipment was going to go and how. But we had to move it.

We rounded up any volunteers again, it still rained and for two days we passed and loaded onto lorries. One of our sponsors had offered warehouse space, which was a godsend, and scenery and equipment was dispatched to goodness knows where.

We had also asked the Council for 'storage cabins' to be put round the edge of the fenced off car park – we had so much stuff. These all had to be packed tight and we left Steve to organise the packing. He was excellent. I think we put a few backs out that week. I did not realise it at the time but the following January I had to see an osteopath for the first time in my life. I had strained muscles in my back and my treatment lasted for nearly six months.

Finally we were out. The insides of the building were being stripped before we had time to take breath. I took a last look at what I knew was the original Stag – it would be very different next year.

That Christmas (1992) was a real holiday for us all for the first time in nine years. No shows on Christmas Eve, Boxing Day, New Year's Day. Just for once we were all able to have a proper break. We really needed it. The move had been exceptionally gruelling physically and mentally – nothing must be lost. By the end of it we were all slightly light-headed, a sort of 'end of term' feeling.

Spring was soon upon us. By then we were busy planning and preparing the re-opening. We had built up such a wonderful following for Stag and the closure had come just as we were at our peak. We knew we would have to work really hard to remind people to come back to us. There is nothing so short as the public's memory. We were earning nothing apart from income from our wardrobe so planning publicity and advertising was always a struggle.

We kept as close an eye as we were allowed on what was

going on over the road. As the Council was in charge of the project we had to be careful not to interfere. Just occasionally it was absolutely necessary and during those months there were some sticky moments when one or other of us would spot a potential disaster. Tempers often frayed, discussions were heated – tact was the order of the year!

Our theatre, bar and cinema were to be improved, altered and expanded. Our old bar room was to be a restaurant and bar, our two small cinemas were to have more seats, one projection box for both and improved screens. We could not afford to have all the seats replaced and there would be Dolby sound in only one screen. The new hall would be able to host conferences, dances, dinners on a small scale, weddings, meetings etc.

The names for the enhanced project taxed our minds. We finally decided on three names which had historical association with the old cinemas in Sevenoaks – The Plaza Suite for the new building, Majestic Cinemas for the screens downstairs, Carlton Bar for the new stage extension and STAG for the project as a whole. After all, many people knew us as Stag, there was no point in making matters more confusing.

We were under quite a lot of pressure to re-open the building in stages. The Council, some Board members and friends full of advice urged us to consider this possibility. Albert, Francis and I carefully pondered the problem. We were painfully aware that Stag needed to earn again, and quickly, but we had to get it absolutely right.

The Plaza Suite would be finished first. We were strongly advised to try and open that to the public whilst the rest of the work was going on. We did consider this as being very possible. As things turned out it was used minimally in advance of the rest of the complex, but only when the adjacent area in the car park ceased to look like a building site.

I refused to have prospective clients taking away a mental picture of chaos and disorganisation, quite apart from cement powder on their shoes. To their credit the Local Authority accepted my reasoning.

All through these months I was in close consultation with Sara, the designer. I think I sat in almost every type of chair in south east England to select the right type with the right seat, back and arms for all shapes and sizes of individuals. They had to be comfortable if one was dining, listening to a lecture, attending a conference or coming to a tea dance.

I did have fun. I travelled with Sara to see glass blocks in buildings in London and we spent hours talking about colour schemes, lighting, loo fittings, bars, ice-cream kiosks, box office and the hundred and one other things which all had to be planned.

Security was an immense subject on its own. Steve, Dennis, Francis and I spent hours trying to decide which locks should go on which doors. This was made even harder by the fact that we were working only from plans. Trying to imagine a typical day in a building which was not even finished was a real challenge.

We were given a date in August 1993 for the 'handover' of The Plaza Suite. The date arrived. It was perfectly obvious that there was still much to be done and we refused to take the building as it stood.

My son Noel, who had trained as a chef at Westminster College, offered me help in deciding the quantities and types of catering equipment. It was just as well I had had a commercial kitchen at The Moorings or I would have been sunk. Between us we pictured the whole building in use with bars open, coffees being served for the theatre and maybe even a wedding or dinner in The Plaza Suite on the same evening. We then had to work out numbers of *everything* from the teaspoons to the salt cellars and it took us days. Our lists grew ever longer and we checked and double checked until we were cross-eyed. The cutlery list alone was awesome and we had to remember to allow for breakages and the occasional disappearance(!) of items. Everything was checked with Bruce Cova's assistant, Debbi Boffa, and the orders were duly placed.

The thirteen months of closure were very strange but rather

delightful for all five of us remaining on the staff. We worked normal hours for the first time ever and had all the Bank Holidays off. It was wonderful to be able to travel freely to theatres around the country to see shows which agents wanted me to buy in for Stag when we reopened. Distance and time were suddenly unimportant. It was nice too to catch up with friends for whom I had little or no spare time in the preceding years.

One of my greatest joys during that period was that I was cast for the female lead in the Sevenoaks Players' production of *Shadowlands* at the Sackville Theatre in Sevenoaks School in September. Here was I, with the time at last to act, but ironically able to do so only on somebody else's stage.

Joan Lloyd was once again the driving force behind the choice of play and was its producer. As always she assembled a formidable cast, with Paul Barnes playing the part of C S Lewis, and a group of dons who were extremely believable. The strange thing was, I nearly didn't audition for that play. I was given a copy to read and found it made me extremely emotional. It was a love story with great sadness woven through the tale. Joy (the part for which I might audition) suffered breast cancer and eventually died of the disease, but her courage and sense of fun throughout was astonishing. It brought it all back to me again and when I put down the book I genuinely felt that I probably would be unable to rehearse such a heart-rending and pertinent story. I had to read the play three or four more times before I agreed to audition.

Once I had taken the decision and been offered the part, I absolutely revelled in it. I had to develop a believable American accent and was hardly off-stage the whole evening, so there was a lot to learn. Would I still be able to learn lines like I used to? Having watched other people's problems with words as they reached middle age, I guessed I would find it difficult, so I started early. I need not have worried. To my relief and surprise, learning the lines was no trouble whatsoever and rehearsals every week were a joy. Paul was a delight to work with. We found the story very moving and beautifully written.

The play was an enormous success. It would have made it perfect for me had it been at Stag – but then if the theatre had been up and running I would not have had time to do it.

The Opening of the Plaza Suite

Our new banqueting and conference suite was finally handed over in late September. Although the area outside made it impossible to let out to the public at that time I decided that we must try and make some money from it by using it ourselves. However, I had no intention of letting out something which I had not tried and tested. The new kitchen equipment was installed but had not been used, and I needed to find out what I might be up against before I tried to 'sell' the place to strangers. It was a completely new venture for us and once again I blessed my experience of running the hotel.

During our closure period the Friends of Stag had been busy raising money for a set of tabs (theatre curtains) for the main stage. Each member of the Friends was asked to raise at least £30. Our supporters were really missing the theatre – suddenly large numbers of people had a big hole in their lives – and the fund raising provided a good opportunity for people to meet again, become motivated and talk about the excitement of re-opening.

I made up my mind to do a dry run in The Plaza Suite. I chose to hold a Barn Dance. It would serve two purposes – raise my £30 towards the tabs and give us the opportunity to test out the new suite. I did a handbill and sent it out to all the Friends explaining it was an 'experiment' and they were the guinea pigs. I said that as everyone was going to have to accept whatever happened they need only pay £7.50 and for that they would get a cooked supper. Noel agreed to be part of the experiment and be in charge of the food. He also offered to write an objective report for me about the kitchen, any problems which might arise and whether there was enough of everything – in general whether the place worked or not. It was only a Barn Dance, but at least it would tell us whether we could hold such events with confidence!

I knew Noel would not gloss over any problems. I also knew that any major crisis would be in very good hands. He agreed to do the work for nothing and I would pay for the food and re-imburse myself from the ticket sales.

The response was astonishing. Everyone wanted to see the new Suite and finally I had to announce that the Barn Dance was full. I was quite sure it was going to be a crush!

The total amount so far raised for the tabs was a few hundred pounds off its target. If the evening went smoothly we might make that final amount – wonderful.

That dance was the greatest fun. No-one minded being a bit squashed at their tables. From that I learned how many the Suite held comfortably for a Barn Dance or something similar. The goodwill and excitement made for a very happy evening. The problems that cropped up did not really take us by surprise. Nothing is ideal and we had already foreseen some difficulties in the arrangement of the building. It transpired that noise from the kitchen flooded into the hall itself, whilst the reverse was not the case. If something had to be timed, the kitchen staff could not hear at all what was going on in the hall and we guessed that would make for some awkward situations later on. There was no money for more communications at that point, and trying to keep kitchen staff silent when they are on a high from having achieved something fairly miraculous at an event was well nigh impossible. Heigh-ho!

We had a large catering dishwasher which Noel and I had chosen after visits to commercial kitchens and my gratitude to our future barman's wife, Maggie, knew no bounds. She was familiar with the operation of this wonderful machine and did the washing up for us. No-one else was available who had used such a piece of equipment before.

Everyone who came that night was amazed at how beautiful

and elegant the Plaza Suite looked. Not everything worked quite as it should (!) but on the whole they were impressed. They couldn't complain because I had warned them! We made about £300 profit that night (I didn't have to pay the hire charge!) so my contribution to the Curtain Fund helped us to place the order.

What excitement – real theatre curtains at last. I loved our open stage, but for me there is nothing quite so thrilling as that magical moment when the house lights dim as the audience wait with bated breath for the curtain to reveal the secrets behind it. Just sometimes a show really needs that breathtaking moment and we would soon be able to have it. Now of course there was the responsibility of choosing the curtains! When it was announced in a newsletter to the Friends that our fund raising target had been reached I had a very friendly letter from my dear friend and Stag's Patron, Sir Desmond Heap. He had strong views about theatre curtains and quite rightly decided to express his opinion before I did anything dreadful. I noted what he said. As always it was very wise. I think he approved of the final design.

The next thing I needed to try was how many people could be accommodated efficiently and comfortably for a three-course dinner in The Plaza Suite.

Again I asked Noel for help and, together with an ex colleague of his from Westminster College and a team of waitresses headed by a very experienced lady, we set a date for another experiment. Again the Friends were offered first refusal – they were so good about being guinea pigs.

Once more the tickets sold almost immediately (124 in total) – it was a very good price but again everyone was told anything might happen – or not – so they knew there was an element of risk. We used seven waitresses that evening, two chefs, a barman, a receptionist and a full-time washer up – that alone gave us a firm indication of the costs involved in running such an event. The problem which I had foreseen from the beginning as being the major stumbling block of that building was very evident that night. Although we could happily seat and serve about 100 people, there was nowhere for them to go between leaving their coats at reception and actually taking their seats for dinner. On that night the goodwill was so great that everyone made do, but it made us doubly aware of our limitations for the future. Ken Davies (the Council's architect) and I had talked over this dilemma in the early days but knew there was no solution at the time. We could only hope that one day, if there was money and space to spare, perhaps we could extend outwards into the car park with a marquee type awning – but that was far away in the future.

Noel, Paul and their staff did an amazing job that evening. Once more they were able to write a truthful report which was to be so useful in the future. Now we had done a three-course meal – about the most difficult thing to achieve – and we had moved up that learning curve.

These two events now gave me more confidence to talk to prospective clients about what was and was not possible. I was determined that Stag should not develop a reputation for poor service in any one part of its building. The only way I could handle this was to be absolutely sure of my ground. As my mother would have said, "never practise in public, dear."

Francis Price and Jane Simpson had been preparing a publicity leaflet for the Suite although we had little spare money. We all trudged for hours round shops and offices delivering them by hand to save postage.

Our very major worry was an opening date for the theatre and cinemas. On the one hand I could not possibly programme anything knowing that completion date was so unpredictable, yet on the other we were constantly being pressed for when we would open and what would be on. Clients were very anxious to perform again in the theatre, were really excited about the prospect of a refurbished building and needed firm dates for their Christmas concerts. I kept everyone at bay for as long as was possible. Finally, and only after some pretty heated meetings, the Council, the building contractor and ourselves agreed an opening date in early December. The Kemsing Singers and the Eynsford Concert Band immediately booked their events but I did stress to them that anything might happen. With an operation as complicated as a place of entertainment (which most builders did not understand) it was bound to be fraught with difficulties.

Having discussed this matter with my colleagues, our feeling was that completion would be at least a fortnight after the date we had been given. We could all see what was going on across the road. There were rumours flying that the building contractor might be in financial difficulty (they were to cease trading a few months after completion), so quite apart from the normal building problems we were very anxious that the project might not be completed at all. We were right in our assumptions. The completion date could not happen as agreed. Very sadly, and for the first time ever in nine years, I had to tell two clients that their concerts could not take place. I made quite sure I delivered the news personally and apologised and explained the circumstances. They were both bitterly disappointed but seemed to understand – I'm happy to say that they have remained clients of ours ever since.

In the early part of 1993 Michael Cormack died. It was an awful shock and I was particularly sad because Michael had been so excited about the refurbishment. It was he who had suggested how our stage could be extended, thus giving us the opportunity to have 'theatre in the round'. I was very pleased to be able to suggest to a willing Board that the new, small stage should be named after him – the Cormack stage.

Throughout the summer of 1993 I had been planning the Christmas Show with the Channel Theatre Company.

Channel had now established an excellent reputation in Sevenoaks and in order to replenish our funds I knew that the Christmas Show had to be all things to all men. We needed not only a show that would woo back those families who had gone elsewhere but one that would appeal to new audiences. We chose *The Plotters of Cabbage Patch Corner.* The final date for the re-opening was given as 22nd December. Just as I had experimented in The Plaza Suite, I decided that if we had two or three performances at cheap prices for schoolchildren it would also give everyone a chance to iron out the wrinkles in the theatre. Technical and office staff would need to be on their mettle, volunteers would find things in new places and all in all everyone would have to be on their toes – ice-cream sales alone would show up any major problems! The advertising was prepared and distributed to schools in the south east, and great emphasis was put on the 're-opening' aspect. In our temporary offices our box office was once again preparing for business but from now on it was to be computerised! It has to be remembered that all box office transactions in the past had been done manually. When we advertised for new box office staff they had to be prepared to squash into our temporary office and be trained in the new system. When we reopened across the road the staff would need to be able to sell tickets – and fast!

Dennis Gilkes was a computer buff and experience had shown us in the last two years or so that theatres were reaping great benefits from having computerised box offices. Marketing could be handled far more effectively, full customer details were to hand and there were numerous other advantages. The advance in technology had also made it possible to speed up the allocation of tickets (the thing which had put me off completely many years before).

Unfortunately, Stag had no money to purchase a system so we talked to the District Council about the idea. It was agreed that Dennis should do a 'paper' on computerised box offices and if it could be proved to be the most beneficial way to go forward, the Council would consider the purchase of the equipment as part of the refurbishment.

Dennis did a splendid job and to our delight the Council agreed a sum to purchase a system. We chose Databox from Dennis's research with other places and the cabling and points for all this had to be incorporated in an almost finished building.

196

Dennis also had to be trained to use it and be able to train others.

To add to all these complications (nice though they were) our 10th Birthday would be on 18th December 1993. I simply could not let the occasion pass without notice, but with everything else happening and the fact that we would not physically be open, it was impossible to plan a special event for that date.

We formed a sub-committee of Patrick Harper, Christopher and Margaret Holgate, John Lurcook, Francis Price and myself. After lengthy discussions we decided to tell our clients (our hirers) that we were celebrating our tenth year and that it would be nice if they could perform 'in celebration of Stag's 10th Birthday'. This most of them did. So instead of one celebration we continued to celebrate off and on for the next twelve months.

We were by now over halfway through November 1993, with our opening five weeks away. The 'lists' reappeared, different ones this time but more of them, and sometimes my brain felt as though it could not hold on to all the information. I was exceptionally lucky that I slept so well. Once my head hit the pillow I was away and I am convinced that that kept me going. I could not have coped, even with all the goodwill and support which surrounded me, had I not been able to sleep at night. It had to be something very worrying to keep me awake and all these pressures were not really a worry, just things that had to be dealt with. As W S Gilbert wrote, and I could often be heard singing it, 'Quiet calm deliberation disentangles every knot'. For everyone's sake I had to *appear* calm no matter how I felt inside – maybe I was a better actress than I thought.

The Greatest Surprise of Them All

One morning in about the third week of November I went out into the hall at home to collect the post. Noel was still living with me at the time and having him around since John died had been the greatest comfort. Among the post was a battered and creased brown envelope with the letters OHMS in one corner, a post office sticker on the front saying 'not known at this address' and the letter itself addressed to our old house which we had left some six years previously. It looked official and my immediate thought was Inland Revenue. I brought my tea from the kitchen and sat at the dining table opening the post. My jaw dropped. The brown envelope was official, very, and informed me that I was to be made a Member of the Most Excellent Order of the British Empire – an MBE.

ME. An MBE. I could not take it in. At that moment I called Noel with what he said was a strangled shriek. When he came hurrying into the room he thought I was having a heart attack. Apparently, I just sat there with my mouth open, holding out this letter but unable to get out any words.

The letter said this information was strictly confidential but I at once rang my other two sons – there was no way I was not going to tell them. I still did not really believe it. The three boys were over the moon – so proud and about as amazed as I was.

I read the letter about another six times before I could accept the truth and on the third time of reading I noticed that it said that if I agreed to accept this Honour then I must reply by return of post. I grabbed the envelope. The postmark was 21 days previously! My heart sank. I was bound to be too late. How ironic it would be if through no fault of my own I missed out on this wonderful opportunity. I lost no time in telephoning London, explained about the mistaken address and was assured that all was well. I could not help having a quiet smile to myself about how the best organised institutions in the world could get things wrong.

Heavens, I had to go to work in a minute and no-one must know of my unbelievable excitement. I probably had a silly grin walking to the office, but people thought I was nuts anyway so I got away with it. Behaving normally with my staff, however, was extremely difficult. They were such a major part of this award that I longed to tell them, but I didn't. Maybe the self-control lessons at the Convent had sunk in after all!

Apparently the announcement would be made in the New

Year's Honours List so on top of all that was happening with the refurbishment, the re-opening, new staff, endless lists, a thousand and one things to organise, there would be this festering secret. I knew nothing at all of the details of Honours Announcements. I had of course been very aware of them, had occasionally read them in the paper and knew several people with Honours but I had no knowledge whatsoever of how people were selected, nor had I ever taken note of the date on which the announcement was made. It would not be long before I found out. I did finally tell Albert, our Chairman, and Francis but it was not until December that I let on even to them. When it came very near to Christmas I made an appointment to call on Sir Desmond Heap and gave him the extraordinary news. His response took me completely by surprise.

"My dear Margaret, about time, we wondered when on earth it would happen."

"What do you mean, when it would happen?" I asked rather puzzled.

"A group of us have been pressing for this to happen for about five or six years. I am absolutely delighted there has been a response at last!"

It was during this conversation with Sir Desmond that the mystery of the mis-addressed envelope was unravelled. Two groups of people quite separately had been trying to secure this Honour for me starting from at least six years before. At that time we had been living in our old address!

Desmond, Albert and Francis kept the secret superbly – so did my sons. Not a whisper was heard and luckily no-one on the staff or any of my clients had the least inkling that I was to be made an MBE. This made the following few weeks much easier for me as I was able to carry on as normally as possible in the circumstances. What it would be like when it was announced I imagined would be exciting, but as New Year's Day by co-incidence fell on a Sunday I (in my ignorance) thought I would have twenty-four hours to celebrate it with my family without anyone else really knowing. How naïve I was!

Opening day was suddenly rushing towards us and there were urgent practical matters to be dealt with. There was little time to dwell on what was to come.

We were interviewing prospective staff without being able to show them what their working conditions would be like but trying to make sure they understood that when we moved back it would be all hands on deck. Everything that had been moved out now had to be moved back, and everyone would be expected to help. Although we had a lift in the refurbished building it only went to the first floor so all the really heavy equipment would still have to be manhandled up many stairs. The prospect of getting back into the building was so exciting that it carried us all along in spite of our dread of the physical work that would be involved once again. We decided that we could not have an 'Opening' until we had got the snags out of the building, so I began to plan a special three day event from Friday to Sunday in the month of February by which time we hoped to have ironed out any problems.

Planning the move back was another nightmare. The first thing that had to be ready was the box office. Dennis had the unenviable job of being in charge of its move back across the road, ensuring that Databox had a couple of days in which to set up the system, that the new staff could practise operating the computers in their new surroundings and that security was in place once we were open. He had a tough time. There was still dust floating in the air, it seemed as though it would never go, last minute things went wrong and tempers were frayed. However, he and the staff worked miracles and were proudly ensconced in our new box office which was, in fact, in almost precisely the same position as the original 1937 cinema box office. It looked very elegant, and for the first time in our history the ladies behind the windows were not frozen by the draught from the front doors as in the old days. Ann Gaston had been one of our staff in those cold, cold days, and to my delight works in our box office to this day. She took to the computers like a duck to water.

Steve Wiltshire, our chief technician, had been given the task of overseeing and co-ordinating the installation of our new telephone system as well as his other responsibilities. It was to be extremely complicated – phones by the dozen! He had a tough time too. On numerous occasions he had gone over to the building and spotted someone laying a cable in a totally unacceptable place. Had it not been for his constant and often unpopular visits to the site there would have been some really expensive errors to undo. How on earth we were going to be able to pay for the upkeep of all this technology we did not know, but we had been up against it before and won through – it was just that this time the figures were much bigger and our good housekeeping would be even more important.

In the months prior to opening one of our directors, Louise Williams, had met Mr Michael Betts, Deputy Chairman of British Telecom. He lived in Otford at the time and through an introduction by Louise (she and her late husband Harry were great supporters of the theatre) we managed to obtain sponsorship for our Christmas Show. What a relief that was! Our first show, which was selling well, carried the added bonus of a cushion of sponsorship money. Francis and Jane milked the publicity angle to the full. Channel Theatre were very pleased and honoured to be the first performers in our new building and Francis's particular responsibility was to see that they would be able to bring in their scenery at the right time, that the show would look good on the stage and that the company would be looked after backstage.

He had his share of problems too. There still seemed to be an enormous amount of building materials around – far too much for us to be able to mount a show. Once again tempers flared and the air, at times, was blue. We also had to organise the return of all the materials and equipment which had been so generously stored around Kent, and we decided that it would be impossible to do the bulk of this before we reopened. We agreed to have a week or ten days in January when we would go dark (closed apart from the admin and the box office) so that we could try and restore order to the building, bring back in the bulk of our scenery and tie up any loose ends.

It was a marathon task. I take my hat off to all those who stuck with us through thick and thin. It was touch and go but luckily the public had no idea of the trials and tribulations being acted out behind the scenes.

The day of moving back came nearer and nearer and excitement was at fever pitch. We had interviewed and taken on one or two more staff but there was no time for the niceties of training them – they were simply going to have to 'muck in'.

I had not quite forgotten about my MBE – it was always lurking somewhere in my mind but it was at the bottom of my list of priorities. There was nothing to be done about it anyway and I would give myself time to enjoy it once we had reopened and Christmas was over.

In the meantime, ice-creams, sweets, popcorn, crisps, drinks and coffee had to be ordered to arrive on precisely the right day. It was no use a delivery turning up early – we would not be in to receive it. The setting up of the orders alone was a nightmare. The ice-cream freezers that arrived twenty-four hours before our opening show were the wrong ones and no-one was interested in changing that sort of equipment five days before Christmas. Our phones were hot – good job Steve had done his stuff!

We moved back. Suffice it to say it was horrendous. Such hard work, such a responsibility for everyone as we were all so proud and wanted the public to be as well. Last minute touches were being made to curtains at fire exits and all the thousand and one things that can only happen a few hours before the doors are opened. The anticipation was huge, we were all extremely tired but exhilarated and thrilled to be 'home'.

We opened with our first performance on Tuesday 21st December 1993 and happiness was everywhere. It was such a wonderful day. Francis and Steve were holding their breath, I was holding my breath, everyone was on their toes because until we did a show and had a house full of people, we were not quite sure whether everything would work.

It was lovely to have so many children in the audience with their particular needs, because we discovered that the toddlers' loo was a godsend but the water in the taps everywhere was too hot! We managed to get the ice-creams out on time, the drinks ready, and for the first time in Stag's history we served tea and coffee in china cups and saucers. That meant washing up. Our new dishwasher in the upper foyer let us down. Luckily not many adults had tea or coffee so our volunteer managed to wash up by hand, but that threw up the next problem. Noise. Previously our polystyrene cups had been thrown away, hence silence, but until we had experienced the clatter of china we had not bargained for the noise.

The Plotters of Cabbage Patch Corner was extremely well received and compliments came flooding in from the public about the new look of the place. What a transformation. It was no longer a grotty old building which was once the cinema. Maybe now members of the public who had not set foot inside before would come out of sheer curiosity. If they did, and we were sure they would, then it was up to us to make sure that they wanted to come back again and again.

I made sure that The Plaza Suite was not busy that Christmas. It had been quite impossible to market it fully anyway, and I wanted to be sure that we gave excellent service when it was open properly. A busy Christmas doing functions would just about have finished us off. Every member of staff was at full stretch with either one or two performances every day.

Cash had to be counted, sweets and ice-creams were disappearing fast, so had to be regularly re-stocked, the public had to be attended to with special care – and on top of it all we were all trying to get our own Christmases organised.

That was the one advantage of having only myself at home. I could work long and unsocial hours and it upset no-one else, but how I wished John could have seen the inside of the building. I was so busy that Christmas Eve that I forgot all

203

about picking up my turkey from Skinners, the butcher opposite the theatre. It was only because Mrs Skinner was kind enough to ring to remind me (even though they were closed), that we had our usual feast on Christmas Day.

This was my third Christmas as a widow but I was very very fortunate that the boys and their partners made sure I was not alone. It fitted in very well with everyone else's plans. I needed to be at the theatre on Boxing Day and the day after so no-one had to worry about me being on my own and everyone else could do their own thing with other 'in-laws' or girlfriends' families – getting it right at Christmas is so often a real difficulty for people that I felt we were very lucky. Of course, we were all looking forward to the following weekend and the announce-ment which would be in the papers.

In the refurbishment we had made plans for a restaurant to work in conjunction with the theatre bar and to be situated in the same room. It would not be ideal, the kitchen of necessity would be tiny, but we needed to create a good atmosphere for patrons and we needed the income.

In the final weeks before we reopened a sub committee ad-vertised for caterers to tender for the position. My son Noel got the job.

I appreciated that it would not be easy for him, in spite of his qualifications. I also knew that he would not fail me in a crisis. Being my son, I realised he would have to be twice as good as anyone else at the job or I would be accused of nepotism. Little did people know quite what the problems were going to be, catering for the public from that very small kitchen. Noel realised – he had seen and heard enough about the rest of the building to understand its pitfalls – but he was looking forward to the challenge.

The restaurant was behind schedule. The kitchen equipment although ordered in plenty of time had not arrived, there was still too much dust around the place, and one or two workmen would suddenly appear to polish off some task or other – the finishing touches seemed to me to drag on for ever.

Planning the 'Gala' Weekend

In the months leading up to the reopening I had been very hard at work planning our 'Gala Weekend' to celebrate not only our ten years but our refurbished building. I wanted something really special for Stag, something which would give us national publicity and announce us and our new building to the world! And of course I had to have it for very little money! I decided to approach the BBC to see whether it would be possible to have something broadcast from the theatre so that our name could be heard by millions (always try for the top!). What I had in mind was something like *Friday Night is Music Night* from The Stag Theatre, Sevenoaks – a live broadcast. With a great deal of persistence I found my contact and briefly told him our story. He was quite cool and explained that a new directive had gone out to all producers of outside broadcasts to the effect that these events now had to cover their costs. I asked him what that meant as I, like many other people, assumed that if the BBC was given a venue and the opportunity to broadcast to the nation, then it did not charge for its services. How wrong I was.

He was pleased to give me a full explanation and it frightened the life out of me. When the BBC took into consideration all the rehearsal costs for the orchestra, the soloists, the transport and the technical requirements of an outside broadcast, the total was in the region of £75 – £80,000! I had no idea, but as soon as I was able to catch my breath I asked how on earth any of these outside broadcasts happened in any theatre – how could they possibly afford them? The BBC man explained that so long as the extra costs were covered by the hirer the BBC met the large part of the total amount. Phew! What a relief! How much then would we have to find? Anything between £10 – £12,000 was the reply. I asked whether, if I managed to get a sponsor, their name would be mentioned and he said the name would appear in Radio Times for one week and would be mentioned twice on the air during the broadcast.

Good news, because I knew exactly who I would like to approach to be our sponsor.

For some years Jeff Adams, Managing Director of United House, had not only been a staunch individual supporter of the theatre but his company had sponsored all the StagTech shows. I talked to Francis immediately. I said that whilst I did not want to encroach on any future sponsorship for StagTech I felt it only right that United House should be given the first opportunity for such nationwide coverage. The company had helped us so much it was only fair and just. Their attitude was so forward looking under Jeff I guessed they would really appreciate the commercial opportunity. Francis was in total agreement and we made a rapid appointment to see Jeff. He was enthusiastic, asked for a few days and to our utter delight responded positively. United House would contribute in a major way to the whole evening and that would make it possible for us to charge a Gala price without having to go to something like £25 per ticket.

When I knew the whole thing was possible I contacted the BBC again and this time spoke to the producer of the programme. He was fascinated by the story of Stag, the BBC had a free Friday in February 1994, I explained that £10,000 was our absolute maximum and within two days he came back to me to say the deal was done. We were on the phone for about 40 minutes that day and by the time the conversation ended not only had I persuaded him to use the interval to promote the theatre and the town of Sevenoaks, but he was going to allow me to suggest most of the items for the programme.

What a coup. I was thrilled. So, the Friday of the Gala Weekend was now in place and my other pet scheme which I had been working on for about three years now had to be achieved.

I am a great fan of Dame Judi Dench. Her performances have always inspired me and I was really keen to bring her to Sevenoaks if she could be afforded. During our closed period I

had travelled one Sunday evening with Noel to see a performance called *Fond and Familiar*. It was in a tiny arts centre and
starred Dame Judi, her husband Michael Williams and John
Moffatt. The place was packed. It was stunning to see those
three stars perform so naturally in a place that was not even half
the size of Stag. I made up my mind that evening, this is what I
must bring to Sevenoaks – the town would love it. If I could possibly arrange that sort of evening on the Sunday of the Gala
Weekend I had only to fill the Saturday to make the three days
exciting for everyone.

I rang the man who was organising the Sunday evening performance. It was very difficult to tie down a date – if any of the
stars was filming or doing a television series even a Sunday was
not a day of rest for them. I told him the story of Stag, about its
tenth birthday and the refurbishment. After many phone calls,
yes then no then yes, the deal was done. What bliss. I was over
the moon. I could not think of anyone I would be more pleased
to have on our stage – it would really seal our grand opening.

The other thought uppermost in all our minds was our amateur clients. They were the real reason behind the theatre in the
first place, they had supported us through some really difficult
times, had been more than helpful when we needed to raise
money – they deserved a night to themselves. The weekend was
looking perfect – a BBC broadcast on Friday, a top-class
Amateur Night on the Saturday and to cap it all beautifully,
Dame Judi Dench and friends on the Sunday, in the round,
using our new stage extension meaning we could seat 690
people – what a way to celebrate!

Our Chairman, Albert Granville, offered to organise the
reception part of the Friday night Gala, I asked Terry Shaw if he
would mastermind the amateur evening, and with those two
major jobs delegated we felt we could just about cope with the
three very full days.

That Rather Special New Year . . .

Christmas came and went, very happily, and our Christmas show continued to sell well. Our new box office staff member, Eleanor Hartland was beginning to settle in with Ann Gaston and although there were teething troubles everyone was so enthusiastic it did not seem to matter too much. I told myself that I might get away with very little fuss on the day my MBE would be announced. New Year's Day fell on a Sunday and our Christmas Show finished on the Saturday. No-one on the staff would know until the Monday.

Saturday 31st December. For some extraordinary reason I woke at about 5am. Goodness knows why but I was really wide awake – so much so that I decided to get up, make a cup of tea, take it back to bed and listen to the radio. The news came on at 5.30am. It was announced that a postman had been included in the New Year's Honours List. I almost dropped my cup – surely someone had made the most terrible mistake – the names would be announced tomorrow wouldn't they? As the programme proceeded the DJ was making jokes about all sorts of people who had been honoured. I had got it all wrong. The announcements are made on 31st December, not 1st January! Not a hope of going back to sleep once the truth dawned. When the paper boy came it took me ages to find my name on the lists – but there it was – official – an MBE.

At 7.45 my phone rang. It was Richard Shirtcliff to congratulate me. I really had had no idea that anyone would even have noticed me among all those names, but from that moment the congratulations came pouring in. By the time I left for the theatre I had had an early morning visit from Francis bearing flowers and quite a few phone calls. I was a little late for work. I felt excited, very shaky and not really sure whether I would be able to cope with all this wonderful feeling and the kindnesses that I was receiving from my friends and relations. Some hope of slipping into the theatre unnoticed. It's quite astonishing how news travels so fast, good or bad, and the day was one of unforgettable excitement. Balloons, flowers, all arrived during the day. At one point in the afternoon when I was on duty during the matinee performance I was called to the telephone in the upper foyer. It was a call from Nick Willmer, ex Board director of Stag and musical director of *My Fair Lady* in 1986.

"Maggie – congratulations – I'm ringing from Holland to say it's about b . . . time."

"From *Holland?*" I squeaked. "How on earth did you know about it over there?"

"I've been looking in the Honours List every year for the past five years or so and this time, there you are!"

The day passed in a haze of happiness and quite extraordinary words of kindness and generosity from my many friends. The whole weekend was the same and by Monday morning the letters were arriving in their dozens – I had had no idea whatever that so many people cared. I was truly surrounded by love and affection. If only John could have shared it all.

It was quite difficult to concentrate but the business still had to be run and we still had audiences to look after. We also still had workmen in the building. They were trying to get the cinemas finished and all sorts of things seemed to be going wrong. We missed all the Christmas holiday cinema business which in its turn had a knock-on effect on our cash forecast. What a blessing that we had sponsorship for our Christmas Show. That at least helped us to pay the salaries at the end of the month (by now considerably increased with our one or two extra staff).

The days flashed by – not without their problems but nonetheless highly enjoyable. So much to do and still so much excitement, about the building, my MBE and the preparations for our Gala Opening Weekend.

At last, and after much tearing of hair, the problems in the cinema were sorted out. We could open – nearly three weeks late and during the month of January, not at all the best time to launch anything. Despite what many members of the public thought about the amount of money that was spent on the refurbishment, there were some harsh facts to face in that we could not possibly do all the things we would have liked (and I don't mean glamorous nonsense). I completely understood and indeed encouraged the view that no money must be wasted on fripperies but that we must do our very best to spend whatever was available in the most sensible way. The cinema unfortunately could not have the amount of money spent on it that it really required. To keep abreast of current trends and try to compete with the multiplexes in comfort alone would have meant ditching all the existing seats and installing new ones – a vast and unaffordable sum.

Our two screens were being increased in audience capacity, which in itself created a technical problem within our new projection room (now one instead of two thus saving on staff). We would have loved to have Dolby sound in both screens for our patrons and I particularly wanted slide projection facilities in order to advertise theatre shows on our cinema screens regularly. None of this was possible. We kept the newest seats we already had, moved all of them into one screen so that at least they would look uniform and purchased new seats for the other cinema. We had to bear in mind the rake and size of the auditorium and I remember a supplier arriving in the car park one day with two or three seats in his van which were at a price we could afford, and sitting in them trying to imagine I was in a cinema. The sun was shining and people parking their cars must have thought we had gone mad.

New screens had to be purchased, the heating and ventilation system had to be completed in the projection box otherwise the projectionist would faint from the heat generated by the equipment and the new carpet had to be laid, although I insisted on keeping the lino between the rows of seats for ease of cleaning. That was a little battle but I had actually cleaned those cinemas and had experienced trying to clean up popcorn squashed into spilt coke. So concerned was I for the cleaning operation that I had gone to a large cinema in Leicester Square one morning when the cleaners were on duty and asked specific questions about how they dealt with such problems. The cleaner I spoke to was succinct.

"Well, ma'am," he said, "it's a nightmare. We have professional companies who come in and regularly disinfect the seats and carpets. When there's a real problem they change the carpets!"

That answer would not serve Stag so I was even more convinced that to keep lino between the rows was the long-term solution even if the audience felt it was not quite so luxurious as they would have liked. We had to be practical.

Our new cinema manager, Linda McPaul, took on her new post with great excitement. However, we had great reservations about her ability to withstand the daily commuting by train from her home in Essex, but she assured us that she did not consider this a problem. As the months went by it became obvious she was not happy in her job. Stag was quite an unusual set-up to someone who had not previously been involved in such a project.

For the first time cinema seats at Stag could be booked in advance on our new computerised box office system and this was extremely popular with our audiences. However, by some mischance, the seats in both auditoria had been replaced one behind the other instead of being staggered. The complaints began to arrive thick and fast.

Our newly angled screens were now showing not quite such a good picture, the induction loop for the hard of hearing was not functioning properly and to cap it all overspill of sound from the stage seemed to be funnelling itself through a new fire exit at the back of the cinemas and ruining everyone's enjoyment. Oh boy, were we under fire. The public who complained simply could not understand how anyone could spend 'so much money on a building and get something wrong'. Our efforts in the cinema had not been good enough. Although there was no more money at the time it was obvious that mistakes had been made and would have to be rectified in due course if we were not to lose all our cinema patrons. All we could do was field the complaints, apologise with a smile and explain that when time and money permitted we would do our utmost to rectify what we could. The morale of the staff had to be boosted quite often in those months. I knew how difficult it was to be at the sharp end – I had had the experience over many years – no-one enjoys it. As long as I didn't crumple everyone was alright and as long as staff could get it off their chest they coped with it very well.

Guy Wrenn, who had been the manager of the cinema long before Stag took it over, returned as our chief projectionist, and I could not have been more pleased. Guy knew so much about the projection equipment in that building, how old it was, where it was unreliable and how it needed to be looked after. He also had contacts for finding spare parts, a thing which was becoming more and more difficult as the equipment aged. He had a tough time too. He hated hearing complaints from patrons saying they could not see or hear properly, and we spent hours doing tests on almost everything. It would have been so nice to provide new technical equipment in the cinemas but it was out of the question. Like the rest of us Guy had to grin and bear it.

In January, immediately prior to our ten days' dark period, Petts Wood Operatic Society brought *Guys and Dolls* into the theatre. They were one of the societies who had been hoping very much to perform the show before Christmas but with the building delays they had had to postpone their performances. Hard for them because it then meant they would have two musicals within the space of about four months as the spring show was already planned and booked. Anyone involved in an amateur society knows exactly what problems that throws up. It was of great help to us to have rent coming in from a large amateur society in our newly refurbished building and the big cast were delighted with the improvements backstage – hot water and more loos!! Audiences were excellent and our refurbished building preened itself in front of a few more thousand people.

We then had our ten 'dark' days, not only to bring back in all those things which were still sitting in warehouses but to sort out the snags which had been thrown up in those two or three weeks after opening. And snags there were. Our restaurant which was hopefully to be such a source of income still could not be opened. Equipment had not arrived and Health and Hygiene rules were such that short cuts could not be taken. Noel was finally able to open on 14th March. The tension was pretty high. He had a tough time too!

No time to do a snagging – we needed the income – and apart from the staff being used twice as guinea pigs, the business opened to the public with the minimum of rehearsal. Simply called the Theatre Bar Restaurant, it could seat thirty-six. It had its own baby grand piano and whenever possible lunchtime patrons were entertained. Its popularity spread, with the intro-duction of pre-show suppers, children's parties and cast parties all providing extra income for the building. Unfortunately it turned out that the extraction unit in the tiny kitchen faced the post office recreation room and we began to get regular com-plaints about the cooking smells. The dishwasher broke down on countless occasions and washing-up, just as eleven years ago, had to be done by hand. The gas often went out, and some-times the lights, but the staff always seemed to cope. The restau-rant flourishes to this day, although Noel has since moved on to other things.

We discovered that the signs which we had so carefully thought out were not adequate. Our new lift, installed at enor-mous cost, was very difficult to locate. Many people complained about still having to walk up the stairs. Such a pity when we thought it had all been so well planned.

Although by now the number of workmen in the building had dwindled, there were still many occasions when workmen would appear to put finishing touches to this and that. They were still working against the clock at the back of the building to complete the workshop/scenery area which we had deliber-ately left to the last (trying to tie in its final thrashings with our 'dark' ten days). Sometimes I would be sitting in the restaurant, ever critical and watching all that was going on, when a workman in overalls, carrying buckets or some such building accessory, dust all over his boots, would suddenly appear from the fire exit from the street, walk straight across the beautiful new carpet between tables occupied by patrons. They did not even ask! It drove me mad and I was forever complaining to the powers that be that it had to stop. There were we, doing our utmost to impress our customers and it was being undone on our behalf. Dust seemed to return all over the building for weeks, but despite all the problems, and there were many, I often sat in the empty auditorium quite overwhelmed by the fact that tatty little Stag had become a real centre of entertainment and something the district could be proud of.

Never had I imagined anything on this scale – ever.

The Gala – February 1994

The advertising for this was well and truly under our belt, tickets were selling fast and it looked as if it would be a glorious feast of entertainment. Terry Shaw consulted me about the amateur night *Fanfare for Stag* on the Saturday evening and asked if I would appear at the very end of the show to the tune of *Hello Dolly* (to which they would sing 'Hello Maggie'!). It would provide a fitting finale that would bring all the performers together on stage. It was after all a triple celebration – the refurbishment, our ten years and my MBE. I was to appear at the top of a staircase and walk down the stairs to the music. I thought I might just be able to manage that. It would be nice to be part of the evening and not just sit out front and watch. Of course I had to find a suitable frock (and make sure this time there was no price tag on my backside). I couldn't make a grand entrance in any old thing – so I took a girlfriend with me to Morris Angel's and we chose a very fitted blue dress with long sleeves which looked made for me and was glamorous enough for a Shirley Bassey entrance!

214

DAY ONE

The plans and preparation for the BBC Broadcast on the Friday night were going very well. The producer had been down to see the theatre and pronounced it most suitable despite the odd workman or two around the place, and I submitted my suggestions for the items in the programme.

I had tried to imagine myself, as a weekly follower of the show, listening on my radio at home. I hoped I had provided a balanced evening's entertainment. I selected mostly big numbers from musicals which had been very successful at Stag during our previous ten years, some ballet music and some opera. I ran through my suggestions with Terry Shaw – his previous experience in the world of entertainment was invaluable – and we finalised the items. The soloists were to be Ramon Romarro and Susan Bullock, the compere for the evening the inimitable Robin Boyle.

All the tickets for this performance had been sold out weeks before and the local press carried much publicity for our Gala Weekend. It took my breath away to hear over the radio on the Friday before our opening that "next week's *Friday Night is Music Night* will be broadcast from The Stag Theatre, Sevenoaks. Return tickets only."

About one week before the great event I recorded at Stag my part of the interval broadcast which would go out over the air. I was very surprised and pleased at how much time I was given to talk about the theatre. What a marketing opportunity – I'd better not blow it. The interviewer had also arranged to speak to three or four other Sennockians who were involved with the arts in the town. They were Roger Woodward, Artistic Director of the Sevenoaks Summer Festival, Jill Hargreaves-Browne who had not only been one of our first pioneers but had run the Sevenoaks Three Arts Festival from its early days, and Dr Philip Headley, then Chairman of the Sevenoaks Music Club and President of the Sevenoaks Players. The technical staff were very excited at the prospect of an outside broadcast – it would be our first ever.

The day dawned, everyone at Stag was in place early waiting for the BBC to arrive. First to come were the technicians with their mobile broadcasting vans, their miles of cable and all the paraphernalia that went with it. The producer arrived at about lpm and the schedule was duly handed out. Precision itself. Everything was timed to the second. From the arrival of the instruments, through arrival time of the musicians, right through the length of the rehearsal (their tea break when we had to have the tea *ready*) to the precise close of the rehearsal. Immaculate and extremely efficient. Technical staff very impressed. Suddenly, amid all this precision, every light in the building went out. We were aghast. It was 1.30pm. Immediate checks were made within the building but it was not just us as we rapidly discovered. Sevenoaks had a major power cut. Here was Stag within hours of its first ever outside broadcast to approximately four million listeners and we were powerless. We could not believe it. Telephone calls flew through to Seeboard. At that moment no-one had any idea where the fault was. Francis explained in capital letters our predicament (in his most charming manner). He said it was of national importance – not just local.

Seeboard have always run a very good system for companies who earn their daily bread by entertaining the public. Anyone in that position is given the most up to date information in order to be able to take a decision as to whether to send patrons home or suggest they remain in the building. When Seeboard heard about the BBC they promised to let us know the minute they had any news. It was frightening. How could it happen, today of all days?

The BBC producer was remarkably calm. He decided to go and have some lunch, told us not to worry (!) and said he would be back in 45 minutes.

Then instruments failed to arrive as scheduled. We later learned that the articulated truck containing most of them had been stolen during the night and was later found dumped somewhere. That little problem had to be solved but fortunately not by us.

The building was pitch dark and cold. The only way we could get any light on to the stage area was to open all the doors including the large double 'get in' door leading from the stage to the car park. Here we were, in February, with doors open to the elements to let some light in. The musicians began to arrive on schedule. They were very mystified that they had to enter the stage through the 'scenery door' and totally puzzled to find us letting in all the cold air. Their immediate impression was "what a strange place – fancy economising on the lights!" It was like the black hole of Calcutta. We kept our fingers crossed that no-one would hurt themselves in the dark. Everyone was cosseted and sat down somewhere safe. We couldn't even make them tea!

I felt quite sick – was it really going to be ruined after all this effort? After what seemed like an eternity Steve Wiltshire was informed that it was a very serious electrical failure. However, after a couple of hours of nail-biting agony (whilst I tried desperately to think of some way of retrieving the evening), the power was suddenly restored. Seeboard had come up trumps.

The impeccable schedule was utterly scuppered. Everyone now felt quite insecure but my staff coped admirably and I really admired the aplomb of the BBC team.

At least there was no time to think about butterflies in the stomach. Thank goodness the tickets had all been sold – our computers in the box office were unable to function and ticket sales were chaotic. Dennis and the box office staff used all their diplomacy with patrons.

But we had a Gala Reception to host, celebrities to receive and as always everything must appear to have gone like clockwork. It brought back a few memories!

In the end, the evening was a huge success. So happy, such a gorgeous programme, though I say it myself, and very thrilling to know that we were broadcasting to the nation. Stag, my little dream of many years ago, now having national airtime.

The BBC kindly provided me with a superb tape of the complete broadcast, including our interviews in the interval. Anyone still reading at this point can borrow it from the box office (I would suggest a donation of £5 towards theatre funds).

What a magical start to our weekend.

DAY TWO

Saturday dawned. We were all elated that the previous evening had gone so well. One or two friends who had moved right away from the district telephoned to say how lovely it was to hear the broadcast the night before. So people really did listen.

Fanfare for Stag this evening. I was extremely relieved I was not in charge of that event. There were so many in the cast that for the first time we had to use The Plaza Suite as an extra dressing room. It took military precision to organise hundreds of amateurs up one staircase and down another (in a place many of them had not even seen) and all without making a noise. I gather that some of them made a fuss – heigh-ho, temperaments will out!

It was a full house and the atmosphere that evening was again so warm, the hundreds of performers seemed really delighted to be playing their part and we had a splendid time. The audience, I believe, expected me to appear only in a glamorous role. When I popped out of the front half of a camel in a sketch about Lawrence of Arabia (Francis was the rear!) it brought the house down.

When it came to the finale I felt almost overwhelmed and not at all sure I could do it. The staircase had no handrails (there hadn't been time), my dress was heavy and my heels were high. I probably looked about as stilted as it was possible to do and there was no way I could shimmy down those stairs. I just walked slowly, very slowly, and tried to smile.

I will never forget that evening.

DAY THREE

Well, here we were – the final and for me the most challenging of our three day event.

218

It was our first performance 'in the round'. All 690 seats had been sold long before and there was a waiting list for returns. The anticipation of using our Cormack stage extension for the first time was tremendous. (How I hoped Michael would be taking a peek).

Dennis had had to work out the lettering and numbering of the seats on the stage itself because we had never done it before. All the seats had to be put out on the Sunday afternoon as late as possible but before Dame Judi arrived. We would then manually stick labels on them denoting their rows and numbers. We had not been able to rehearse it, so tension was quite high.

Steve had not 'lit' the stage extension before, we had no idea what it would sound like with 690 people sitting there and the only thing I had tried out was standing in the middle of the stage and 'delivering' some lines to an imaginary audience all around me. It felt as though it would work well.

Our volunteers had never been on duty in such a seating arrangement. Ticket holders hopefully arriving at the right door had to be guided to their seats, ice-creams had to appear in new positions as well as their old ones and all in all the whole thing would be an experiment. The setting was very simple. A large rug centre stage. A table with three chairs at three separate points to enable each section of the audience to have full benefit of the stars.

Francis, Steve and Peter Fleming had much work to do during the day on that Sunday. Dennis was to arrive late afternoon with some volunteers to do the chairs and I was going to be there during the afternoon to check on all aspects of everything.

In our refurbishment programme we had had installed a hydraulic lift built into the floor of the stage. It went through the orchestra pit and down to the workshop, thus enabling us to bring up pianos (no more six men), pieces of scenery and heavy props without all that hassle. It was particularly useful that weekend because we had never coped with three such different performances on consecutive days. With our very limited staff we could not possibly have managed without this wonderful addition to our facilities.

At about 3 o'clock my phone rang at home. It was Francis.

"Maggie, are you free to come up and have a look, there are one or two things we need to sort out."

He was perfectly calm and thinking nothing of the call I went to the theatre. Albert Granville our Chairman was there and I was slightly puzzled. Albert was always very supportive and involved but I could not quite understand his presence on a Sunday afternoon. I went on to the stage and noticed that the huge lid of the lift was in its raised position.

"Are you going to tell her, Albert, or shall I?" asked Francis.

"Tell me what?" I asked.

Albert's beautifully sonorous voice echoed across the stage.

"Maggie, the lift is stuck."

Our new, beautiful toy was well and truly stuck. Despite everything that Francis, Steve, Peter and Albert had tried, nothing would shift it. We had 690 people coming and Dame Judi and friends due to arrive at five.

No need to describe the ensuing conversations.

"Have you thought of . . .?"

"Yes."

"What about . . .?"

"No good."

Francis had a maintenance number and an emergency number. *But it was Sunday.* No reply from the maintenance number. The emergency number was a mobile phone and had been switched off. Yellow Pages revealed a number somewhere miles away in Kent but no-one answered that either.

We stayed remarkably cool. Francis, Steve and Peter continued to call the emergency number and eventually someone responded. I think the air was pretty blue from what I heard later, but in the meantime Dennis and volunteers had arrived. In order to minimise the panic I suggested we started getting out the new seats and numbering them even if the lid of the lift was taking up three-quarters of the stage!

Dame Judi telephoned to say she would be a little later than 5 o'clock as she had been filming all day and was slightly behind schedule – thank heaven!

An engineer finally arrived at about 4.30. It was not long before the lift lid was back flat on the floor in its proper place. What a nightmare.

I sent up many silent prayers that afternoon.

Dame Judi arrived suffering from an extremely heavy cold. She was very impressed with the 'star' dressing room. Francis made her his usual cup of tea and discussed the shape of the evening. She was very excited to be at such a 'pioneering' performance in the theatre, although she said she had not realised it was to be in the round. My explicit explanation of the arrangements had apparently not reached her ears. However, she was so professional and, when her two fellow actors John Moffatt and Richard Pascoe arrived, they simply whizzed through the framework of the performance with the utmost aplomb.

The performance, called *Fond and Familiar,* was a selection of Victorian and Edwardian prose, poetry and music and each actor took turns to perform. They handled the in-the-round superbly. When one had finished his act he would turn to his colleagues and they all moved to the next chair thereby giving the whole audience the opportunity of seeing each star full face.

The thing the audience did not know was that because Dame Judi had such an appalling throat her cough sweets had been placed at unseen but easily accessible points around the table. I was seated on the stage – I had to test it out didn't I? – and as I knew about the cough sweets I marvelled at the very skilled way in which she managed to take the lozenges without the public realising.

It was a delightful and very funny evening and from a technical point of view it worked excellently. During the interval it was really strange to see members of the audience in the main auditorium waving to their friends on the stage and vice versa – it created a very special atmosphere. John Moffatt and Richard

Pascoe were extremely popular with everyone and of course Judi Dench received roars of appreciation. Her rendition of slightly saucy Victorian ballads was a lesson to behold and that evening I learned a great deal more about delivery and timing. I felt very privileged to be able to watch.

The Friends of Stag had arranged a 'meet the stars' party after the show in The Plaza Suite but it was such appalling weather that only about 35 people stayed on. Peter Othick greeted Dame Judi but I think because of her bad throat she was quite relieved that she did not have to stay for very long talking to hordes of strangers. I had a large brandy with Peter that evening before I went home.

I was so happy just to have had her in the building – Dame Judi Dench at Stag – the culmination of three days' artistic endeavour.

That had been some Gala Weekend!

Everyone applauded our efforts over those three days. Council Officials, committees, our clients, our audiences, all had really appreciated what we had achieved and I knew in my heart that we could not have wished for more or done better. Staff, volunteers and performers had done us proud and for that I was very, very grateful and told them so.

We had now used the refurbished building to its utmost. We knew the limitations, were aware of possible problems and felt that in the future nothing could be quite so difficult as that first time. How fortunate we were to get away with it – as far as the audiences were concerned everything ran smoothly, the place looked stunning and the staff were all smiling. That's what show business is all about.

I admit that at times I genuinely wondered how on earth we had managed everything. I occasionally questioned why I slept so well and how could I cope with such demands on my energy?

My answer I am sure was because deep down – although I *loved* it – I had taken the decision to give it all up before it gave me up. I was able to pour every ounce of energy and enthusiasm into every occasion, deal with every problem however moment-ous and still not lose my cool. In my mind I knew that this relentless but very exciting life could not continue indefinitely. I had seen things happen to other people, knew the dangers of ruining the very thing I had nurtured so carefully and was absolutely determined that my project should not suffer because I was too greedy to hand it over when the time was right. I was completely happy about my decision and once having made it, before the refurbishment even began, I had no intention what-soever of changing my mind. My instinct had served me well all these years and there was no reason to believe it would let me down now.

Of course I could not make my decision known. The theatre was in a major period of transition, I was working very hard to integrate new staff into what had been a very close-knit team and I was running a business which had changed gear upwards in a very major way. I did eventually confide in Albert and Francis.

During all these weeks of excitement I was naturally won-dering when I would be asked to go to Buckingham Palace. One or two of my 'honoured friends' were very worried because they were sure I would be able to take only two guests. Horror – how on earth could I possibly choose any two of the three boys – they were equally important. I said nothing to them at all. My joy and relief when the invitation finally arrived saying I was allowed 'three guests' was unbounded. It would be simply per-fect to have them all there.

One evening in late February I arrived home from the theatre. Noel sat me down and asked if I could take any more excite-ment.

"Why?" I asked, wondering what on earth was coming.

He explained that he had written to the BBC, ITV and Carlton television telling them the brief history of Stag and that I had been awarded an MBE. He really had not thought anything would come of it but to his astonishment Meridian TV had phoned him to say that they would like to shoot some film of the refurbished building and also do an interview with me.

I could not believe it. When I had recovered from the shock I realised what an enormous publicity boost this would give the theatre. For two or three days we waited in anticipation, half expecting it to be called off at any minute as so often happens with television companies. Two evenings later the phone rang. I answered it and a voice said "It's Meridian Television, may I speak to Noel please."

They actually fixed a date for the filming and an interview. We had to prepare something interesting to film. Showing a refurbished building might be pretty boring and would no doubt be watched by a few million people – so it had to be planned. We arranged for students from West Kent College to come and help us out by staging a rehearsal. In addition it so happened that on the arranged day we had a 'get-in' for a ballet company. We were able to film real work in the theatre. The whole affair appeared to me to be extremely haphazard and informal. A crew of two plus the interviewer, no help or advice with my appearance and a very laid back attitude altogether. They wanted a shot of me arriving for work and this had to be done four or five times as one or two pedestrians that morning decided to join in and apparently ruined the filming. Sevenoaks had no idea as to what was happening.

That morning went by in a whirl. I was suddenly sat down in the auditorium and with virtually no preparation launched into my interview about the theatre and the part I had played in its realisation. Albert made a brief appearance and members of the staff looked particularly busy. We tried to make it as interesting as possible.

Knowing what normally happens with these types of items I guessed that would be the last we would hear of it. No-one seemed to be very sure what it would be used for. The contact Noel had had with Meridian was a free-lance producer and he wanted it for the final edition of a series for which he had been responsible called *Monday People* which formed part of *London*

Tonight. I wasn't going to fret about it anyway – we had probably gone to a lot of trouble for nothing – I had plenty of other things to deal with that were more pressing.

Little did I know what had been going on behind my back!

The Investiture – 8th March 1994

The appointed day was Tuesday 8th March. We were requested to arrive at the Palace between 10.00 and 10.30am. What a difficult time of the day to drive to London and be sure of one's time of arrival!

The weather was extremely kind. Sunny but breezy and not at all cold. Barry came to the house early and would drive to London with Noel and myself. We were to meet Kim at the gates of Buckingham Palace at the appointed time.

Noel had arranged with the *Sevenoaks Chronicle* to send a photographer to the house to take pictures before we left. The boys looked extremely smart and were as excited as I was. I was ready in adequate time for the photographer (the hands shook a little putting on the face!) and we watched for her from the window. No-one showed up so we left for London. We discovered afterwards that the photo session had been 'overlooked'.

The journey was excellent. As we neared the Palace we could see the queue of cars waiting to enter. Kim suddenly appeared, also looking extremely smart. As he jumped in the police were examining the car under the bonnet and in the boot. Crowds were gathered at the railings and it was very thrilling to be driving through those gates with everyone looking to see if we were famous – if they had only known!

By this time I was beginning to get the collywobbles. It had been one thing imagining this day but it was quite another actually being there at the Palace. The Investiture would be taken by HRH The Prince of Wales as Her Majesty the Queen was travelling back from her tour of the West Indies that day. Somewhat ironic that it was the Prince I had written to all those years ago asking for his support for some little theatre in Sevenoaks.

We all made our way towards the steps leading up to the entrance and it was there that I had to part from the boys. Now I really did feel alone and I heard the guests being asked to hand over their cameras to the staff. I walked up the steps feeling very excited. John would have been tickled pink – I hoped he was keeping an eye on things for me.

Uniforms flashed and sparkled everywhere, the furnishings were quite breathtaking and I tried very hard to absorb it all and keep it in my memory. Every person on duty was so helpful and yet full of fun, realising our nervousness and explaining in detail precisely what would happen and when. The demonstration of how not to bow and curtsey had us in giggles very quickly and for an instant I felt quite at home – this was just like any other rehearsal really – or so I told myself.

We assembled in the Portrait Gallery. It was suddenly overwhelming to realise that the portraits hanging on the walls were the real ancestors of the actual people living in this house – history sprang to life in a way which I had not experienced before.

I mentioned to one of the staff that I would be quite happy being left in there all day, there was so much to see.

The sequence of presentation was 'rank of order' and the MBE's were the last group. We did not have to wait too long and during that interlude I met individuals who had done quite amazing things and had come miles for the presentation. Some had had to draw lots in their families, poor things, to decide who should attend, others who had made journeys from the Hebrides had had to limit the family attendance for lack of funds to pay for accommodation in London. I realised how very fortunate I was not to have had all those complications.

Staff were on duty every few yards during our progress to the Ballroom and it became more and more nerve-racking and yet exciting the nearer we approached. A few yards from the Ballroom doors a hook was placed on my jacket. I had been wondering how medals could be pinned on everyone in the time allowed.

I had no idea where the boys would be seated or even whether they would be able to see my great moment, but as I reached the outer door of the Ballroom to await my turn I suddenly spotted their three faces in the fifth row. Three great big grins and one tiny wave.

The Ballroom was magnificent. What a stage set that would make! Giant chandeliers and the Band of the Coldstream Guards playing on the balcony put the finishing touch to the whole spectacle.

I could see Prince Charles very clearly now, and oh heavens, it was my turn next.

Please God don't let me wobble!

My name was announced loudly and clearly (that man could project!), the citation was read out and I walked forward to accept my MBE. His Royal Highness lifted my medal from its box, shook my hand and placed the MBE on its hook. How simple and how clever. He asked precisely what I did and I explained briefly. I also reminded him that I had written to him so many years previously requesting his help. He told me never to give up and to carry on the excellent work.

As soon as he shook my hand again I knew the interview was over (we had been told). I took my four steps backwards and made my curtsey. No – I didn't wobble.

One particular memory will remain with me always: the kindness in the Prince's eyes and the way in which he watched every recipient intently until they had turned away and moved off in the direction of the door out of the Ballroom. Not one of us was made to feel that HRH could not wait to get on with the next individual and get the whole thing over with. That left a very deep impression.

As soon as I reached the opposite corridor on the other side of the Ballroom my medal was unhooked, the hook removed, the medal placed in a box and I was free to join the other guests at the back of the room to enjoy what remained of the ceremony. It was gorgeous. I thought I would burst with the emotions that were taking over. I listened to the band and so wanted to dance.

I opened my box and there was my MBE – so pretty and still quite unbelievable.

When His Royal Highness had finally finished and had left the Ballroom we had a family reunion. We were all so happy – what a splendid time we had had.

Noel seemed somewhat preoccupied as we made our way out. He appeared to want us to get to the courtyard fairly quickly. I was really past caring by this time and we strolled out into the sunshine watching the crowds of happy people and delighted to drink in everything that was going on.

As we walked down the final flight of steps to the courtyard, I saw two people standing alone facing the Palace. One held up a TV camera with ITV in large letters and the other a huge white board .

On it were the words "DURRANT-HOLLAMBY". Totally unaware of what it was all about I just felt slightly irritated that someone had spelt our name incorrectly. It took one or two double takes to realise that they were looking for me (hence Noel's preoccupation).

They really had turned up and were waiting for me. I did not think I could take any more excitement – the boys would have to deal with it.

Apparently ITV were covering the Investiture that day and had agreed to do an interview with me for Meridian Television which they hoped to put out that night on *London Tonight*. It was all too much – what organisation had been going on behind the scenes and what secrets those boys had kept!

The interview seemed to be fine although I clearly remember having to hold on to my hat in the breeze. I just prayed that I had not said anything facile because I was much too excited to think on my feet. The boys were asked to pose with me at the end of the interview and I stood there proudly displaying my medal in its box.

We noticed that ITV then moved on to interview Jim Swanton who had also been honoured that day. He looked a very happy man.

We could have had 'official' photos taken but by now the queues for these were very long and we decided against it. A husband and wife near us took the same decision so we did a swap. The wife took our picture and Kim took theirs. I only hope they have as lovely a memory as I have.

We finally walked back to the car parked in the outer court-yard on a complete cloud and drove out of Buckingham Palace and down the Mall to the Savoy Hotel where I had booked lunch for us and where we were to meet with Barry's wife Winnie and Kim's girlfriend Anne Marie.

Someone was really looking down on us that day. As we drove into the forecourt of the Savoy, one or two Rolls were parked and the liveried doorman opened our doors and ushered us into reception. Kim and Noel said they would go and park the car and be back as soon as they could. Barry and I sat down gratefully, having greeted the girls, and expecting at least a ten-minute delay whilst the other two parked the car, but to our surprise they returned almost immediately. The Savoy's doorman, for a small favour, had allowed them to park the car in the forecourt – what a nice man.

The lunch was impeccable. There were a number of tables in the room seating families and parties like ours with an award sitting in its box in pride of place on the table and the atmo-sphere was terrific. We thoroughly enjoyed the occasion. Lunch lasted a considerable time!

Finally we had to leave Kim and Anne Marie in London and the rest of us started our car journey back to Barry and Winnie's house where Winnie's parents had been baby-sitting the two little granddaughters.

Noel did a running commentary almost all the way home because he had his eye on the time – we had to be back in front of a television for 6pm. At each hint of the smallest traffic jam he changed his route and the journey back was very exciting and quite different. I did not really believe we would appear on TV, certainly not at peak viewing time, but I said nothing.

We arrived at the house with about five minutes to spare.

Winnie's parents already had the TV on and had been watching the news. Lots of cuddles with the granddaughters, hugs and kisses all round and the youngest granddaughter, Sophie, wearing my large hat askew. I flopped out on the sofa, completely and utterly pooped. All I wanted was a cup of tea.

Suddenly there was a "Ssssh!" from someone and the voice on the television announced that "today a woman from Kent has been rewarded . . ."

We were stunned into silence. There on the screen for all the world to see was a picture of three very happy sons and their mother in the forecourt of Buckingham Palace. We could not believe it. The item then went on to show the film they had made at Stag together with my interview. An amazing amount of air-time.

Nothing could quite top a day like that.

The Final Months

About three weeks after all this excitement I received a letter from The World Government of the Age of Enlightenment asking me if I would accept the Maharishi Award for that Spring for the County of Kent.

I was totally nonplussed. The only Maharishi of whom I had any knowledge at all was the one who had been pictured with the Beatles all those years ago. Why me? How did they know about me?

My letter requested that I attend a Presentation Ceremony in deepest Paddock Wood. I made one or two tentative inquiries. I had never practised Transcendental Meditation and I simply did not understand why I had been chosen.

My enquiries revealed that twice a year individuals are invited to accept an award on behalf of The World Government for their services to their County. I was to be honoured in such a way. Apparently, a local teacher of Transcendental Meditation knew about the success of the theatre and had recommended me for this particular honour.

I was invited to take a guest. I asked Albert Granville to accompany me as Stag's Chairman but he had a prior engagement. His wife Jocelyn agreed to accompany me and offered to drive.

It was a foul evening. Pouring with rain, very windy, and we got completely lost. It is very easy to get very lost in the identical country lanes around Paddock Wood and we had to stop and ask the way. By this time we were late and I was anxious. Very embarrassing and rude to be late when you are an honoured guest.

I need not have worried. The lady who received us at the front door was very, very pleasant, extremely relaxed and friendly, and I was relieved to see she was dressed just like one of us. I'm not sure what I had expected, it was completely foreign territory to me, but I should not have been so silly.

Everyone was absolutely delightful. Happy without being over the top, extremely kind and full of praise for the apparent happiness and joy I had given so many people by founding the theatre. We were served a delicious and enticing buffet supper, the house was very large but not grandly furnished and the atmosphere was completely relaxed and very genuine.

The Maharishi's personal assistant had flown over from the United States to address the group of people present and we learned that awards were given in the Spring and Autumn to individuals recommended by one of their members. There were about five other people from all walks of life receiving awards that evening.

One man rose to his feet and explained that he was a retired District Commissioner in the Police. He said that Transcendental Meditation (TM) had restored his sanity after the vagaries and horrors of police life. He said he had spent many weekends with his wife in this particular house simply being 'quiet' and that he could not recommend it highly enough. It set me thinking.

I listened to everything that was said and found it very believable – after all, one of the greatest blessings of my life had been to be able to relax when I needed to, often with the help of deep breathing taught me when young, and in my humble view TM was simply a furtherance of that gift. However much I had had to wheel and deal for the theatre I had determined to keep an open mind. Who was I to say something did not work when it was patently obvious that it did for a large number of people. We had a delightful evening. I was given a large certificate bearing the following words:

"It is with great joy and appreciation that the World Government of the Age of Enlightenment presents to you the Maharishi Award: the expression of the highest esteem of the community. Through your creativity and success in life you have demonstrated the potential for success inherent in the life of every individual. Your life is a shining example and your influence an essential contribution to the continuing tradition of success in your community. All those who know you and know of your achievements are inspired in their own lives to rise to higher levels of achievement. You are an ambassador of success and your success is a ray of light in this rising Age of Enlightenment. The World Government of the Age of Enlightenment honours the outstanding men and women whose achievements demonstrate this ability to enhance the quality of individual and community life and thereby inspire the rising world consciousness of the Age of Enlightenment."

I have to confess that I never really read those words properly until many months after I had left the theatre. I found it very difficult to associate what was said with what I had done, but one thing did occur to me. When one thinks about it, we all know people who have done very difficult things and I know from my own experience that it is perfectly possible for each one of us to achieve things for ourselves *if we really want to.*

I also know that none of the achievements could have happened without undying support from many other people and I just wished they could have shared the happiness of both my MBE and my Certificate – they deserved to.

232

Exit – stage left

During late 1994 I announced to the Board of Directors my wish to hand over my job within the next year. I believe they were quite shocked. I explained my reasons. I had never pretended to be someone who relished the thought of running a big business, and for me Stag had now become big business involving all those processes and procedures which I disliked most – staff meetings, endless jargon, regulations and all the things which companies had to keep up with in the current climate. And it was going to get worse. I had had the most exciting time during the last eleven years but I knew my limitations. I felt sure I had steered the business onto a very firm base and although everything was by no means perfect I knew it needed fresh blood, enthusiasm and new ideas. I also had someone in mind to take over from me.

Stag still had strict financial limitations, salaries were still very low. My instinct told me that it needed someone who was passionate about it, who would love to be absorbed in the running of it and yet someone who could afford to work for a small salary. If this person could also already be known in the district and a familiar face to our audiences, that must be the answer.

Terry Shaw seemed to fit all those requirements. After many weeks of meetings, talks with Directors and endless discussions with Terry, himself obviously very enthused by the whole prospect, it was finally agreed. The matter was of course confidential. New staff still learning their way around did not need the worry of a different boss. We were still integrating hard and there was work to be done.

I knew that no individual could continue doing all the jobs I had done over the previous years – the business was now too big. We had appointed a young man to become our House Manager. His name was Karl Davey. He was very experienced in the theatre and had come to us from the West End. He was hot stuff on computers and he and Dennis Gilkes had a lot in common. He was very popular with the volunteers and endeared himself to members of the public. We all had high hopes that he would become a 'right-hand' to whoever was running the business.

Terry Shaw was interviewed formally by the Board along with many others. He was already a Director and had been on the Board for about a year. He was finally appointed in 1995. It was agreed that he would work alongside me during the month of April and take the reins from 1st May.

I finally gathered my courage to call the staff together in the auditorium. I told them of my decision. I think it fair to say that they were very shocked and surprised and a little upset. I made it quite clear to them that I felt it was the right time to hand over, that it was my decision and mine alone, that no-one had put me under any pressure but that I could not bear the thought of reaching a point when people might say "When on earth is she going to give up?"

I found that meeting one of the most difficult and emotional occasions of my life.

I had no doubts whatever that what I was doing was right for both me and the theatre, but it was still hard to do. I exited very quickly, walked back up the stairs to my office and shut the door. Both Albert and Francis had known what I was going to tell them all. I left them to answer the inevitable questions.

Things then moved at a rapid pace.

April Fools Day (that was unintentional) saw Terry arrive and we worked closely together for the whole of that month. The relief for me was fantastic. I gradually began to feel this enormous weight lifting off my shoulders. People were telling me that I looked better already – I can't imagine what I must have looked like before.

The Directors threw a party for me using the Plaza Suite and my beloved stage. We had a delightful evening with many, many old friends, including my original partner in crime, Hugh

Barty-King, and his wife. So much had happened since 1966. Look where we were now.

On my last Friday my staff threw a lunchtime party for me and it was really warming to see some ex members of the cinema staff with their wives as well who had all given up precious spare time to come and see me off.

What a day of emotions that was. However, nothing could make me feel I was doing the wrong thing. Stag had to move ever onward and upward.

What was I going to do with myself? I had not the least idea. All I knew was that in the words of the King in *The King and I* – I had done my 'utmost best'.

Now it was someone else's turn.

Chairmen and Members
of the Board of The Stag Theatre

CHAIRMEN SINCE 1980

1980 – 1987	Margaret Durdant-Hollamby MBE
1987 – 1991	Patrick Pascall
1991 – 1993	Dr Kenneth Brown
1993 – 1996	Albert Granville CBE
1996 –	Brian Pearce OBE

In the years since 1980 the following people have served on the Board:

Tom Blackmore, Sally Burrows, Nick Dean,
Barry Durdant-Hollamby, Albert Granville, Ray Gulliver,
Jill Hargreaves-Browne, George Knott, Geoffrey Lambert,
John Marsh, Mark Pyper, Ray Russell, Peter Scoble,
Peter Seldon, Terry Shaw, Richard Shirtcliff,
Peter Strother Smith, John Tanner, Nicholas Willmer,
Peter Wilson, Ian Wood.

THE BOARD OF STAG AT TIME OF PUBLICATION

Chairman:	Brian Pearce OBE
Secretary:	Patrick Pascall
Directors:	Jeff Adams
	Tom Blackmore
	Margaret Durdant-Hollamby MBE
	Elizabeth Heard
	David Hodgkinson
	Sheila Smith
	Mrs Pam Walshe
	Louise Williams

Some Facts and Figures
about the project

The idea for a theatre in Sevenoaks was conceived in 1966. It took seventeen years to find a suitable site and get planning permission.

In 1982 Stag Theatre Ltd was registered as a charity. Registered Charity No 282111.

In 1983 the lease of the cinema in the London Road was purchased on Stag's behalf by the Sevenoaks District Council for the sum of £250,000.

The Stag Theatre was opened on 18th December 1983 in what was the old dress circle of the cinema. The auditorium seats 455. The two cinemas downstairs remained in independent ownership.

In 1989 the Board of Stag took over the control of the two cinemas on the ground floor.

In 1992 the Sevenoaks District Council agreed to spend approximately £1m to refurbish the whole building and create a new hall to the rear of the theatre.

From 30th November 1992 the building was closed for thirteen months.

Completely refurbished, Stag reopened in December 1993.

In 1994 Margaret Durdant-Hollamby was awarded the MBE.

The refurbishment had cost almost £3m.

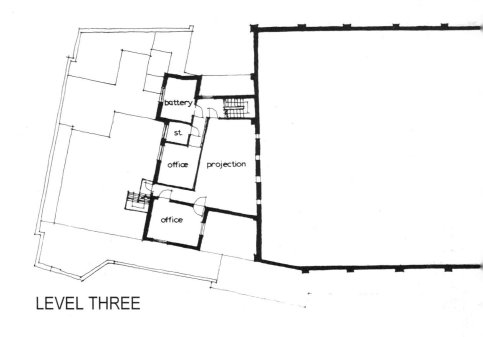

LEVEL THREE

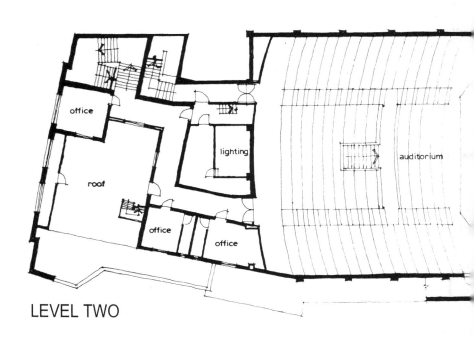

LEVEL TWO